MIND CONTROL, WORLD CONTROL

by

Jim Keith

MIND CONTROL, WORLD CONTROL

"Only the small secrets need to be protected. The big ones are kept secret by public incredulity."
—Marshall McCluhan

"If both the past and the external world exist only in the mind, and if the mind itself is controllable—what then?"
—George Orwell

MIND CONTROL, WORLD CONTROL
by Jim Keith

© 1997 Jim Keith

ISBN 0-932813-45-3

Printed in the United States of America

Published by
Adventures Unlimited Press
One Adventure Place
Kempton, Illinois 60946 USA

Second Printing
July 1998

Other Books in the Mind Control/Conspiracy Series:
MIND CONTROL, WORLD CONTROL
NASA, NAZIS & JFK: The Torbitt Document
MIND CONTROL, OSWALD & JFK: Were We Controlled?
INSIDE THE GEMSTONE FILE: Howard Hughes, Onassis & JFK
LIQUID CONSPIRACY: JFK, LSD, the CIA, Area 51 & UFOs

For Donna

Thanks are due many: The Keiths and Angells, who make it worthwhile. David Hatcher Childress for free reins and the guts to commission this book. Ron and Nancy Bonds, good friends, who more than anyone have furthered my recent work. And for the many friends who assisted, including the George Pickard family, the Ron Brown family, Ron Keith, Len Bracken, James South, Adam Parfrey, Kenn Thomas, Jim Moore, Jerry Smith, Len Bracken, David Crowbar, Paul Larson, Peter Thompson, G.J. Krupey, Matt Love, Paul Schaefer, Erich Agen, Charmaine Ferreira, Tim Cridland, Sarah Salmon, and John Driessler.

DEFENSE INTELLIGENCE AGENCY

PSYCHOTRONIC WARFARE: SPIRITUAL ACCESS

Prepared by U.S. Army
Medical Intelligence Office
DST-03447/82/018

Top: A Defense Intelligence Agency brief on
"Psychotronic Warfare." Bottom: An enlarged
x-ray of a brain implant.

TABLE OF CONTENTS

Top: H.G. Wells. Bottom: John Foster
Dulles.

Introduction:
WAR FOR THE MIND

Since the beginning of recorded history men have lusted for control of their fellows—the impulse seemingly part of the makeup of the half-ape, half-angel we call human. Until modern times brute force, propaganda, and religion were the most successful methods for the manipulation of human beings, but by the turn of this century coercive methodology had advanced far beyond the sword, the inflammatory slogan, and the stick and carrot of heaven and hell.

Now, in the 20th century, scientists in the pay of governments and other monied interests have made technical breakthroughs that render actual mind control feasible, and on a nigh-universal scale. Invasive control techniques have been fine-tuned to the point where the controllers are literally able to get inside our heads and to command us. They are able to tinker with our humanness, to manipulate it, to destroy it if they choose. They are able to use high tech networks of electronic entrainment and broadcasting whose nature has not even been hinted of in the mass media —since the mass media itself is employed in the same manner, for the manipulation of the populace. Even the subject of mind control in the media is mentioned only in the context of science fiction, or is derided as the delusions of the crazy "aluminum foil hat crowd," never mind that those guys might be on to something.

Now the powerful in their quest for a totalitarian state are provided with unprecedented access and control of our minds and humanity, to do with as they wilt. The means for the creation of worldwide slavery are in sight, and the implementation of this technology progresses day to day. The signs are all around us.

Many suspect that there is an overarching philosophy that has been engineering the crises and chaos of the latter portion of the 20th century, and I believe they are right. There are forces working behind the scenes, working to promote a New World Order not significantly different than the nega-utopian

Worldstate described in George Orwell's *1984*. If this elite is cold-blooded enough to have calculatedly created war, famine, and designer disease, as many suspect they have, what qualms would discourage them from creating worldwide mind control? This book is meant to portray certain aspects of the history of world mind control, its evolution, and the political currents that have historically dictated its directions. I will not pretend that it is definitive or the last word on the subject, and it is probably not even the last word I will have to say on the topic. The book is, however, intended to offer perspective on the present day that is rarely provided in the controlled mainstream media.

I have accessed a wide variety of sources—some mainstream, some controversial—in order to try to get to the secret programs and influences that have long dictated our thinking, our behavior, our welfare. I believe that some, although certainly not all, of those programs and influences have been revealed here, and that this information will assist future researchers in delving into these matters. I have quoted my sources throughout the book, both for the skeptic who disbelieves what I have to say, as well as for the interested reader who would like to research these topics more thoroughly. When I am speculating, as opposed to relying on solid fact, I have tried to make this clear. The truth is startling enough without getting into fantasy.

Although the subject matter of this book is for the most part unrelievedly grim, I have not intended to create inertia, to "tell how bad it all is" and to immobilize the readership with fear about the horrible state everything is in. My hope is to do just the opposite: to galvanize the reader into action. I have attempted to provide information that may be helpful for taking control back from those who would dictate our lives, and for that control to be returned to the individual, and I have also provided contact addresses of allied individuals and groups at the back of the book.

Ultimately, the American people are like Gulliver, restrained by the Lilliputians' most fragile of threads. It is time for the giant to awaken and to rip off his bonds. I hope the informa-tion in this book helps.

Chapter 1:

THINGS TO COME

It was the first decade after the turn of the century, in the lull before the storm of the first World War, and many who lived then have reflected on what seemed to be a golden, untroubled time. William Howard Taft was inaugurated as 27th president of the United States. Mary Pickford, the first film star, was featured in silent films by D.W. Griffith. Picasso painted his "Harlequin," and Matisse coined the word "Cubism." The first permanent waves were being worn by beauties as they strolled the streets of London.

Behind the scenes in the world, in the industrial boardrooms, ornate drawing rooms, and in the offices of government other activities, not quite so idyllic, were afoot. For this was a time of massive, covert consolidation of power by the monied elite, and the activation of long-term plans of control that would affect the world until the present day.

This was the time of the creation of the Federal Reserve, the FBI, the institution of the federal income tax in the United States, and, with the League of Nations, the first stirrings towards a global government. Powerful men were obsessed by the idea of increasing their power and in advancing the technology of control to enable them to do so, and they were burning the midnight oil to turn those dreams into reality.

It was the time of meetings held to brainstorm the New World Order in groups like the Round Table, the Coefficients Club, the Fabians, and the Skull and Bones society. The New World Order, that term so often bandied about by politicians and conspiracy writers, is the long-term plan to create a one-world oligarchical government on this planet. It is not really in question that such a plan exists—except among those who have not taken the time to study the documentation, or those whose interests dictate that it should be denied.

The Round Table/City of London financier focus is one group behind the New World Order—certainly not the benighted lumpens whom they have pretended to champion—and their plans for world control have been carried out by the universities, the bankers, the politicians—wielding in particular a tangle of international intelligence agencies and the psychiatric frontmen who would later be mobilized by such groups as Tavistock and the National Institute of Mental Health (NIMH). Throughout this century the members of the Open Conspiracy have busied themselves worldwide, spreading the New World Order virus, all in the interest of the domination of the elite.

Amazingly enough, the battle plan of the New World Order controllers can be clearly read in the works of a science fiction writer, a man who came up from humble beginnings in Britain to hobnob in his adult life with the movers and shakers of the elite. Herbert George Wells, more than just the latter day Jules Verne that he is presented as in the history books, was head of British Intelligence during World War II, and his mistress was Maura Benckendorff, a woman who has been called "perhaps the Soviet Union's most effective agent-of-influence ever to appear on London's political and intellectual stage." H.G. Wells knew whereof he spoke when extolling the plans of the New World Order.

Wells acted as a publicist for the real planners who worked behind the scenes. He was a front man for the Cecil Rhodes Round Table elitist secret society—Rhodes himself an agent for the Rothschilds' banking conglomerate who left his fortune to Lord Rothschild in his third will. The Round Table later branched out to spawn the influential Council on Foreign Relations and other groups perhaps not as powerful, but more well known in our time. Wells was an intimate of the Rothschild-allied Sassoons, who had made their fortune from opium shipping, and he was often seen at Sassoon fetes attended by the likes of Edward VII, George Bernard Shaw, and the young Winston Churchill.

Rhodes stated in 1890 in a letter to W.T. Stead, "What an awful thought it is that if we had not lost America, or if even now we could arrange with the present members of the United States Assembly and our House of Commons, the Peace of the world is secure for all eternity. We could well hold your federal parliament five years at Washington and five years at London. The only thing possible to carry this idea out is a secret one (society) gradually absorbing the wealth of the world to be devoted to such an object..."

Elsewhere, Rhodes stated it even more plainly. His objective was: "The extension of British rule throughout the world, the perfecting of a system of emigration from the United Kingdom and of colonization by British subjects of all lands wherein the means of livelihood are attainable by energy, labour and enterprise... and the ultimate recovery of the United States of America as an integral part of the British Empire."

Rhodes set out to accomplish this task and, through his own labors and those of his successors, has almost succeeded. [1]

It is a matter of high strangeness that within the pages of books written by H.G. Wells in England in the 1920s and 1930s—one of them science fiction—that the actual future battle plans of the controllers jump off the pages with crystal clarity. Here is an unmistakably clear picture of the New World Order, along with a clear statement of its plans.

Although H.G. Wells is primarily known for his works of science fiction, such as *The Time Machine* (1895), *The Invisible Man* (1898), and *War of the Worlds* (1898), he also wrote a number of works which overtly propagandized for the overthrow of existing nation-states and the creation of a one-world government. These books include *The Open Conspiracy: Blueprints for a World Revolution* (1928), *The New World Order* (1940), and *The Shape of Things to Come: The Ultimate Revolution* (1933).

While all of the above books are eye-opening when it comes to understanding the future as foreseen by the controllers, it is Wells' novel *The Shape of Things to Come* (and the movie he scripted that was based upon it, the title shortened to *Things to Come*), that provide the best overall view—past, present, and future—of the New World Order.

Again: Interestingly, deceptively, the book is presented as a work of science fiction, but within its pages is Wells' best guess of how the New World Order would come to pass, from a 1930s perspective.

While primarily a work of propaganda that pushes the one-world worldview of Wells and other internationalists during the first half of this century, the book is particularly revealing in that it also exposes many of the strategies that are to be employed.

Wells' introduction to the book is titled, "The Dream Book of Dr. Philip Raven." In a familiar ploy of the science fiction of the time, the book is introduced as the factual work of a Dr. Raven, a deceased friend of Wells, and a member of the Geneva

13

Secretariat coyly described as having "unusual opportunities for forming judgments upon the trend of things." Wells maintained that Raven wrote the book using the curious technique of transcribing during his waking hours a book of future history that he read during his nightly dreams. This is the fictional vehicle by which Wells sounds the clarion call for the New World Order.

The dream book purports to be a work of history, written from the perspective of a citizen of a future utopian world-state. Wells terms the book "a Short History of the World for about the next century and a half" and an "Outline of the Future."

He commences his reverse history with a reiteration of actual events up to his own time, describing how the evolution of communications and transportation has brought the human race into closer contact than ever before—global village stuff—although he comments that "Distribution, paper supply, and news services had fallen into the hands of powerful groups able and willing to crush out any... inimical schools of public suggestion. They set about stereotyping the public mind."

Not surprisingly Wells places the City of London—the international center of banking culture—and its financial credit as responsible for knitting together world economic life over the previous hundred years. With these innovations in communications and finance, but also with the frustrations and wars inherent (so he says) in the existence of independent national states and sovereignties, came about the gradual dawning of the idea of the World-State.

Wells muses, "By this time (1919) there was indeed quite a considerable number of intelligent people in the world who had realized the accumulating necessity of a world government, and a still larger multitude... who had apprehended it instinctively and sentimentally, but there was no one yet who had the intellectual vigor to attack in earnest the problem of substituting a world system for the existing governments." He also describes a one-world government as "manifestly the only possible solution of the human problem."

Like many another wealthy individual advocating a one-world state for the "common good," Wells did not believe that commoners were capable of running that world-state. He described democracies as exercising "a political fiction of a very extraordinary kind: that every subject... was equally capable of making whatever collective decisions had to be made." And so this New World Order would be run by the few, by those upper-crust and white racialist Englishmen and their anglophilic American associates, the men that Wells saw as being capable of doing so.

Referring in the book to the Versailles Peace Conference that followed World War I, Wells points to American President Woodrow Wilson as being "the most susceptible to the intimations of the future... But it is doubtful if at any time he realized that a world pax means a world control of all the vital common interests of mankind."

Within a litany of bright ideas leading up to the acceptance of the one-world-state, Wells notes Wilson's abortive League of Nations, precursor to the U.N., but mourns its failures and regrets that the League, where "The World-State had appeared dimly and evasively, as an aspiration, as a remote possibility... had no executive powers, no certain revenues, no army, no police, and practically no authority to do anything at all." Wells warns the builders of the world-state not to make that mistake again. They would not.

Wells even indicates the presence of conspiratorial factions involved in the creation of the unified world order during the twentieth century, the sort of men that he cozied up to in real life in London's exclusive clubs. Wells says that, "strange Mystery Men were dimly visible through a fog of baffling evasions and mis-statements, manipulating prices and exchanges. Prominent among these Mystery Men was a certain Mr. Montagu Norman, Governor of the Bank of England from 1920 to 1935."

Not surprisingly, this is the same Montagu Norman who was a rabid pre-war partisan of Hitler, and who participated with Hjalmar Schacht, with American intelligence, with Wall Street, and with the Rothschild/Warburg/Schiff banks in the creation of Adolf Hitler and the Third Reich. "Another big obscure financial force in the war and post-war periods," Wells goes on, "was the complex of great private banking ganglia, of which Morgan and Co., with its associated firms, was the most central and most typical."

Wells marks the transition from the date of his actual writing of his book, the early 1930s, to his elitist, technocratic vision of the future with a section about the coming war—World War II, that is—and what he sees as its terrible aftermath, titled, "The Days After Tomorrow: The Age of Frustration."

H.G. Wells was not the only person during the post-World War I period to see that another devastating world war was nearly inevitable. Wells has World War II beginning in 1940 in Poland, over an imagined slight taken by a Nazi over the actions of a Pole of Jewish origin. He characterizes World War II as it was, as an orgy of world violence, and has the fighting end in 1949—staying remarkably close to the actual dates of the conflict—only to be followed by another scourge, that of rampant disease, "The Raid of the Germs."

Given the present-day climate of AIDS, Ebola, Mad Cow disease, and other resistant viral strains—and the persistent rumors of the military engineering of those same diseases—perhaps Wells' dating in this particular should have been moved forward a few years.

In Wells' scenario, years of terrible war and disease result in the near-total disintegration of society. Wells places the final break-up of the nation-states and "America in Liquidation" at 1966, when "the great patchwork of empires and nationalist states, set up during the Age of European Predominance, lost its defining lines, lost its contrasted cultures and its elaborated traditions, and ceased to divide the allegiance and devotion of men of goodwill."

Wells was no prophet as regards his timeline, only a science fiction writer privy to the plans of men with an interest in promoting the coming of the dictatorial world-state. His crystal ball is somewhat cloudy on certain details. Obviously his prediction of the destruction of civilization did not come to pass as an immediate result of World War II, although it is easy to see how Wells might not have foreseen the coming nuclear stalemate which brought about the protracted "cold war" between the U.S. and the USSR.

Wells places responsibility for the creation of the New World Order in the lap of scientists of the future, the group he dubs the "Technocracy." Citing a fictional future book by an author named DeWindt, he says the New World Order, "sustained by multitude of nuclei on DeWindt's pattern scattered throughout the whole world, very much as the Bolshevik political organization had been sustained by the Communist Party, came into existence and spread its ever-growing network about the planet without an immediate struggle. Its revolutionary nature was understood by few people other than its promoters."

Wells dates the formal institution of the Technocracy—the New World Order, by any other name—at the "Second Conference of Basra" in the year 1978. Although his timeline is faulty, the tactics of gradual ideological assimilation that he describes are time-honored and immortalized in the slogan of the Socialist Fabian Society that Wells belonged to: "Proceed slowly," while the thesis-antithesis-synthesis that culminates in the Technocracy is the product of Hegelian thinking. This is the philosophy as well as the method by which the Wellsian vision of the New World Order has come to pass in our own time—come to pass in virtually everything but its formal institution, and in planetary "mopping up" operations.

Exactly where did Wells obtain his information of the plans of the elite? It is interesting that Wells is particularly fond of the adjective "illuminating" when describing an idea he particularly likes, in *The Shape of Things to Come*. He describes President Wilson's one-worldism as "one of the most illuminating events in the early twentieth century." Before a New World Order can be formed, "scattered flashes of understanding had to ignite a steadier illumination."

Is this proof of his card-carrying membership in a group linked to the infamous Illuminati secret society, founded by the German Weishaupt, and alleged by many to be the power behind the institution of the New World Order? Hardly. But it would be a mistake to totally dismiss such clues. The Illuminati, the Freemasons, members of the Skull and Bones and related and offshoot groups have been particularly fond of what they term "revelation of method," secret handshakes, in-group references, and cant language to reveal their presence to their cohorts and to befuddle the "profane" masses. There are solid connections between illuminist groups, the Rhodes Roundtable, the Nazis, British intelligence... and, well, Wells. It is not impossible that Wells is doing just this.

Another explicit statement of the intentions of the New World Order can be read in Wells' nonfiction book *The Open Conspiracy*, published in 1928. The specific directives of Wells' proposed Open Conspiracy program, again identical with what has come to be known as the New World Order, were:

"1. The complete assertion, practical as well as theoretical, of the provisional nature of existing governments and of our acquiescence in them;

"2. The resolve to minimize by all available means the conflicts of these governments, their militant use of individuals and property and their interferences with the establishment of a world economic system;

"3. The determination to replace private local or national ownership of at least credit, transport, and staple production by a responsible world directorate serving the common ends of the race;

"4. The practical recognition of the necessity for world biological controls, for example, of population and disease;

"5. The support of a minimum standard of individual freedom and welfare in the world;

"6. The supreme duty of subordinating the personal life to the creation of a world directorate capable of these tasks and to the general advancement of human knowledge, capacity, and power."

This is the multiple-pronged New World Order scheme in black and white, and while it sounds pretty good on paper, what it doesn't say is paramount: it is a plan to demolish national boundaries and constitutions, and to consolidate control—total control—in a tiny aristocratic governing body. Gone will be the constitutional safeguards that Americans have come to take for granted—gone will be any safeguards at all, any protections whatsoever for the human cogwheels subject to this vast totalitarian scheme.

The New World Order plan would later be furthered by such offshoot groups as the Council on Foreign Relations, the Trilateral Commission, the Club of Rome, the Tavistock Institute, and the Bilderbergers, and realized in the form of such institutions as the United Nations, the International Monetary Fund, and the World Bank. None of these groups or their individual members have acted entirely on their own, but instead are an evolving hydra with many heads. Their actions have always been coordinated in a unified manner, and their shared objective has always been total control of the world. [2]

NOTES:

1. Knuth; Lockhart, Robin Bruce, *Reilly: The First Man*, (Penguin Books, New York, 1987); Wilgus, Neal, *The Illuminoids*. (Sun Publishing Co., Santa Fe, 1978); Sutton, Antony C. *America's Secret Establishment*. (Billings, Montana: Liberty House Press, 1986); Chaitkin, Anton, "British Psychiatry: From Eugenics to Assassination," *EIR (Executive Intelligence Review)*, October 7, 1994; White, Carol, *The New Dark Ages Conspiracy*. (New York: New Benjamin Franklin House, 1984); Dobbs, Zygmund, *Keynes at Harvard*. New York: Probe Research, Inc., 1969; Robertson, Pat, *The New World Order*. (Dallas, Texas: Word Publishing, 1991)

2. Wells, H.G., *The Open Conspiracy: Blueprints for a World Revolution*. (London, Victor Gollancz, 1928); White; Higham, Charles, *Trading With the Enemy*. (New York: Dell, 1983; Chaitkin; White)

Chapter 2:

LODGE BROTHERS AND LITTLE HITLERS

While the one-world elitists in England were scheming for control of the planet, and for the suppression and elimination of "the masses" by one means or another, their American brethren—and brethren they were, in a deal reportedly cut in 1897 to apportion the business of the world—were thinking along the same lines. [1]

In these early years of the 20th century, British Round Table controllers and—acting at a command level in the U.S.— members of the German-spawned Skull and Bones society, worked in concert with the Rockefellers and others to pour huge sums of money into American and German coffers for the research of psychiatry, psychiatric genetics, eugenics, euthanasia, and other means of controlling and "perfecting" what they conceived of as an otherwise imperfect human race, at least in terms acceptable to the elite.

Although it may seem obvious, political and economic imperialism are almost always linked to an imperialism of the mind. In the early 20th century, embryonic studies of biology, eugenics, and the human mind were massively funded to be utilized, not for the overall improvement of the human condition, but for domination of the many by the few, for the "good" of the State.

Skull and Bones is the Yale-based American chapter of a German secret society that is in all probability linked to the famous Illuminati, founded on May 1, 1776, by Adam Weishaupt, Professor of Canon Law at the University of Ingolstadt, and referred to internally as "The Order."

Samuel Russell was the founder of Russell and Company, that shipped opium from Turkey to China in the 19th century.

Numerous of the dominant "Eastern Establishment" families in American affairs to the present day made their fortune in opium shipping. Russell bought out the Perkins Syndicate in 1830, that had previously dominated the American opium shipping market. Among Russell's employees were Warren Delano, Jr. (the grandfather of Franklin Delano Roosevelt), John Cleve Greene (who financed Princeton University), and Joseph Coolidge (his son was the organizer of the United Fruit Company, alleged to be Mafia-associated and involved in drug smuggling, while his grandson was one of the co-founders of the Council on Foreign Relations).

The American Skull and Bones group was founded in 1833 at Yale University by Samuel Russell's cousin, General William Huntington Russell, and Alphonso Taft. In 1831-32 Russell studied in Germany, at that time a hotbed of the Hegelian/ Prussian system that declared the jackbooted state as supreme and the individual as merely a cell in the greater organism.

While in Germany, Russell apparently was contacted by the Bavarian Illuminati or an offshoot group. Skull and Bones was incorporated in the U.S. in 1856, as the Russell Trust, and like the Illuminati is also known as "The Order." Internal documentation of Skull and Bones places the beginnings of its German predecessor group at about the time that the Illuminati was suppressed by the Bavarian Elector. [2]

"The Order [Skull and Bones]," according to historian Antony C. Sutton, "has either set up or penetrated just about every significant research, policy, and opinion-making organization in the United States, in addition to the Church, business, law, government and politics. Not all at the same time, but persistently and consistently enough to dominate the direction of American society. The evolution of American society is not, and has not been for a century, a voluntary development reflecting individual opinion, ideas and decisions at the grass roots. On the contrary, the broad direction has been created artificially and stimulated by The Order." [3]

Part of the New World Order plan, reflected in the views of the people who have promoted it, has always been eugenics: the elimination of "useless eaters" and "inferior races" who are seen only as an impediment in the road of the almighty State. Their aim is a new synthesis in which the only solution for what they consider an overpopulated Earth is for massive depopulation programs to be instituted, and for most of the persons left on the planet to subsist in a virtually pre-industrial tribal state. Aborigines, but aborigines with laptop computers. The controllers, naturally, would not be so burdened by hardship, but would serenely float above society like members of Wells' Technocracy, skimming the cream.

Eugenics as a subject had been disseminated by the English psychologist Francis Galton, beginning in 1883. Again seeing the State rather than the individual as the supreme measure of man, and taking off from Darwin's theory of natural selection, Galton proposed that, through selective intervention through breeding programs and the suppression of less desirable breeding stock, society might be brought up to an overall higher condition.

In 1904 the University College in London established the first chairs in Eugenics and Eugenics in Working Society in London. This led to the creation of the Galton Laboratory for National Eugenics in 1907. The ideas of eugenics, euthanasia, and sterilization for those judged inferior were heartily supported in London, specifically by the "upper crust" of the populace who were eager to do something about the bothersome lower classes. Eugenics philosophy and programs were soon received with approval worldwide, however, including in America.

In 1911, when Judge Kenesaw Mountain Landis ordered Standard Oil broken up, John D. Rockefeller, the first American to amass a billion dollars in assets—equivalent to roughly one hundred billion dollars today—responded by starting the Rockefeller Foundation. The at-the-time astronomical sum of $300 million was transferred into the account of the foundation, and administered by trustees who were family members and employees of the family.

John D. Rockefeller had, in the 1860s, started on his way in the oil business with a boost of British capital. Rockefeller was soon notorious for using violent methods for increasing his wealth. In *The Robber Barons*, Matthew Josephson talks about those methods:

"Where the Standard Oil company could not carry on its expansion by peaceful means, it was ready with violence; its faithful servants knew even how to apply the modern weapon of dynamite. In Buffalo, the Vacuum Oil Co., one of the 'dummy' creatures of the Standard Oil system, became disturbed one day by the advent of a vigorous competitor who built a sizable refinery and located it favorably upon the waterfront. The offices of Vacuum conducted at first a furtive campaign of intimidation. Then emboldened or more desperate, they approached the chief mechanic of the enemy refinery, holding whispered conferences with him in a rowboat on Lake Erie. He was asked to 'do something.' He was urged to 'go back to Buffalo and construct the machinery so it would bust up... or smash up, to fix the pipes and stills so they cannot make a good oil... And then if you would give them a little scare, they not knowing anything about the business. You know how..." The foreman's reward would be a lifelong annuity, and "in due time a small explosion took place in the independent plant." [4]

The Rockefellers also used more sophisticated forms of espionage. John D.'s brother William Rockefeller employed in his business a British intelligence officer named Claude Dansey who, prior to World War I, had been involved in reorganizing the U.S. Army intelligence service. Dansey's protegé General Marlborough Churchill, a relative of Winston Churchill, was given the task of organizing and directing the American intelligence services. After the war, Churchill ran the "Black Chamber," an espionage group with stated allegiance to the State Department and the U.S. Army, but with implicit servitude to the New York monied elite. General Churchill was also responsible for creating the Macy Foundation, which would later be a major conduit for the funding of the CIA's MKULTRA mind control research of the 1950s and later.

In order to change his image as the most despised blackguard of the era, John D. Rockefeller took on the services of Ivy Lee, the top advertising man of the day. Lee suggested that Rockefeller start giving away large amounts of cash. Lee was still in the employ of the Rockefellers when, in the 1930s, he was given the specific assignment by Standard Oil President Walter C. Teagle and Hermann Schmitz of the German I.G. Farben company to supply intelligence on America's reaction to the Nazis, and to concoct and disseminate pro-German propaganda to the Americans. This was no fluke. Rockefeller holdings, including Standard Oil, were extensively intertwined with those of the Nazis, and contact and commerce—including shipments of oil—continued throughout World War II. [5]

Relations with Germany were not so inflamed when Rockefeller monies funded the Kaiser Wilhelm Institute for Psychiatry in Munich, Germany (initially endowed by the Krupp munitions manufacturing family, and James Loeb, brother-in-law of Paul Warburg, the architect of the Federal Reserve in America), to the tune of 11 million marks. The Rockefeller Foundation, in 1925, also provided a grant of $2.5 million to the

22

Institute, and furnished other large grants to the institution throughout the Hitler era.

Also funded by the Rockefellers was the Kaiser Wilhelm Institute for Anthropology, Eugenics, and Human Heredity. These institutions were run by Swiss psychiatrist Ernst Rudin, who was assisted by Otmar Freiherr von Verschuer and Franz J. Kallmann. [6]

James Loeb was a relative of the Warburg banking family, key among the elite controllers in London, and a business partner of William Rockefeller. The Rockefellers and the Warburgs had initially bankrolled the pivotal American Harriman family in their enterprises, channeling monies provided by Sir Ernst Cassell, banker to the British royals. The Rockefellers, the Warburgs, and the Harrimans are familiar faces, appearing again and again during the creation of the primary social control mechanisms of this century, including eugenics and psychiatric mind control.

These families acted in collusion with the Round Table groups founded by Cecil Rhodes, himself a Freemason and operative of the Rothschild banking family, as well as the Skull and Bones society in America.

Although the Rhodes Round Table groups were originally financed primarily by the Rhodes Trust, since 1925 substantial funding has been provided by the Carnegie United Kingdom Trust, whose first president (1902-05) was Bonesman Daniel Coit Gilman—a man key in the subversion of American education—and organizations associated with J.P. Morgan, the Rockefellers, the Whitneys, and the Lazards.

Factually, one of the New World Order's early projects was the creation of the Third Reich. Nazism, in fact, differs very little from the New World Order philosophy except in its emphasis on German nationalism.

After Hitler's ascent to chancellorship in 1933, sponsored by many of the men who lusted after a New World Order, psychiatric institutes controlled by Ernst Rudin were incorporated into the Nazi machine. Rudin became head of the Racial Hygiene Society, and Rudin and his staff, in the Task Force on Heredity chaired by SS chief Himmler, instituted the German sterilization law, based upon existing American laws of the Commonwealth of Virginia.

Far from being an anomaly of the Nazi regime, the horrific eugenics and psychiatric programs instituted in Germany during this time were only a reflection of studies and proposals that were in vogue in Europe and America. It has only recently been revealed that thousands of persons deemed physically or morally unfit continued to be sterilized after World War II—until the middle 1970s—in Sweden, France, Denmark, Finland, and other European countries. Hitler's Reich, however, provided a political climate in which eugenics plans could achieve a particularly ghastly fruition.

Otmar Vershuer, assistant to Ernst Rudin and the director of the Kaiser Wilhelm Institute for Anthropology, Eugenics, and Human Heredity in Berlin, was in turn assisted by a name more familiar to us: Josef Mengele. Vershuer procured funds for Mengele's inhuman research programs at Auschwitz. There, many arrivals at the camp filled out questionnaires from the Kaiser Wilhelm Institute, before a wide variety of frankensteinian experimentation was performed on them. Thousands were tortured and murdered, with body parts shipped to the Rockefeller-financed Kaiser Wilhelm Institute.

Mengele was captured and identified in an Allied prisoner of war camp in 1945, and although his captors knew the nature of his crimes at Auschwitz, he was released. His organizational senior Vershuer also eluded punishment; he was simply hired by a Rockefeller-funded eugenics organization, the Bureau of Human Heredity in Denmark. Rudin's assistant Kallman testified on Rudin's behalf at de-Nazification proceedings, and both men were later involved in the creation of the American Society of Human Genetics, which later organized the currently high profile and highly subsidized Human Genome project that may turn the description of mankind as sheep into more than a metaphor.

In 1936 another player became apparent in the field of psychiatric genetics and mind control experimentation, one hardly whispered of in other exposés of the subject: the Scottish Rite of Freemasonry. The Scottish Rite's loyalties are and have always been with the New World Order vision of one-world government, and the loyalties of at least a certain faction of the men promoting the New World Order have always been to Freemasonry. Glimmerings of the New World Order strategy can in fact be traced back to the days of their predecessor Rosicrucians—not to be confused with the mailorder AMORC currently seen in UFO and psychic magazines—and such early works as Bacon's *New Atlantis.*

In 1936, Dr. Nolan D.C. Lewis, the Scottish Rite's Field Representative of Research on Demential Praecox (incurable insanity), and director of the New York State Psychiatric Institute, was overseeing 14 projects funded by the Supreme Council of the Scottish Rite Northern Supreme Council. At the time of these Freemasonic psychiatric projects, the Duke of Connaught, son of the German Coburg Prince Albert and Queen Victoria, and brother to Nazi sympathizer King Edward VII, was the grand master of the "Mother Grand Lodge" in England. He was also linked to a racialist "shadow government" called the Broederbond that, according to the *Philadelphia Inquirer,* ruled South Africa until recent times, and was only exposed in the 1990s.

Although very little information is available on these Freemasonic psychiatric projects, details on one provide a telling conjunction between the Freemasons and the Nazis. A protegé of Nazi eugenics head Ernst Rudin, psychiatrist Franz J. Kallmann, was forced from his job in Germany when he was discovered to be half Jewish. Kallmann's character can be gauged by the fact that he had argued at the International Congress for Population Science in Berlin in 1935 that, not only should schizophrenics be sterilized, but the same mutilation should also be performed on their apparently healthy relatives.

Kallmann moved to New York and smoothly transitioned into being the director of research at the New York State Psychiatric Institute, an institution headed by the Freemasons' Dr. Lewis. Kallmann was paid by the Scottish Rite of Freemasonry to study 1,000 schizophrenics to prove that mental illness was inherited genetically. The study was published in the U.S. and in Germany in 1938. The preface to the study thanked the Scottish Rite and Rudin. Kallman's report was used as part of the scientific justification for a program launched by the Nazi's infamous T4 Unit, named after its address, Tiergartenstrasse 4, Berlin. Operatives of T4 were reportedly responsible for murdering over 200,000 mental defectives. [7]

NOTES:

1. Knuth, E.C., *The Empire of the City.* (The Noontide Press, 1983)
2. Sutton, Antony C., *America's Secret Establishment.* (Billings, Montana: Liberty House Press, 1986); Anonymous, *Skull & Bones: The Very Heart of the Shadow Government,* May 1996, obtained on the Internet, copy in the author's possession
3. Sutton
4. Knuth; Chaitkin, Anton, "British Psychiatry: From Eugenics to Assassination," *EIR,* October 7, 1994; Josephson, Matthew, *The Robber Barons.* Cited in Allen, Gary. *The Rockefeller File.* (Seal Beach, California: '76 Press,

1976)

5. Andrew, Christopher, *Secret Service: The Making of the British Intelligence Community.* (London, Sceptre Books, 1986); Chaitkin; Allen; Higham, Charles, *Trading With the Enemy.* (New York: Dell, 1983); Hillel and Henry, *Of Pure Blood.* (New York: Pocket Books, 1976)

6. Schreiber, Bernard, *The Men Behind Hitler;* Chaitkin; Weindling, Paul. "The Rockefeller Foundation and German Bio-medical Sciences, 1920-1940", in *Science, Politics and the Public Good: Essays in Honour of Margaret Gowing,* (London: McMillan Press, 1988)

7. Chaitkin, Anton, *Treason in America.* (New York: New Benjamin Franklin House, 1984); Oglesby, Carl, *The Yankee and Cowboy War.* (New York: Berkley, 1977); Sutton; Chaitkin, Anton, "British Psychiatry: From Eugenics to Assassination"; Santa Monica *Outlook,* July 24, 1990; Hillel and Henry; Perloff, James, *The Shadows of Power.* (Appleton, Wisconsin: Western Islands, 1990)

Adam Weishaupt, founder of the Bavarian Illuminati in 1776.

Chapter 3:

TAKING THE "PSYCHE" OUT OF PSYCHOLOGY

Among the basic studies consulted by Rockefeller-funded scientists and others interested in social control at the beginning of this century were those of the official Prussian state psychologist Wilhelm Maximilian Wundt, professor of psychology at the University of Heidelberg. It's fascinating that Wundt's grandfather is mentioned in the Illuminati Provincial Report from Utica (Heidelberg) of September 1782, as being the member known as "Raphael." [1]

During the period before Wundt's ascendancy in the field, psychology was considered to be, simply enough, the study of the soul or mind (psyche). Wundt was to change all that, defining and propagandizing for the materialistic viewpoint that would disinform the work of successors like Pavlov, Skinner, and Watson.

Wundt took a chair in philosophy at the University of Leipzig in 1875, establishing the world's first psychological laboratory, creating the psychological journal *Philosophical Studies,* and redefining psychology for this century. Wundt stated with characteristic modesty, "The work which I here present to the public is an attempt to mark out a new domain in science." Wundt was to remain at the University of Leipzig until his death in 1920.

Wundt's doctrine might be characterized as science meets the Hegelian sturm und drang. One of the primary under-pinnings of the New World Order is that its strategy for world conquest originates in the philosophy of Hegel. Hegel was a professor of philosophy at the University of Berlin, and his works formed the basis for both Marxist dialectical materialism and fascist Statism.

Hegel's stated belief was that Man is subordinate to the State, and only finds fulfillment in obedience to the diktats of the State. As he said, "The State is the absolute reality and the individual himself has objective existence, truth and morality only in his capacity as a member of the State." This philosophy can be and has been used for the justification of any number of atrocities committed upon the human race, and provides an unexamined sub-stratum to the philosophies of many politicians today. If only the omelette (the State) is important, what does it matter if we lose a few million eggs (humans) in the process of cooking up the dish?

Hegel was the originator of the theory of the "dialectic," the idea that conflict determines history. According to Hegel, a force (thesis) dictates its own opposing force (antithesis). These forces in conflict result in the creation of a third force: a synthesis. Out of this synthesis the process begins again. Marx later revised the theory of the dialectic, insisting that only material events were relevant, and that the dialectic was inherent in matter, thus divorcing the idea from metaphysics, at least to his own satisfaction.

From the theory of the dialectic comes the realization that the creation of conflicts can create determined outcomes, or syntheses. Those who promote the New World Order, again and again, are seen to be using the theory of the Hegelian dialectic to bring it about. They are manipulating events, creating conflicts, creating wars, and destroying the lives of untold millions in the bargain. The New World Order is the desired synthesis of the controlling forces operant in the world today.

Naturally, the Hegelian system goes completely against the grain of most people, particularly in the West, who view the individual as the true sovereign. Thus the real enemies are not America vs. the Soviets, or the political Left vs. the Right, but those who would manipulate the yin and yang of history.

To return to Wundt: Like Marx, he maintained that unless a thing could be scientifically quantified, there was no point in considering it or including it as a factor in scientific investigation. All psychological studies should be based upon physiology: body reactions. Wundt essentially redefined psychological studies as studies of the brain and nervous system, and redefined man as an animal without a soul, thus legitimizing at least for his associates and their employers the treating of man as such. This, no doubt, was a welcome rationalization for the controllers who could now happily slaughter whomever they pleased without fear of ultimate spiritual retribution or accounting.

Wundt said, "it truly appears to be a useless waste of energy to keep returning to such aimless discussions about the nature of the psyche, which were in vogue for a while, and practically still are, instead, rather, of applying one's energies where they will produce real results."

According to researcher Paolo Lionni, "For Wundt, will was the direct result of the combination of perceived stimuli, not an independent, individual intention as psychology and philosophy had, with some notable exceptions, held up to that time."

Wundt's rejection of the intangibles of life, such as soul, mind, and free will, have influenced psychiatry and psychology up to the present day. And now you know why shrinks look so weird and often have nervous tics. They have been taught that they do not have a soul. [2]

According to one chronicler of the history of psychology, after Wundt's theories became popular,

"Naturally Leipzig became the Mecca of students who wished to study the 'new' psychology—a psychology that was no longer a branch of speculative philosophy, no longer a fragment of the science of physiology, but a novel and daring and exciting attempt to study mental processes by the experimental and quantitive methods common to all science. For the psychology of Leipzig was, in the eighties and nineties, the newest thing under the sun. It was the psychology for bold young radicals who believed that the ways of the mind could be measured and treated experimentally—and who possibly thought of themselves, in their private reflections, as pioneers on the newest frontier of science, pushing its method into reaches of experience that it had never before invaded. At any rate they threw themselves into their tasks with industry and zest. They became trained introspectionists and, adding introspection to the resources of the physiological laboratories, they attempted the minute analysis of sensation and perception. They measured reaction-times, following their problems into numerous and widespread ramifications. They investigated verbal reactions, thus extending their researches into the field of association. They measured the span and the fluctuations of attention and noted some of its more complex features in the 'complication experiment,' a laboratory method patterned after the situation that gave rise to the astronomer's problem of the 'personal equation.' In their studies of feeling and emotion they recorded pulse-rates, breathing rates, and fluctuations in muscular strength, and in the same connection they developed methods of recording systematically and treating statistically the impressions observed by introspection. They also developed the psychophysical methods and in addition made constant use of resources of the physiological laboratory. And throughout all their endeavors they were dominated by the conception of a psychology that should be scientific as opposed to speculative; always they attempted to rely on exact observation, experimentation, and measurement. Finally when they left Leipzig and worked in laboratories of their own—chiefly in American or German universities—most of them retained enough of the Leipzig impress to teach a psychology that, whatever the subsequent development of the individual's thought, bore traces of the system which was recognized at Leipzig as orthodox." [3]

The essence of Wundt's research was that man was a machine, albeit a soft one. Wundt also went along with the Hegelian axiom that man was simply a cog in the greater machine of the State. Was it just a coincidence that Wundt and his cohorts, funded by and working with the Prussian military and political establishment, provided the justification for treating humanity as individual pieces of nearly valueless machinery, to be tinkered with or destroyed at will?

Wundt, along with other Hegelians, rejected the moral equation in dealing with mankind—thereby putting man in a test tube—and by doing so opened the door to many of the atrocities that followed in this century, including the horrors of mind control. Another mainstay in the arsenal of elitist mind control research was the work of Ivan Petrovich Pavlov, who studied physiology at Leipzig in 1884, five years after Wundt had a laboratory there, and first worked at the St. Petersburg Military Medical Academy in Russia. In 1906 Pavlov cut holes in dogs' cheeks and inserted tubes to measure salivation. A bell was rung just before food was given to the dogs, and after a period of time it was observed that the ringing of the bell alone would increase the rate of the dogs' salivation.

The observation that responses could be so precisely conditioned was then brainstormed to apply to the mental processes of humans—and Pavlov's successors, the shrinks and social controllers, have continued ringing their bells, selectively keeping us drooling ever since. [4]

Shortly after Pavlov was driving dogs crazy in Russia, John B. Watson at Johns Hopkins University—the Hegel hotbed for the

30

United States—was doing the same thing to humans. Watson, the founder of what is known as the behaviorist school of psychology—but is really only research following in the dark shadow of Wundt—believed that complex forms of behavior could be programmed into humans. He conducted one experiment in which a young boy, "Little Albert," was given a white rat to play with. After the boy became accustomed to the rat, Watson would beat on the floor with a steel bar every time the rat was brought in. The boy was understandably terrified by such lunatic behavior, and eventually reacted with terror every time the rat was given to him, and finally, whenever any small furry animal was around him.

Dr. Watson himself drooled over the possibilities of this kind of mechanical conditioning of human beings: "Give me the baby, and I'll make it climb and use its hands in constructing buildings of stone or wood... I'll make it a thief, a gunman or a dope fiend. The possibilities of shaping in any direction are almost endless... Men are built, not born." Watson later became a highly successful advertising executive, although there are no records available of what happened to Little Albert. [5]

In the late 1930s, Harvard psychologist Burrhus Frederick (B.F.) Skinner, an unapologetic student of Wundt's theories, and a member of U.S. Army intelligence, fine-tuned the art of human control into what he termed "operant conditioning," becoming a guru to generations of mind shapers that followed. His simple (and quite familiar, by this time) notion was that the reinforcement of a repeated negative stimulus (punishment) or positive stimulus (reward) formed the basis for learned behavior.

Skinner's early experiments produced pigeons that could dance, do figure eights, and play table tennis. His experiments did not stop with pigeons.

Skinner's most famous invention, aimed at producing a "socialized child," was the environmentally controlled "Skinner box," a crib-sized container into which he put scores of children, including his own. His ultimate aim was not only to control the behavior of isolated persons, but to gain insights into how to control society as a whole. [6]

Skinner's most explicit statement of his philosophy, ultimately one of world control, is contained in his book *Walden Two,* written in 1948. The book describes a perfect communist utopia run along behaviorist lines.

In *Walden Two* society is run by Frazier, a straw man designed to dramatize Skinner's beliefs about human conditioning. Below Frazier in the pigeon-pecking order are six Planners, who in turn run Managers, who are held responsible for the "controlees" who perform the menial tasks of daily life. Members of the *Walden Two* society follow a puritanical "Code of Conduct," that applies to virtually every aspect of day-to-day life, including the forbidding of midnight snacks. Education is a subset of "human engineering," and children are turned over to the group by the parents. "Home is no place to raise children," drawls Frazier, his philosophy one that has seemingly been adopted by many current-day shrinks and social workers.

The essence of *Walden Two* is the application of positive and negative reinforcement to create a smoothly running state, free of such unwanted encumbrances as crime and choice.

Skinner followed up his vision of *Walden Two* in 1971, with his vastly hyped nonfiction book *Beyond Freedom and Dignity*, awarded the honor of being the most important book of the year by the *New York Times.* "What is needed is more control, not less," Skinner reminded us. [7]

It may be revelatory that throughout his life, Skinner was interested in mechanical contraptions, even working for years on a perpetual motion machine. His view of the composition of human beings was no less mechanical—a vision which characterizes the philosophies of most psychiatrists to this day. This atheist/materialistic viewpoint, again, provides a justification for the atrocities which are daily committed in the name of science: How can it be unethical to tinker with, or even destroy a human, if in fact he is really only a machine?

With B.F. Skinner, the philosophy of psychosocial control was finely honed. Although many psychologists today insist that the behaviorist's vision of a controlled world is crude and outdated, and that a docile society cannot be engineered by science, they protest too much. The behaviorist doctrine—forecast by Hegel, invented by Wundt, and fostered by a legion of followers in science and education—is firmly in place in the halls of academia and in the offices of population-shaping worldwide, and are being applied at every level of society. The elite could not be happier if the whole world was placed in a Skinner box.

NOTES:

1. Sutton, Antony C., *America's Secret Establishment*, (Liberty House Press, Billings, Montana, 1986); Lionni, Paolo, *The Leipzig Connection*. (Sheridan, Oregon: Delphian Press, 1988)

2. "Hegel, Georg Wilhelm Friedrich." New York: Funk & Wagnalls *New Encyclopedia*, 1973; Lionni

3. Heidbreder, Edna, *Seven Psychologies*. (New York: D. Appleton-Century Company, Inc., 1933)

4. Lionni; Bowart, Walter, *Operation Mind Control*. (New York: Dell Paperback, 1977); "Pavlov, Ivan Petrovich," *The Encyclopedia Americana*, (New York, Americana Corporation, 1963)

5. Watson, John B., quoted in Bowart; Packard, Vance. *The People Shapers*. (New York: Little, Brown, 1977)

6. Bowart; Packard; Judge, John, "The Secret Government," *Dharma Combat* number 10

7. Packard; Skinner, B.F., *Walden Two*. (New York: Macmillan Company, 1962)

Colonel Sir Claude Dansey, spymaster for the Rockefellers.

Top: Aldous Huxley. Bottom: John Rawlings
Reese, Tavistock controller.

Chapter 4:

HEY TEACHER, LEAVE THOSE KIDS ALONE!

One of the major world arenas in which Hegelian philosophy and the materialistic anti-psychology of Wundt has been applied is that of education.

In 1819 in Prussia the first compulsory schooling for children was instituted. According to educator John Taylor Gatto, society in Prussia was divided "into children who will become policy makers; children who will become assistants to policy makers (the engineers, architects, lawyers, and doctors); and the children who will be the vast, massed, used.

"Prussia sets up a three-tier school system, in which one half of one percent of the population is taught to think. They go to school called academie. Five and a half percent of the population go to Realschulen, where they partially learn to think, but not completely, because Prussia believed their defeat at the hands of Napoleon was caused by people thinking for themselves at times of stress on the battlefield. They were going to see to it that scientifically this couldn't happen. The lowest 94%, (that's some pyramid, right?) went to volkschulen, where they were to learn harmony, obedience, freedom from stressful thinking, how to follow orders. They worked out a system that would in fact guarantee such results. In the volkschulen, it was to divide whole ideas (which really simultaneously participate in math, science, social thinking, language and art) into subjects which hardly had existed before, to divide the subjects further into units; to divide the time into small enough units of time. With enough variations in the course of a day, no one would know what was going on." [1]

In the middle of the last century a member of the secret Skull and Bones society, following in the Prussian tradition, set in motion an American educational revolution that has subverted the entire system toward the goals of the New World Order. That man was Daniel Coit Gilman, first president of Johns Hopkins University and of the Carnegie Institution. Gilman studied Hegelian philosophy at the University of Berlin in 1854-55. Also at the University of Berlin during this time was the earlier mentioned Wilhelm Wundt, who was key in applying Hegelian-styled psychology to the world.

Gilman came from a family of Bonesmen and, after he returned from Germany, in 1856 became treasurer of Skull and Bones. Simultaneously, Gilman became assistant librarian at Yale, and was appointed to the position of head librarian two years later.

During the same period Skull and Bones covertly took over the administration of Yale University, with the presidency of the school from that period forward turned over to a succession of illuminized Bonesmen. According to *The Iconoclast* (October 13, 1873),

"They have obtained control of Yale. Its business is performed by them. Money paid to the college must pass into their hands, and be subject to their will. No doubt they are worthy men in themselves, but the many whom they looked down upon while in college, cannot so far forget as to give money freely into their hands. Men in Wall Street complain that the college comes straight to them for help, instead of asking each graduate for his share. The reason is found in a remark made by one of Yale's and America's first men: 'Few will give but Bones men, and they care far more for their society than they do for the college.' The Woolsey Fund has but a struggling existence, for kindred reasons... Here, then, appears the true reason for Yale's poverty. She is controlled by a few men who shut themselves off from others, and assume to be their superiors..."

Gilman met with Frederick T. Gates, who ran Rockefeller's foundations, and he implored him to set up the Southern Educational Board, merging the Slater and Peabody funds. Gilman called the foundation the General Education Board—signaling his intentions. The organization was later renamed The Rockefeller Foundation. [2]

Gilman was the first president of Johns Hopkins University, and he carefully chose for the faculty members from the Skull and Bones and other groups of the Hegelian stripe. Among those was G. Stanley Hall, the first of Wundt's American students

36

to make a mark. Hall's training in Leipzig was paid for by a loan from a member of Scroll & Key, sister society to Skull and Bones at Yale. In Leipzig, Hall immersed himself in Hegelian-inspired psychological studies taught by materialist psychologists like Hartmann, Helmholtz, and his greatest influence, Wundt. Returning to America in 1883, he took over the psychological laboratory at the new Johns Hopkins, and started the American Psychological Association and the *American Journal of Psychology*.

According to Hall, "The psychology I taught was almost entirely experimental and covered for the most part the material that Wundt had set forth in the later and larger edition of Physiological Psychology." [3]

In 1889 Hall was chosen as the first president of the newly established Clark University in Worcester, Massachusetts. Hall was the mentor of one of the most influential names in American education of this century: John Dewey.

Dewey studied under Hall at Johns Hopkins, moving on to teach at the universities of Michigan and Minnesota. Another major influence upon Dewey was the Hegelian philosopher George Sylvester Morris, who had received his doctorate from the University of Berlin. According to Dewey, echoing the sentiments of his Prussian mentors,

"There is no god, and there is no soul. There are no needs for the props of traditional religion.

"With dogma and creed excluded, then immutable truth is also dead and buried.

"There is no room for fixed, natural law or permanent moral absolutes." [4]

Dewey published the first American textbook on Hegelian philosophy as applied to the Wundtian psychological innovations in his book *Psychology*. In 1895 he joined the faculty at the Rockefeller-funded University of Chicago, heading the philosophy, psychology, and teaching departments, and establishing an education laboratory called the Dewey School, later known as the Laboratory School of the University of Chicago.

Dewey followed the Wundtian example in his insistence that education was not the teaching of mental skills such as reading and writing, but in the channeling of raw experiences to the evolving mind of the child; a sort of psychic Skinner's box version of education. The traditional role of the teacher as educator was replaced by the teacher as shrink, socializer, eugenicist and herald of the coming world superstate.

Dewey believed that the purpose of public schools was to "take an active part in determining the social order of the future... according as the teachers align themselves with the newer forces making for social control of economic forces." [5]

Dewey also remarked that "The school is primarily a social institution. Education being a social process, the school is simply that form of community life in which all those agencies are concentrated that will be most effective in bringing the child to share in the inherited resources of the race, and to use his own powers for social ends. Education, therefore, is a process of living and not a preparation for future living." [6]

For Dewey, the issue was always how the child related to the State, rather than how the State related to the child.

Another student of Wundt, who was to prove to be perhaps the most successful popularizer of the new psychology that abolished the psyche, was James McKeen Cattell. Cattell was Wundt's assistant in Leipzig in the years 1883-86, receiving his Ph.D. from the grand old man in 1886. Lecturing in Cambridge in 1887, Cattell met and was converted to Social Darwinism by Darwin's cousin, the English psychologist Francis Galton, the man responsible for the popularization at the beginning of this century of the science of eugenics and selective breeding.

In 1887 Cattell established at the University of Pennsylvania a psychological laboratory of the Wundtian mold, then moved on in 1891 to head the new psychology department at Columbia University. Cattell was tremendously influential in disseminating the new overtly materialistic psychology, and did so by establishing a host of magazines, including *The Psychological Review, Science, Scientific Monthly,* and *School and Society.* He also published reference works including *American Men of Science, Leaders in Education,* and *The Directory of American Scholars,* an effective strategy for screwing Wundtian-school psychologists into the mainstream of American thought.

Another of Cattell's questionable feats was the abolition of the use of phonics methods for teaching reading. Cattell popularized the "Look-Say" method of teaching reading, a technique that according to some sources had been invented by Thomas Hopkins Gallaudet for teaching the deaf. Although Gallaudet was not a member of Skull and Bones, two of his sons attended Yale and were initiated into the secret society.

Following upon the insight of Gallaudet in teaching the deaf, Cattell came to the conclusion that the direct memorization of words would increase literacy if applied to normal students. Experience in subsequent years has not proven this to be the case, obviously, and one byproduct of Cattell's advocacy of the "Look-Say" theory is that as we approach the 21st century millions of American adults cannot read or write at all.

The whole story about Gallaudet may in fact be a sanitization of what actually happened. Educator John Taylor Gatto attributes the "Look-Say" method to the Prussian system of schooling, where this system of not-teaching-reading was used essentially to disadvantage all but the privileged class. Gatto says, "So they figured out that by replacing the alphabet system of teaching reading we teach sounds. (The Prussian System was a whole sentence system, rather than a whole word system. You memorize whole sentences.) If they could get the kids and keep them from reading well for the first six and seven years, then it didn't matter after that. They had broken the link between printed information." [7]

Possibly the most effective Trojan horse for injecting the Wundtian theory of man-as-machine into the American educational establishment was an individual, James Earl Russell, who studied under and received his doctorate from Wundt in 1894. Russell became dean of the New York College for the Training of Teachers, which he would run for thirty years while heavily weighting its faculty with practitioners of the Wundtian school, at the same time turning it into the largest institution for the training of teachers in the country.

Another luminary in the shrink-wrapping of American education was Edward Lee Thorndike, who studied with Wundtians Armstrong and Judd at Wesleyan University, graduating in 1895. Thorndike moved on to Columbia University, where he specialized in studying animals in "puzzle box" mazes, finally finding his niche at Teachers College under Russell.

According to Thorndike, teaching was "The art of giving and withholding stimuli with the result of producing or preventing certain responses. In this definition the term stimulus is used widely for any event which influences a person,—for a word spoken to him, a look, a sentence which he reads, the air he breathes, etc. etc. The term response is used for any reaction made by him, —a new thought, a feeling of interest, a bodily act, any mental or bodily condition resulting from the stimulus. The aim of the teacher is to produce desirable and prevent undesirable changes in human beings by producing and preventing certain responses. The means at the disposal of the

39

teacher are the stimuli which can be brought to bear upon the pupil, —the teacher's words, gestures, and appearance, the condition and appliances of the school room, the books to be used, and objects to be seen, and so on through a long list of the things and events which the teacher can control." [8]

Thorndike further stated,

"Studies of the capacities and interests of young children indicate the advisability of placing little emphasis before the age of six upon either the acquisition of those intellectual resources known as the formal tools —reading, spelling, arithmetic, writing, etc. —or upon abstract intellectual analysis...

"Despite rapid progress in the right direction the program of the average elementary school is too narrow and academic in character. Traditionally the elementary school has been primarily devoted to teaching the fundamental subjects, the three R's, and closely related disciplines... Artificial exercises, like drills on phonetics, multiplication tables, and formal writing movements, are used to a wasteful degree. Subjects such as arithmetic, language, and history include content that is intrinsically of little value. Nearly every subject is enlarged unwisely to satisfy the academic ideal of thoroughness. That the typical school overemphasizes instruction in these formal, academic skills as a means of fostering intellectual resources... is a justifiable criticism... Elimination of unessentials by scientific study, then, is one step in improving the curriculum." [9]

The emphasis by Thorndike and his fellows on the "socialization" of the student—in fact the subjugation of the student to the social order—as opposed to the teaching of specific skills, is another factor that has led to a general breakdown of literacy in the United States, while at the same time providing no noticeable increase in the ability to socialize—in fact, obviously the contrary.

Thorndike believed that, "Education is interested primarily in the general interrelation of man and his environment, in all the changes which make possible a better adjustment of human nature to its surroundings."

This is another important aspect of Thorndike's and all of the other latter-day Wundtians' philosophies. Man is an animal who must adapt to the environment, that is, the social system and political regime, rather than adapting the environment to his own vision. Man is to be conditioned to accept the circumstances that he finds himself in, not learn to change them. Again, the controlling elite have no qualms about

40

changing society or the environment to conform to their own whims—even if it takes 'dozing a rainforest—it is only the rebellious public-schooled who must have the devastating defect of individuality brainwashed out of them. The socialization techniques used by the Wundtians create robots, not sociable people.

Working out of the Teachers College at Columbia University and the later-established Lincoln School, and dependent upon a steady infusion of Rockefeller money, the major lights in the field of Wundtian psychology, including Thorndike, Cattell, Russell, and Dewey, kick-started "educational" psychology, remaking the face of American schooling. And many of these disciples of Wundt were very straightforward in proclaiming that the purpose of educational psychology was the creation of a New World Order.

By the 1950s the Teachers College was indisputably the most powerful force in education in America, with approximately one third of all school presidents and deans, and one fourth of all American teachers accredited there. It must have been reassuring to the Rockefellers and their ilk to see that materialistic psychology and education had won, and was now accepted as the norm in American school systems.

NOTES:

1. Gatto, John Taylor, "Origins & History of American Compulsory Schooling," an interview conducted by Jim Martin, *Flatland* magazine number 11

2. Sutton, Antony C., *America's Secret Establishment.* (Billings, Montana: Liberty House Press, 1986); Mullins, Eustace, *The Curse of Canaan.* (Staunton, Virginia: Revelation Books, 1987)

3. Hall, G. Stanley, Cited in Sutton

4. Dewey, John. Cited in Ralph A. Epperson. *The New World Order.* (Tucson, Arizona: Publius Press, 1990)

5. Lionni; Sutton; Dewey, John. Quoted in Allen, Gary, "Hands off our Children!," *American Opinion,* volume XVIII, No. 9, October, 1975

6. Dewey, John, *My Pedagogic Creed,* cited in Sutton

7. Gatto

8. Thorndike, Edward L., *The Principles of Teaching Based on Psychology.* (New York: A.G. Seiler, 1925)

9. Thorndike, Edward L., and Arthur I. Gates, *Elementary Principles of Education.* (New York: Macmillan, 1929)

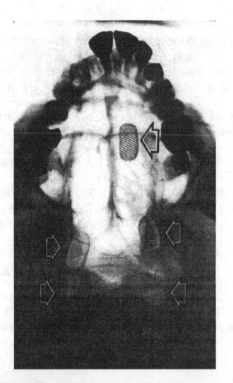

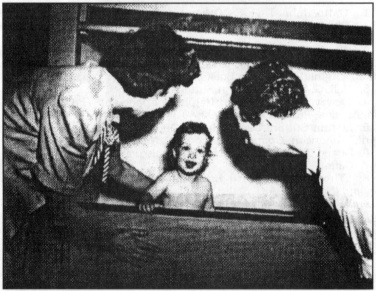

Top: X-ray photos of brain transmitters. Bottom: Dr. and Mrs. Skinner view daughter Debbie in a "Skinner box." Debbie committed suicide in her 20s.

Chapter 5:

TAVISTOCK

The Tavistock Insitute for Human Relations, known by insiders as the "Freud Hilton," has been a major nexus for the worldwide psychological manipulation that has taken place over the last 50 years. The Tavistock story—at least the public version of it—begins immediately after World War II, when members of British military intelligence created the Institute. In its own literature Tavistock is described as an organization of "dynamic psychiatry" which was intended to practice what they term "societry" on the planet as a whole—and what I term world mind control.

British military intelligence itself, in the persons of many of its chief players, has been aimed at a one-world government since its inception. British Secret Service directors on an almost one-for-one basis have been advocates of Fabian socialism. [1]

It is alleged that Tavistock was set up much earlier than its announced inception, over 20 years prior in 1921, by Major John Rawlings Reese, on the orders of the Round Table's Royal Institute of International Affairs (also known as Chatham House). The RIIA, along with the American Council on Foreign Relations, had been founded in 1919 during the Versailles Peace Conference, both being early New World Order executive arms.

Reese was the man who dreamed of "building a society in which it is possible for any member of any social group to be treated [psychiatrically], without resort to legal means, and even if they do not desire such treatment." At the end of World War II, Reese called for the creation of "psychological shock troops" who would fan out from the Tavistock Institute to engineer the future direction of society. [2]

In 1932 Tavistock was put under the directorship of the German psychologist Kurt Lewin. Lewin was a founder of the National Training Laboratories and director of the Harvard

Psychological Clinic, and—an odd qualification for a psychiatrist, I think—one of the key players in the original creation of the OSS in America.

Lewin is credited with much of the original Tavistock research into mass brainwashing, applying the results of repeated trauma and torture in mind control to society at large. If terror can be induced on a widespread basis into a society, Lewin has stated, then society reverts to a *tabula rasa,* a blank slate, a situation where control can easily be instituted from an exterior point.

Put it another way: By the creation of controlled chaos, the populace can be brought to the point where it willingly submits to greater control. Lewin maintained that society must be driven into a state equivalent to an "early childhood situation." He termed this societal chaos "fluidity."

Tavistock's focus in the early days was on strategic warfare studies, in particular of Germany, with emphasis on the re-education of that errant New World Order colony. During World War II many of the Institute's members, including its founder, Reese, ran the British Psychological Warfare Directorate and subsidiary organizations based in the United States. After World War II Tavistock can functionally be considered to have become a part of Britain's Psychological Warfare Bureau, now working on projects dealing with the brainwashing of populations. [3]

Tavistock is governed by what it calls an invisible college, echoing antique occultist terminology and reminding one that British intelligence was founded by Freemasons and remains deeply Freemasonic to this day. The original use of the term "invisible college," prior to the announced creation of Tavistock, was Reese's reference to an informal association he had created of all the psychiatrists then working in the British military.

For funding, the Tavistock Institute relies on large grants from anonymous benefactors—with no doubt a substantial portion coming directly from the Crown—along with grants from the Rockefeller Foundation, the Ford Foundation, the Carnegie Institute, the World Health Organization, and the British Home Office. Tavistock is also interlinked worldwide with a vast network of other organizations and think tanks, including UNESCO, WHO, the World Federation for Mental Health, and the Rand Corporation. Tavistock is simply a front group for the psychological imposition of the New World Order on the planet, and its main philosophic tool is the Hegelian dialectic framed in the terms of Lewin.

The Rockefellers have always been prominent in deciding the course of Tavistock. According to the official chronicler of the group,

"The Rockefeller Foundation, before making us a grant, would need to be satisfied, not only by our policies... but also with the persons to carry them out." [4]

In a Tavistock-funded profile of the group, it is stated that the role of the institute has been:

"(a) The invention of the command psychiatrist as a medical-social role carrying out reconnaissance in a large structure and defined group, leading to the ascertainment and recognition of critical problems in the sphere of human relations and management.

"(b) The invention of social psychiatry as a policy science permitting preventative technical intervention in large-scale problems...

"(c) The fashioning of a whole series of military institutions which concretely and effectively implemented the policies advocated.

"(d) The invention of new types of therapeutic communities.

"(e) The invention of cultural psychiatry...

"Capability nurtured in the Tavistock for the psychiatrist to work with lay personnel—in this case the military—in a collaborative partnership. In other words, the strategy of command psychiatry and the developments to which it led were psycho-dynamically conceived and based."

Tavistock, born from the collaboration of the international monied elite, military intelligence, and the materialistic psychiatric community, refers to its self-admitted "military" orientation as Operation Phoenix—again, a Freemasonic symbol that it shares with the infamous Vietnam War assassination program. One is reminded of the Freemasonic legend " *Ordo Ab Chao*," Order Out of Chaos, which could just as easily describe the Tavistock method of destroying a target subject, or a target population, prior to reprogramming; the Tavistock modus operandi.

Throughout the Tavistock literature—either official or Tavistock-inspired—they reiterate their "global vision" and make it clear that the institute is intended to work its long-term "society" on the world regardless of the wishes of individuals who inhabit it.

One of the most successful of Tavistock-offshoot organizations is what was originally known as the   National Training

Laboratories (NTL), and now the NTL Institute for Applied Behavioral Sciences, founded in 1947. Located in Bethel, Maine, the mission of the NTL is to give Lewin-inspired "group dynamics" sessions to American leaders. Again, during group sessions "dissonance" or stress is introduced to destroy the individual's previous beliefs, and then a new, group-oriented personality is coaxed forth. This is the primary technical method used by a myriad of Tavistock-influenced "sensitivity" groups like Alanon and Esalen.

Since the 1950s, NTL has processed the majority of America's corporate leaders in its programs, while simultaneously running the same programs for various segments of the government, including the Navy, the Department of Education, and the State Department. None dare call it mind control. [5]

Eric Trist, the chairman of Tavistock's governors, in 1963 described his and Tavistock's work on mass brainwashing, delineating in detail his theory of "social turbulence," based upon the theories of Hegel, although again, Trist is far more quick to cite Lewin.

Trist postulated that the administering of a series of traumatizing shocks upon a society would destabilize it, lowering the overall character of the society's reasoning. Trist suggested that by late 1963 the world had moved into a condition of "permanent social turbulence" that would serve to usher in a new condition of society, a new paradigm, and a new possibility for remaking the face of the planet.

The nature of the permanent social turbulence that Trist foresaw is further defined in a book published in 1975 by one of Trist's associates, Fred Emery. The book, *Futures We Are In*, likens the condition of current day society to the violent punk welfare state of Anthony Burgess' novel, *A Clockwork Orange*, written in the 1960s.

Emery, in reflection of Trist, also trumpets Hegel. He describes the first stage of the breakdown of society as being "superficiality," in which previous societal values are questioned and discarded. He uses as an example of this the death of the Judeo-Christian paradigm.

The next inevitable state is "segmentation," in which societal institutions break down, resulting in a reversion to paranoid groups of individuals hostile to each other.

The next stage in the breakdown of society would be the launching of a fascist movement akin to the Nazis.

The final and most disrupted state of society is termed disassociation, in which the individual becomes the entirety of society for himself, and is isolated from other members of the group. The dominant culture of the society becomes "fantasy and superstition." According to Trist, the current "wired society" where the main interaction of the individual is with electronic media is only a metaphor for disassociation. Cyberpunks, New Agers, and couch potatoes, take note. It is interesting to note that the same progression can be seen in the microcosm with the induction of the multiple personality, an oft-asserted goal of intelligence agency brain-banging.

In May 1967 at Queen Elizabeth's palatial estate in Deauville, France, a conference was convened. It was intended to update participants on ongoing projects of the Tavistock network. This was the "Conference on Transatlantic Technological Imbalance and Collaboration," sponsored by the Scientific and Technological Committee of the North Atlantic Assembly and the Foreign Policy Research Institute. Among the projects mentioned at the conference were the collaboration of Emery and Trist on "social turbulence," and the SRI-Tavistock "Images of Man" project.

Participants in the conference included Tavistock's Harland Cleveland; Willis Harman of the Tavistock offshoot Stanford Research Institute; Dr. Zbigniew Brzezinski, the future Carter national security advisor and the Trilateral Commission's founding executive director; and Fred Emery, who had earlier delineated the stages of societal disintegration in his *Futures We Are In*. Other participants were Dr. Aurelio Peccei, later to head the zero-growth fixated Club of Rome, then chairman of the Economic Committee of the Atlantic Institute, an important NATO think tank; and Sir Alexander King and Sir Solly Zuckerman, advisors to the British crown.

Fleshing out the hologram of elitist New World Order planning is the information that Brzezinski is believed by many in Western intelligence organizations to be a KGB mole, recruited by British Round Tabler and Rothschild-Warburg agent William Yandell Elliot. Henry Kissinger is also linked to this group, reportedly after being recruited to a KGB homosexual blackmail ring focused on the EICOM G-2 headquarters in Oberammergau, Germany, at the end of the second world war. Kissinger was a member of the U.S. Army 970th Counterintelligence Corps, involved in creating the Nazi "rat lines" that enabled many prominent Nazis to escape prosecution at the end of World War II.

Kissinger's reported mentor was Fritz Kraemer of the Pentagon plans division, who also groomed Alexander Haig. Kraemer's secret life during WWII, according to deceased conspiracy researcher Mae Brussel, was that of a special lieutenant to Hitler. What does it matter whose side you are on, the controllers might say? Both sides in the World War, or for that matter the Cold War, only served to foster the synthesis of the New World Order. [6]

The principles that were agreed on at the Tavistock conference will sound very familiar to those who have been following the reshaping of human institutions and values by the New World Order. These include the belief that man should not dominate nature, but instead become a part of it, with no more rights and privileges than, say, the purple-assed baboon in the wild. Governments are obsolete and will be replaced by other, more encompassing institutions. Mankind is moving into a de-industrialized post-technological society, an "information age," the Age of Aquarius; again, aborigines with laptop computers.

The primary impetus towards the evolution to the post-technological society are the repeated shocks and chaos taking place, including such events as the Kennedy assassination, the Vietnam War, and the assault on traditional institutions and thinking by the psychedelic counterculture.

This philosophy was described exactly by Dr. William Sargent of the Tavistock Institute in 1957 in his book *Battle for the Mind—A Physiology of Conversion and Brain-Washing*. Again, the idea is that the micro reflects the macro: the occultist dictum, "As above, so below."

Sargent said, "Various types of beliefs can be implanted in many people after brain function has been sufficiently disturbed by accidentally or deliberately induced fear, anger, or excitement. Of the results caused by such disturbances, the most common one is temporarily impaired judgment and heightened suggestibility. Its various group manifestations are sometimes classed under the heading of 'herd instinct,' and appear most spectacularly in wartime, during severe epidemics, and in all similar periods of common danger, which increase anxiety and so individual and mass suggestibility."

Out of the Tavistock conference also came Zbigniew Brzezinski's 1968 book *The Technotronic Age*, that posits an information society whose basis of competition is replaced by "amusement focus" based on "spectator spectacles (mass sports and TV) providing an opiate for increasingly purposeless masses... New forms of social control may be needed to limit the indiscriminate exercise by the individual of their new powers. The possibility of extensive chemical mind control... will call for a social definition of the common criteria of restraint as well as utilization." And some think that Guy DeBord's *Society of the Spectacle* isn't literal.

In the Technotronic Age, the "nation state as a fundamental unit of man's organized life has ceased to be the principal creative force: International banks and multinational corporations are acting and planning in terms that are far in advance of the political concepts of the nation-state."

Brzezinski also says of the "Technotronic Age" that, "At the same time the capacity to assert social and political control over the individual will vastly increase. It will soon be possible to assert almost continuous control over every citizen and to maintain up-to-date files, containing even the most personal details about health and personal behavior of every citizen in addition to the more customary data.

"These files will be subject to instantaneous retrieval by the authorities. Power will gravitate into the hands of those who control information. Our existing institutions will be supplanted by pre-crisis management institutions, the task of which will be to identify in advance likely social crises and to develop programs to cope with them.

"This will encourage tendencies through the next several decades toward a Technotronic Era, a dictatorship leaving even less room for political procedures as we know them. Finally, looking ahead to the end of the century, the possibility of biochemical mind control and genetic tinkering with man, including beings which will function like men and reason like them as well, could give rise to some difficult questions."

A book written at the same time by the conference chairman, Aurellio Peccei, was titled *The Chasm Ahead*, and it too echoed the prevailing elitist themes: Peccei reiterated that a one-world government was the only solution to the problems of the world. Also required was that Russia and the U.S. would have to enter into partnership in global planning and enforcement—a theme that has become increasingly obvious in recent years with the *Spetznaz* setting up shop in Peoria and Tulsa, and Clinton trying to lease the Long Beach Naval Yards to the mainland Chinese. [7]

One of the footsoldiers of Tavistock—currently fallen from grace at least in the eyes of the American people—is, believe it or not, Newt Gingrich. The truth about Newt exists much in contradiction to his image as a staunch upholder of Republican ideals and conservative family values. Gingrich is in fact another Trojan horse whose mentor is the "futurist" Alvin Toffler. Toffler's book *The Third Wave* describes the current technocratic takeover of the world, the acquisition of virtually all wealth by a tiny elite, and the relegation of the vast majority of the populace to a Third World foraging in the garbage heaps of the rich.

According to Gingrich, speaking to a crowd of yuppies at a congress on "Democracy in Virtual America," "In the mid-to-late-'60s, I read Drucker's *The Age of Discontinuities*, Boulding's *The Meaning of the Twentieth Century*, Bell's *Beyond Post-Industrial Society*—all of which were precursors to the first popularizer of this notion, which was *Future Shock*, which was written basically a quarter of a century ago. Now, those four books described everything we're living through for all practical purposes... and nothing has changed for a quarter of a century... I've worked with the Tofflers for 20 years in trying to figure out this interesting question. Since this is all intellectually obvious, why can't we break through?"

Toffler is a protegé of Kenneth Boulding, who is one of Tavistock's leading lights in the United States, and according to his wife founded the revolutionary Students for a Democratic Society (SDS). Boulding and his wife were responsible for much bridge building between the Fabian "societrists" of Tavistock and the New Left in the 1960s.

Gingrich revealed his not-so-hidden roots when he mentioned the "anticipatory democracy" project in his introduction to *The Third Wave*. "A/D," as it is termed, was a project fielded by Tavistock in the 1960s intended to bring about a New Age shift toward anything but traditional values, unless it is the Wellsian "Open Conspiracy" traditional values of the elite controllers. Among the later projects that would be created by participants in the "A/D" project would be the Malthusian Club of Rome and the Carter administration's Global 2000 plan.

Gingrich was ushered into the Tavistock orbit in 1965 when, as an undergraduate at Emory University, a professor at Georgia Tech introduced him to the work of Boulding and Toffler. After getting his Ph.D. at Tulane, Gingrich took a teaching job at West Georgia State College, outside Atlanta, the East Coast node of the "humanist psychology movement." One of Gingrich's closest associates was the anything-but-Republican Jimmy Carter, who put Newt in charge of an A/D pilot project called Goals for Georgia. It was only later that Gingrich got his calling as a banner-waver for the New Right. [8]

NOTES:

1. Dicks, Henry Victor, *Fifty Years of the Tavistock Clinic.* (London, England: Routledge & K. Paul, 1970); Douglas and Thompson, "New attempt to cover up the English side of the Bolshevik's 'Trust', *EIR*, June 5, 1987; Wolfe, L., "The Tavistock roots of the 'Aquarian Conspiracy', *EIR*, January 12, 1996
2. Dicks; Zepp-LaRouche, Helga, *The Hitler Book.* (New York: The Schiller Institute, 1984); Wolfe
3. Dr. John Coleman, *Conspirator's Hierarchy: The Story of the Committee of 300.* (America West Publishers, Carson City, Nevada, 1992); Zepp-LaRouche; Dicks
4. Dicks
5. Dicks; Wolfe
6. John Judge, "Nazis in the White House: The Reagan Administration & the Fascist International, *Overthrow,* Fall 1985, and "Good Americans", *Dharma Combat* number 11
7. Coleman; Sutton and Wood, *Trilaterals Over Washington.* (Scottsdale, Arizona: The August Corporation, 1978)
8. *Anticipatory Democracy—People in the Politics of the Future,* Clement Bezold, ed. (New York: Random House, 1978); Steinberg, Jeffrey, "Anticipatory democracy," *EIR*, January 12, 1996

Walter Bowart's controversial 1978 book.

RADIO 'MATADOR' STOPS WIRED BULL

Continued From Page 1, Col. 5

our understanding of the mind."

"We are in a precarious race," he said, "between the acquisition of many megatons of destructive power and the development of intelligent human beings who will make intelligent use of the formidible forces at our disposal."

Based on His Experiments

Dr. Delgado's contention that brain research has reached a stage of refinement where it can contribute to the solution of some of these problems is based he said, on many of his own experiments.

These have shown, he explained, that "functions traditionally related to the psyche, such as friendliness, pleasure or verbal expression, can be induced, modified and inhibited by direct electrical stimulation of the brain."

For example, he has been able to "play" monkeys and cats 'like little electronic toys" that yawn, hide, fight, play, mate and go to sleep on command.

And with humans under treatment for epilepsy, he has increased word output sixfold in one person, has produced severe anxiety in another, and in several others has induced feelings

The New York Times

STUDYING BEHAVIOR: Dr. José M. R. Delgado in his office at Yale University School of Medicine.

Switzerland used a similar set-up to stimulate various cerebral regions in conscious cats. He showed that elect could influence posture, balance, such basic psych tions as fear and

For some still reason, those te

those films a of all the an the behavior

This permits tive assessmen social interact: quantification havioral profi said. This is portant when modifications i of the group stimulation of sponse in one animals.

For example several specifi brain can indu in a monkey. tive data on havior, as we others in the more precisel of various, s effects of el tion on individ social behavior

Some of the

With such Delgado has

¶Monkeys w a button that to the brain member of calms it down animals can b trol one anothe

¶A monkey,

Top: 1965 New York Times article on Delgado.

Right: Delgado in 1995. The humanist magazine Free Enquiry described him as "one of the most noted researchers on the brain."

Top: José Delgado of Yale University's School of Medicine faces a charging bull… Bottom: …and stops it cold, using a "stimoceiver," which sent a radio signal to its brain through an implant. These photographs appeared on the front pages of newspapers around the world, including the New York Times (May 17, 1965).

Above: Two photos of Delgado's mind control implants.

Chapter 6:

SHOCKTROOPS

In 1944, while World War II still raged, Lord Montagu Norman resigned from his position at the Bank of England. Norman, a man prone to repeated mental problems and hospitalizations, and who had been a staunch supporter of Hitler prior to the war, announced the beginning of the British National Association for Mental Health, which was in fact only a renaming of the National Councils of Mental Hygiene, a group that had been heavily involved in pushing eugenics programs prior to the war. With Hitler's downfall, eugenics had an extremely unsavory odor that needed to be deodorized with a name change. Certainly eugenics never vanished, as witness, for example, the thousands of women involuntarily sterilized in Sweden and other European countries until the mid-1970s. The NAMH functioned as a Tavistock-front organization which would soon become the controlling body for world psychiatry. [1]

An examination of the officers of NAMH provides clues as to its direction: Richard Austen Butler, the pro-Nazi deputy foreign minister to Lord Halifax, became president. Lord Halifax's son-in-law, the Earl of Feversham, became chairman. Vice chairman was Norman's wife, Priscilla Reyntiens Worsthorne Norman, a vocal proponent of eugenics programs and the Nazis, who had assisted German rearmament by releasing 6,000,000 British pounds in Czech gold to the Germans after the occupation of Czechoslovakia. Otto Niemeyer, Norman's assistant at the Bank of England, became treasurer of the organization. Perhaps the group should have been titled the Nazi Association for Mental Health?

In 1948 an International Congress on Mental Health at the Ministry of Health in London was convened by Norman. The Congress was hosted by the British National Association, whose patron was the Duchess of Kent, widow of the Grand Master of Masons and mother of the Grand Master of Masons to follow. A World Federation for Mental Health was formed at the Congress, with Brigadier General Dr. John Rawlings Rees, head of the British psychological warfare department and of the Tavistock Institute, named president. Co-director of the World Federation was Dr. Frank Fremont-Smith, chief medical officer of the Rockefeller-spawned Josiah Macy Foundation that would later be the primary funnel for CIA MKULTRA mind control funding.

According to Nina Ridenour, technical coordinator of the U.S. delegation to the Congress, "The World Federation for Mental Health... had been created upon the recommendation of the United Nations' World Health Organization and UNESCO because they needed a non-governmental mental health organization with which they could cooperate."

The vice presidents of the Congress, again, provide a sense of its direction: Dr. Hugh Chrichton-Miller was a founder of Tavistock, and vice-president of the C.G. Jung Institute in Zurich. The blatantly anti-Semitic Jung himself was another vice president of the Congress. Dame Evelyn Fox was a leading light of the British eugenics movement. Lord Thomas Jees Horder was president of the Eugenics Society of Great Britain. Dr. Winfred Overhulser was a high-ranking representative of the Scottish Rite Masons, and reportedly linked to German spy activities in the U.S. Dr. Alfred Frank Tredgold was a member of Britain's Ministry of Health Committee on Sterilization.

Providing additional insight into the goals of the manipulators of the WFMH are statements of Dr. G. Brock Chisholm, first director and later head of the World Health Organization of the United Nations. Chisholm delivered an address to psychiatrists and government officials in Washington, D.C. in 1945, confiding:

"What basic psychological distortion can be found in every civilization of which we know anything? The only psychological force capable of producing these perversions is morality—the concept of right and wrong. The re-interpretation and eventual eradication of the concept of right and wrong are the belated objectives of nearly all psychotherapy." [2]

Chisholm also said that, "The people who have been taught to believe whatever they were told by their parents or their teachers are the people who are the menace to the world." [3]

Given these sentiments, that right and wrong do not exist and that parents are the persons least fit for educating their children, can any excesses and crimes of the "mental health" field be a surprise? [4]

The words of a declaration issued by the National Institute for Mental Health in the United States further reveal that psychiatry has its masters, even beyond the Nazis, Tavistock, British aristocracy, and the Freemasons:

"Principles of mental health cannot be successfully furthered in any society unless there is progressive acceptance of the concept of world citizenship. World citizenship can be widely extended among all peoples through applications of the principles of mental health... At a major turning point in world history there is an obligation on social scientists and psychiatrists to attempt this new formulation."

By 1961, the NIMH, under the direction of Masonic controller Robert Felix, had distilled a group of psychiatrists, neuropsychologists, chemists, and others, including many participants in the CIA's infamous MKULTRA program, into the American College of Neuropsychopharmacology. One segment of the college, the Study Group for the Effects of Psychotropic Drugs on Normal Humans, held a 1967 conference to chart out the directions mind control would follow until the year 2000.

The Evans-Kline Report, authored by MKULTRA mind control psychiatrists Wayne O. Evans, director of the U.S. Army Military Stress Laboratory, and Nathan Kline, eugenicist and Columbia University psychiatrist, reported that the group "concluded that the present breadth of drug use may be almost trivial when we compare it to the possible numbers of chemical substances that will be available for the control of selective aspects of man's life in the year 2000."

The study theorized, in obvious reflection of the Tavistock Institute's plan, that American culture is "moving toward a 'sensate society'. A greater emphasis is being placed on sensory experience and less upon rational or work-oriented philosophies. Such a philosophical view, coupled with the means to separate sexual behavior from reproduction or disease, will undoubtedly enhance sexual freedom.

"It seems obvious that the youth of today are no longer afraid of either drugs or sex. Again, the philosophers and spokesmen for the *avant-garde* advocate the personal sensory experience as the *raison d'etre* of the coming generation. Finally, we are moving into an age in which meaningful work will be possible only for a minority: In such an age, chemical aphrodisiacs may be accepted as a commonplace means to occupy one's time...

"If we accept the position that human mood, motivation, and emotion are reflections of a neurochemical state of the brain, then drugs can provide a simple, rapid, expedient means to produce any desired neurochemical state that we wish.

"The sooner that we cease to confuse scientific and moral statements about drug use, the sooner we can rationally consider the types of neurochemical states that we wish to be able to provide for people."

Shades of *Brave New World.*

In 1975, NIMH funded an overall evaluation of behavior modification approaches. Its conclusions were—surprise!—that these techniques should be applied to the general population of the world, and to larger numbers than ever before. [5]

At about the same time, the Association for the Advancement of Psychotherapy, in their *Mankind 2000* report, introduced the following dark vision:

"In the organization of a civilization of the future we anticipate that the individualistically-oriented man will become an anachronism. Indeed, he will be viewed as a threat to the group organization as well as to his fellow man. Hence, as stated, he in all likelihood will have few individual expectations. While such a picture may not be pleasant to contemplate, when viewed with our present orientation and value judgement, we would be amiss were we to deal with unrealistic imageries that would blind us to future reality..."

"The new world of the closed, automated system will necessitate a radical change in political, technologic, and social thinking. All too often, however, we remain bound by the conventional tenets and wisdom of past generations... The cybercultural revolution is altering all this. It differs radically from previous innovations because now man has devices that will largely supplant his labor and certain activities of his mind." [6]

NOTES:

1. Chaitkin, Anton. "British Psychiatry: From Eugenics to Assassination," *EIR,* October 7, 1994; Dicks; Higham, Charles, *Trading With the Enemy.* (New York: Dell, 1983)

2. Chaitkin; Chisholm, Dr. G. Brock, *Psychiatry,* February, 1948

3. Chisholm, Dr. G. Brock. Speech, Conference on Education, Asilomar, Calif. Sep. 11, 1954

4. Chisholm, Psychiatry

5. *Mental Health and World Citizenship,* Int. Cong. On Mental Health, London, 1948

5. Packard, Vance, *The People Shapers.* (New York: Bantam Books, 1977. pg. 29)

6. Less, Stanley and Wolf, William, *Mankind 2000*; Chaitkin

Chapter 7:

OSS ORIGINS

In 1940, President Roosevelt's special emissary General William "Wild Bill" Donovan returned from the Mediterranean burning with a conviction. He told Roosevelt that, "neither America nor Britain is fighting the new and important type of war on more than the smallest scale. Our defenses against political and psychological warfare are feeble, and even such gestures as have been made toward carrying the fight to the enemy are pitifully inadequate."

So goes the story of the beginning of the Office of the Coordinator of Information (COI), that was to evolve into the Office of Strategic Services (OSS), and in turn, the Central Intelligence Agency (CIA). Donovan's COI took the idea of the "Secret Vote"—what has come to be termed "black funding" or "black operations"—from the British, allowing the organization and its successor organizations almost complete latitude in its psychological warfare projects.

In June, 1942, the COI morphed into the OSS. A period of time passed between the formation of the OSS and the issuing of its charter due to Donovan's insistence that the psychological warfare unit of the organization should head up the operation. The Joint Chiefs of Staff finally agreed, saying that "All plans for projects to be undertaken by the Office of Strategic Services will be submitted to the Joint U.S. Chiefs of Staff through the Joint Psychological Warfare Committee for approval. The Joint Psychological Warfare Committee will take final action on all internal administrative plans pertaining to the Office of Strategic Services."

The OSS existed for three years and, according to Walter Bowart, in *Operation Mind Control,* "it developed psychological warfare into an effective weapon against the minds of civilian and military populations foreign and domestic alike. To wage effective psychological warfare the OSS needed background information on United States citizens. Thus the burglary of private files was sanctioned."

An early proponent of mind war was George Estabrooks, of Colgate University. Estabrook contacted the Department of War early in World War II and proposed the use of hypnosis in warfare. Although the government took Estabrooks up on his offer, he destroyed his diaries covering the years 1940-45, and was unwilling to talk much about what he had done. Eastabrooks is, however, said to have intimated to associates that he had researched the creation of hypnotically programmed couriers and the hypnotic induction of split personalities.

Estabrooks became loose-lipped on one occasion when, in 1968, he chatted with a reporter for the Providence Evening Bulletin. According to the article that resulted, "Dr. Estabrooks said that the key to creating an effective spy or assassin rests in... creating a multiple personality, with the aid of hypnosis, a procedure which the good doctor described as 'child's play'. Estabrooks even offered the suggestion that Lee Harvey Oswald and Jack Ruby 'could very well have been performing through hypnosis.'" Estabrooks quite possibly would have been in the position to know. [1]

One of the top secret projects that the OSS participated in during its formative years was the development of a "truth drug" to break down resistance in spies and POWs. This project was run in conjunction with the Freemasons, and supervised by Superintendent Winfred Overhulser, the Scottish Rite's chief psychiatrist, at St. Elizabeth's Hospital in Washington, D.C., along with a research team composed of Harry J. Anslinger, head of the Federal Bureau of Narcotics, and Dr. Edward Strecker, then president of the American Psychiatric Association. The study assessed the uses of mescaline, scopolomine, peyote, and barbiturates, but settled upon a mixture of marijuana and tobacco, attempting to perfect a concoction that would stimulate a "state of irresponsibility." OSS scientists then came up with a potent extract of marijuana called "TD." Its results were noted in an OSS report:

"TD appears to relax all inhibitions and to deaden the areas of the brain which govern an individual's discretion and caution. It accentuates the senses and makes manifest any strong characteristics of the individual. Sexual inhibitions are lowered, and the sense of humor is accentuated to the point where any statement or situation can become extremely funny to the subject. On the other hand, a person's unpleasant characteristics may also be heightened." The results obtained with TD, however, were inconsistent, and research was reported discontinued. [2]

John Marks writes in his seminal *The Search for the Manchurian Candidate* that members of Overhulser's working group included secret agents inside the U.S. government's Manhattan Project to develop an atomic bomb, as well as informers inside the FBI. [3]

On Halloween, 1944, President Roosevelt asked Donovan to work out the details of an intelligence service that would operate after the end of the war. In November, Donovan submitted his plan, constructing the organization so that it bypassed the Joint Chiefs of Staff and reported directly to the president. On September 20, 1945, the OSS was terminated by executive order.

Although Donovan was primarily responsible for the creation of the COI and the OSS, due to his dislike for traditional organization he was cut off from participating in the creation of the CIA. The man who would take over control of the CIA was Allen Dulles.

NOTES:

1. Bowart, Walter, *Operation Mind Control.* (New York: Dell Paperback, 1977); Cannon, Martin, "Mind Control and the American Government," *Lobster 23;* Bowart

2. Cannon, Martin, "The Controllers: A New Hypothesis of Alien Abductions", *MUFON UFO Journal,* Number 270, October, 1990; Lee and Shlain, *Acid Dreams.* (New York: Grove Press, 1985)

3. Marks, John, *The Search for the Manchurian Candidate: The CIA and Mind Control.* (New York: Times Books, 1979)

Frank Olson, an early victim of MKULTRA.

P. A. LINDSTROM, M.D.

July 27, 1983

Mr. R. Naeslund
Ervallakroken 27
12443 Bandhagen
SWEDEN

In response to your most recent letter regarding the roentgen films I can only confirm that some foreign objects, most likely brain transmitters, have been implanted at the base of your frontal brain and in the skull.

The risk of such implantations is considerable and the risk of chronic infections and meningitis when the implantation has been made through the nose or the sinuses are real issues.

In my opinion, there is no excuse for such implantations if the patient has not been fully informed about the procedures, the purposes, the risks, the method of anesthesia, etc., and then gives a clear written consent.

I fully agree with Lincoln Lawrence, who in his book on page 27 wrote: "There are two particularly dreadful procedures which have been developed. Those working and playing with them secretly call them R.H.I.C. and E.D.O.M.--Radio-Hypnotic Intracerebral Control and Electronic Dissolution of Memory."

Many years ago I had some discussions with Delgado. He asked me to apply my ultrasonic technique for his particular purpose of altering patient's behavior but I declined because we had entirely different aims and approaches. However, I found Delgado to be an intelligent but somewhat strange man.

Best wishes!

P. A. Lindstrom, M.D.

PAL/mjt

Chapter 8:

GREY EMINENCE

The major operations of mind control in the 20th century have been initiated by agents dedicated to the New World Order. Bolstering this proposition is information on the background of Allen Dulles, the director of the CIA at its outset and during the period of its greatest involvement in mind control research.

Allen Dulles and his brother, John Foster Dulles, stood at the pinnacle of American government and strategic planning during the 1940s and 1950s—while at the same time being among the most influential agents for the New World Order. Both brothers were brought into the State Department prior to World War I by their uncle, Secretary of State Robert Lansing. According to the Dulles family biography, "Robert Lansing was... so pro-English that he even took elocution lessons to perfect the English accent he was cultivating."

Lansing was good friends with British spy Alex Gaunt, and "Allen [Dulles]... thought Gaunt was one of the most exciting men he had ever met, and he made up his mind that one of these days he would become an intelligence operative just like him—except for the accent, of course." [1]

Lansing brought both of the Dulles brothers into the Paris peace negotiations, an affair guided by members of the Rhodes Round Table group. Other members of the Wilson delegation were Bernard Baruch, J.P. Morgan's Thomas Lamont, and Paul Warburg. It is alleged that the 14 points of the peace plan were formulated at a secret meeting of the Grand Orient Freemasonic Lodge of France and the International Masonic Conference, on June 28-30, 1917. Whether that is true or not, on the American side, President Woodrow Wilson was accompanied by Colonel E.M. House, the consummate one-worldist who was the engineer of Wilson's domestic and foreign policies, who chose his cabinet, and ran the State Department.

House offended Wilson by excluding him from some of his negotiations conducted behind closed doors—this is known—but the nature of those negotiations may have been revealed by the allegation that the Versailles Peace Conference was actually conducted in three tiers: the public conference, covered by the press; secret conferences of the Big Four; and a third tier of Masonic conferences conducted behind closed doors.

It is also alleged that, to guarantee his continued efforts in the creation of a League of Nations, Woodrow Wilson was given a bribe of one million dollars in gold and gems, and that his subsequent nervous breakdown was based on his belief that he would have to return the money after the failure of the League. [2]

House was an intimate of major international bankers, and persuaded Wilson to lobby for the League of Nations, the precursor to the United Nations. In 1916, upon House's urging, Wilson created the first President's Brain Trust to formulate plans for a world government. House headed up the committee, with 150 members including Norman Thomas (later to be head of the American Socialist Party), and the Dulles brothers.

At the Paris conference the Dulleses made the acquaintance of members of the Round Table, and a dinner party was arranged by House and held at the Majestic Hotel, in Paris, with the Dulles Brothers, other Americans in the Wilson camp, and English members of the Round Table. An agreement was made to form a group "for the study of international affairs." John Foster Dulles acted in 1920 as an agent of the group in setting up the Council on Foreign Relations in New York.

According to a 1953 CFR publication: "The Royal Institute of International Affairs and the Council on Foreign Relations were founded in 1920 as a result of discussions between members of the British and American delegations at the Peace Conference in Paris in 1919. The two institutions, though completely independent, have developed their work along parallel lines in Britain and the United States."

With funding from J.P. Morgan, Rockefeller, and members of the Round Table, the CFR acquired its headquarters at Harold Pratt House, 58 East 68th Street, in New York. [3]

At Versailles, Dulles was able to fulfill his ambition of working in espionage, by meeting T.E. Lawrence, "Lawrence of Arabia," and gaining entree into British intelligence circles. Lawrence ran the British Intelligence Arab Bureau, whose head at the time was Harry St. John Philby. Philby's son, Cambridge Apostle Harold "Kim" Philby coordinated both British and American intelligence agencies beginning in 1949, training officers for the CIA and staying in contact with Allen Dulles on a daily basis. Philby later defected to the Soviet Union when his role as a

Soviet mole functioning in both British and American intelligence was discovered.

In 1921 Allen Dulles was posted to Berne, Switzerland by his uncle, Secretary Lansing, where he took over the roll of chief of intelligence in the American ligation. In Switzerland, Dulles was met by his cousins, members of the Mallet family. Dulles' uncle, Petit Dulles, had married the Swiss-American Julia Mallet-Prevost. Both the Prevosts and the Mallets were uniquely powerful families in international politics and finance, holding hereditary seats in the "Council of 200" ruling Geneva, Switzerland. This group, with the British royals, formed a joint committee of spymasters working for the aristocracy that went back to at least the 18th century. The Mallet-Prevosts were also responsible for injecting the Scottish Rite of Masonry into the United States. [4]

By the mid-1920s, Dulles was tapped to be the First Secretary of the American Embassy in Berlin. Dulles was also a director of the Schroder Bank, that handled Hitler's personal funds. In June 1920, American army Captain Truman Smith was brought in to the Berlin mission as a "military observer." In 1922, after Mussolini, in the pay of British intelligence, had taken over Italy, Captain Smith was dispatched by the embassy on a mission to Munich.

According to his 1964 report of the visit, "I talked at length about National Socialism with the Munich consul, Mr. Robert Murphy (later a very distinguished American ambassador), General Erich Ludendorff, Crown Prince Ruprecht of Bavaria, and Alfred Rosenberg. The latter became the political philosopher of the Nazi party.

"On this visit I also saw much of Ernst F.S. Hanfstaengl, of the well-known Munich art family. "Putzi" was a Harvard graduate and later became Hitler foreign press chief. Hanfstaengl states in his 1957 memoirs, *Unheard Witness,* that it was I who brought him into contact with Hitler. This may well be so, but the actual facts of this introduction are not firmly fixed in my memory.

"My interview with Hitler lasted some hours. The diary I kept in Munich indicates that I was deeply impressed by his personality and thought it likely that he would play an important part in German politics. I must confess, however, that I did not see him as the future ruler of Europe." [5]

The memory of another who was present was somewhat sharper. As related by Smith, "Fourteen-and-one-half years later —on March 3, 1937—he accompanied Mr. Hugh Wilson, our newly appointed ambassador to Germany to the chancellor's palace... for his initial reception by Adolph Hitler. Smith together with other members of the embassy staff entered a large formal reception hall to be presented to the fuhrer-chancellor. The embassy staff... passed down the reception line... When Smith's turn came, he shook hands with Hitler and was about to pass on, when he felt a hand grasp his sleeve. 'Have I not seen you before?' Hitler asked. I was somewhat surprised but answered immediately, "Yes, Mr. Chancellor, in Munich in 1922.' 'Oh yes,' replied Hitler, 'you introduced me to Hanfstaengl.'"

There are other aspects of Smith's memory which seem to have dulled over the years. The German-American Hanfstaengl, a friend of Franklin Roosevelt, noted in his 1957 memoirs that he had been assigned by Captain Smith to join Hitler's movement, and to promote Hitler's rising star. As Hitler succeeded in Germany beyond anyone's expectations, Hanf-staengl and his highly-placed American connections served as press agents to the world for Der Fuhrer. Hanfstaengl, according to one credible account, was the man who provided access to the *Reichstag* when conspirators set it afire—the aftermath of the fire being that Hitler was able to claim a Communist revolution and to seize totalitarian control of Germany. After he fell out of favor with the Nazi regime, Hanf-staengl worked as an American psychological warfare advisor. [6]

Although the thought is only speculative, in 1918 Hitler had been gassed in World War One, and was removed from the front lines to a hospital in Bavaria. A Doctor Forrester, cited as "the father of modern hypnosis" was brought in and treated Hitler for what was thought to be hysterical blindness. At about that time Hitler dreamed that he would be prominent in politics and would rise up to control Germany. Although there is probably no way of verifying it as this late date, Hitler may have been, as researcher John Judge puts it, "one of the earliest psycho-patsies." [7]

John Foster Dulles, newly graduated from Princeton, was hired by the law firm of Sullivan and Cromwell, where he would later become the chief executive. Sullivan and Cromwell were the premier lawyers to the Eastern Establishment, as well as representing a host of German cartels including I.G. Farben, central in the prosecution of Germany's war. John Foster Dulles was one of the primary organizers of American funding for Hitler through international elitist financier Hjalmar Schacht, who later ran the Nazi economy. He was also the lawyer for Richard

Merton, the founder of I.G. Farben. [8]

The Dulles family had been among the key players in the international eugenics movement, advocating, according to John Foster Dulles, that "it is only by eliminating the lower members [of the human race] that a higher average is maintained." [9]

John Foster Dulles' business partner, Council on Foreign Relations and Bonesman Averill Harriman—later to be thought of as the elder statesman of the Democratic Party—was the son of robber baron railroad man E.H. Harriman. Averell Harriman ran the private banking firm of Brown Brothers, Harriman, heavily staffed with Bonesmen including Prescott Bush, the father of Bonesman George Bush. As an example of his devotion to the Illuminati cause, Harriman chose 322, the Skull and Bones secret number, for the combination on his briefcase when he had carried secret messages between London and Moscow in World War II.

Among the major accomplishments of Harriman, guided by Skull and Bones, was financial and diplomatic support for the Soviets—at the time quite illegal by dint of regulation of the State Department. Harriman had possessed large business holdings in both Russia and Germany since the early days of the century, and was also involved in RUSKOMBANK, the first Soviet commercial bank, whose first vice president was Skull and Bonesman Max May of Guaranty Trust. Harriman and other Bonesman also owned a large percentage of the Union Bank, which was key in supporting Hitler in the early days. Out of the eight directors of Union Bank, six were Nazis or members of Skull and Bones.

Harriman would later be in the thick of organizing CIA mind control programs, creating the Psychological Strategy Board (PSB) in 1951. [10]

The Harrimans, again, were represented by Sullivan and Cromwell, and were the single most prominent Eastern Establishment promoters of eugenics, a study later to be furthered through the horrific programs of Hitler's psychiatric and medical establishments. Harriman's mother had bankrolled International Eugenics Congresses and the Eugenics Records Office in New York, that had called for the sterilization of 15 million Americans by 1980, in order to create the "perfect man." Averill Harriman himself had contributed large sums to eugenics causes. [11]

The director of the Psychological Strategy Board was Gordon Gray, a Naval Intelligence officer, who later became a close ally of Bonesman George Bush. Another close Harriman associate was Bonesman Eugene Stetson, who had been assistant manager for George Bush's father, Prescott Bush, at Brown Brothers, Harriman in New York. Stetson organized the H. Smith Richardson Foundation, an organization involved in CIA MKULTRA mind control funding, particularly in financing the testing of psychotropic drugs at Bridgewater Hospital in Massachusetts, alleged to have been the center of some of the most horrific MKULTRA experimentation.

The H. Smith Richardson Foundation later was involved in the Iran-Contra affair, where it functioned as a "private donors steering committee" in tandem with the National Security Council. In later years the Foundation ran the Center for Creative Leadership training "leaders of the CIA." [12]

As the careers of Allen and John Foster Dulles and their friends had been in many ways integrated with Nazi interests, so it was with the formation of the CIA. After the defeat of Stalingrad in January 1943 the German general staff were unified in their belief that the war was lost. Deputy Fuhrer and head of the Nazi Party Martin Borrmann and Hermann Schmitz, chief executive of I.G. Farben, developed a plan whereby large numbers of Nazis would flee Europe and hunker down in hideouts around the world, waiting for that bright day when they might take another shot at world power. The first step in this plan was the transferal of large amounts of Nazi loot to safe positions, this including three tons of gold, large quantities of other precious metals and stones, and perhaps a billion dollars in currency.

Hitler's "favorite commando," Otto Skorzeny, was put in charge of moving Nazi assets and in the creation of "rat lines," escape routes to Nazi colonies around the globe. An estimated 5,000 members of Hitler's SS and Gestapo were exfiltrated through Catholic monasteries, in a plan concocted by Papal Chamberlain and Knight of Malta Luigi Parelli. Assisting in the project was the U.S. Army Counter Intelligence Corps (employing Henry Kissinger) and the Office of Naval Intelligence. [13]

General Reinhard Gehlen, in charge of the Third Reich's military intelligence in Eastern Europe and the Soviet Union, and utilizing fascist organizations in Eastern Europe, had an even bolder plan for continuing his influence after the end of World War II. Using his top aides, the most important of his intelligence files were stripped, with the rest burned. Fifty-two crates of files were buried in the Bavarian Redoubt, in a mountainous region called Misery Meadow.

Within two weeks of the war's end, Gehlen walked into an Army command center in Bavaria, and announced "I am head of the Section Foreign Armies East in German Army headquarters. I have information to give of the highest importance to your government." Gehlen was ignored and sent to the prison camp at Salzburg, but within a month someone had taken notice and he was brought to Augsburg for interrogation. Soon after that, Gehlen's associate Hermann Baun was forming up what would be called the "Gehlen Org," and Gehlen himself was flying to the U.S., dressed in an American military uniform to escape detection, to confer with top American military officials.

On August 24, 1945 Gehlen stepped out of a U.S. Army transport plane at Washington National Airport, and was driven to Fort Hunt, located outside of Washington, D.C. At Fort Hunt an agreement was worked out between Gehlen, Allen Dulles, and others, whereby Gehlen's intelligence organization would be grafted almost intact onto the OSS, giving birth to the CIA.

Gehlen's Org, it is said, was initially funded by Dulles to the tune of $200 million and, minimally supervised and working out of a fortified stronghold in Bavaria, grew to control the entirety of the West German intelligence service. Gehlen's intelligence agency also dominated NATO, providing an estimated 70 percent of the intelligence provided to that organization on the Soviet Union and Europe. Thus, American intelligence was infiltrated by the Nazis, who found their association with men like the Dulles brothers, Harriman, and George Bush to be friendly and of a strangely familiar nature. [14]

Key to the CIA's MKULTRA and other mind alteration programs—both scientifically and philosophically—was the Nazi connection. From the 1930s until the end of World War II, Nazi psychiatrists in Germany had been horrifically implementing the Darwinian "eugenics" philosophy that they had inherited from the West, from men like the Englishman Francis Galton, a cousin of Charles Darwin. The basics of this philosophy dealt with the improvement of hereditary qualities of a race. This can be accomplished, per the eugenicists, in a number of ways, including selective mating and the sterilization of mental defectives and members of "inferior" races.

During this period it is reported that at least 300,000 mental patients were exterminated in Germany. After the war the psychiatrists involved in these extermination programs were not punished. In fact, some of the most prominent workers in psychiatry, chemical warfare, and mind control-related areas were imported to the U.S. to work in the scientific establishment and the military under Project Paperclip, through which as many as 5,000 German scientists were sneaked into the country, with others immigrating later.

Among the Nazis imported to the U.S. were Karl Tauboeck, who had been the chief plant chemist at I.G. Farben's Ludwigshaven factory, and who was the Nazi's expert on sterilization drugs and had done work that paralleled the OSS and CIA in attempts to formulate a "truth drug"; Friedrich Hoffman, who discovered a paralysis drug based on conch shell venom; and scientists Theodore Wagner-Jauregg, Karl Rarh, and Hans Turit, who were specialists in poison gases like Tabun and Sarin (the latter allegedly the gas of choice of Japan's AUM cult). Another Nazi imported to the U.S. was Dr. Huburtus Strughold, who had overseen murder and torture of inmates at the Dachau concentration camp. Strughold was employed by NASA and later lauded by that organization as the "father of space medicine."

Another Nazi employed by the U.S. after the end of the war was former SS Brigadier General Walter Schieber, described by one army officer as "the prototype of an ardent and convinced Nazi who used the Party to further his own ambitions." Schieber worked for over ten years at the Chemical Division in West Germany on chemical warfare and the production of nerve gas. Many Nazis scientists, some of whom like Schieber could not be brought to the U.S. because of their notoriety, were employed in chemical warfare research in West Germany. [15]

Combing the 7,104 entries in the 1957 edition of the Biographical Directory of the Fellows and Members of the American Psychiatric Association, 1,125 came from Germany and Eastern European countries. [16]

It is instructive to note that CIA mind control scientists, like the Nazis, used certain target groups for experimentation, including ethnic minorities, foreigners, mental patients, prisoners, sex deviants, addicts, and the terminally ill.

Another connection of the Nazis, the British, and chemical mind control deserves to be mentioned in passing. Although the mere thought that a mass chemical drugging of the population could ever take place is ridiculed in the popular media, that was not the position of Charles Eliot Perkins, one of America's top industrial chemists. Perkins was dispatched by the U.S. government to assist in taking over the German industrial giant I.G. Farben after World War II. In a letter that Perkins wrote to the Lee Foundation for Nutritional Research in Milwaukee, Wisconsin on October 2, 1954, he stated,

"I have your letter of September 29 asking for further documentation regarding a statement made in my book *The Truth About Water Fluoridation* to the effect that the idea of water fluoridation was brought to England from Russia by the Russian Communist, Kreminoff.

"In the 1930's Hitler and the German Nazis envisioned a world to be dominated and controlled by the Nazi philosophy of pan-Germanism... The German chemists worked out a very ingenious and far-reaching plan of mass control which was submitted to and adopted by the German General Staff. This plan was to control the population in any given area through mass medication of drinking water supplies. By this method they could control the population of whole areas, reduce population by water medication that would produce sterility in the women, and so on. In this scheme of mass control, sodium fluoride occupied a prominent place.

"We are told by the fanatical ideologists who are advocating the fluoridation of water supplies in this country that their purpose is to reduce tooth decay in children, and it is the plausibility of this excuse, plus the gullibility of the public and the cupidity of the public officials that is responsible for the present spread of artificial water fluoridation in this country.

"However—and I want to make this very definite and very positive—the real reason behind water fluoridation is not to benefit children's teeth. If this were the real reason there are many ways in which it could be done that are much easier, cheaper and far more effective. The real purpose behind water fluoridation is to reduce the resistance of the masses to domination and control and loss of liberty...

"In the rear occiput of the left lobe of the brain there is a small area of brain tissue that is responsible for the individual's power to resist domination. Repeated doses of infinitesimal amounts of fluorine will in time gradually reduce the individual's power to resist domination by slowly poisoning and narcotizing this area of brain tissue and make him submissive to the will of those who wish to govern him...

"I was told of this entire scheme by a German chemist who was an official of the great Farben chemical industries and was also prominent in the Nazi movement at the time. I say this will all earnestness and sincerity of a scientist who has spent nearly 20 years' research into the chemistry, biochemistry, physiology and pathology of fluorine—any person who drinks artificially fluorinated water for a period of one year or more will never again be the same person, mentally or physically." [17]

NOTES:

1. Mosley, Leonard, *Dulles: A Biography of Eleanor, Allen, and John*

Foster Dulles and their Family Network. (New York: The Dial Press/James Wade, 1978)

2. Hansen, Harry, "The Forgotten Men of Versailles," *The Aspirin Age, 1919-1941.* Ed. Isabel Leighton. (New York: Simon and Schuster, 1949); Smoot, Dan, *The Invisible Government.* (Dallas, Texas: The Dan Smoot Report, 1962); Mullins, Eustace, *The Curse of Canaan.* (Staunton, Virginia. Revelation Books, 1987)

3. Hansen; Smoot; Wilgus, Neal, *The Illuminoids.* (Sun Publishing Company, Santa Fe, 1978)

4. Chaitkin, Anton, *Treason in America.* (New York: New Benjamin Franklin House, 1984.); Mullins; Pincher, Chapman, *Too Secret, Too Long.* (New York: St. Martin's Press, 1984)

5. Smith, Truman, *Berlin Alert, The Memoirs and Reports of Truman Smith.* (Stanford, California: Hoover Institution Press, 1984); Perloff, James, *Shadows of Power.* (Appleton, Wisconsin: Western Island, 1990)

6. Smith; Sutton, Antony C., *Wall Street and the Rise of Hitler.* (Seal Beach, California: '76 Press, 1976)

7. Judge, John, "The Secret Government," *Dharma Combat* magazine, number 10

8. Rauh and Turner, "Anatomy of a Public Interest Case Against the CIA," *Hamline Journal of Public Law and Policy,* Fall 1990; Chaitkin, Anton, "British Psychiatry: From Eugenics to Assassination," *EIR,* October 7, 1994; Chaitkin, *Treason in America;* Sutton, Antony C., *Wall Street and the Rise of Hitler,* ('76 Press, Seal Beach, California, 1976)

9. Chaitkin, *Treason in America*

10. Isaacson and Thomas, *The Wise Men.* (Simon and Schuster, New York, 1986); Chaitkin. *Treason in America*

11. Isaacson and Thomas; Chaitkin, *Treason in America*

12. *Skull & Bones: The Very Heart of the Shadow Government,* obtained from the internet at alt.conspiracy

13. Judge, John, "Nazis in the White House, The Reagan Administration & the Fascist International," *Overthrow,* Fall 1985

14. Scott, Peter Dale, "How Allen Dulles and the SS Preserved Each Other," *CovertAction Information Bulletin,* undated reprint; Oglesby, Carl, "The Secret Treaty of Fort Hunt," *CovertAction Information Bulletin,* Fall, 1990; Oglesby, Carl, *The Yankee and Cowboy War.* (New York, Berkley, 1977)

15. Cannon, Martin. "Mind Control and the American Government", *Lobster* magazine, issue 23; Lee and Shlain, *Acid Dreams.* (New York: Grove Press, 1985); Hougan, Jim, *Secret Agenda.* (New York: Random House, 1984)

16. Prouty, Fletcher, *Free Thinking,* newsletter of the Freedom of Thought Foundation, volume 1, number 4, March 1995

17. Perkins, Charles Eliot, letter reprinted in *The American Mercury,* undated issue, reprinted in *Contact,* January 31, 1995

Chapter 9:

ENTER THE CIA

In the late 1940s mind control experimentation was initiated in narcohypnotic techniques, as well as in the administering of drugs with contradictory effects to induce a "twilight zone" state. Among the drugs that were most commonly used in this kind of research were Desoxyn and Pentothal, Seconal and Dexedrine. CIA experimenters fixed intravenous hookups in both of the subject's arms, monitoring the effects of the drugs and regulating their flow. The idea, according to laborers in the CIA's mind fields, was to create a sudden cathartic expulsion of the feelings and thoughts, and the communication of any information that the subject might be hiding. [1]

In 1947 the Navy instituted Project CHATTER, run by Dr. Samuel Thompson, a Navy commander and psychiatrist, with G. Richard Wendt, chairman of the Psychology Department at the University of Rochester being the functional head of the program. CHATTER is reported to have been a relatively unsuccessful truth drug project that ended in 1953. At about the same time the Army was involved in THIRD CHANCE and DERBY HAT. [2]

The mindset of the CIA at its inception is reflected in a top secret report submitted to President Eisenhower in 1954. The report called for, "aggressive covert psychological, political, and paramilitary organization more effective, more unique, and if necessary, more ruthless than that employed by the enemy... We... must learn to subvert, sabotage, and destroy our enemies by more clever, more sophisticated, and more effective methods than those used against us..." [3]

According to John Marks, "In 1949 the Office of Scientific Intelligence (OSI) undertook the analysis of foreign work on certain unconventional warfare techniques, including behavioral drugs, with an initial objective of developing a capability to resist or offset the effect of such drugs. Preliminary phases included the review of drug-related work at institutions such as Mount

Sinai Hospital, Boston Psychopathic Hospital, University of Illinois, University of Michigan, University of Minnesota, Valley Forge General Hospital, Detroit Psychopathic clinic, Mayo Clinic, and the National Institute of Health."

"This first project," Marks states, "code-named Project BLUEBIRD, was assigned the function of discovering means of conditioning personnel to prevent unauthorized extraction of information from them by known means. It was further assigned to investigate the possibility of control of an individual by application of special interrogation techniques, memory enhancement, and establishing defensive means for preventing interrogation of agency personnel."

The black-budget BLUEBIRD, run by Morse Allen, was intended to create an "exploitable alteration of personality" in agents, POWs, refugees, and defectors, and CIA employees of the program were dispatched around the world to procure rare botanicals, herbs, and drugs that might be of use. The primary agency involved with BLUEBIRD was the Joint Intelligence Committee, the same group responsible for the Project Paperclip importation of Nazis into the U.S.

At least a thousand soldiers were fed up to 20 doses of LSD under the auspices of BLUEBIRD. Other documented BLUEBIRD projects involved the dispatching of a team to Tokyo in July, 1950 for the interrogation of suspected double agents, and the use of "advanced" techniques on North Korean prisoners of war in October, 1950.

In August, 1951 BLUEBIRD was renamed ARTICHOKE and transferred from the Office of Scientific Intelligence (OSI) to the Office of Security (OS). Additional LSD experiments were done by the CIA under the auspices of ARTICHOKE, using Agency volunteers and, verified by CIA memoranda, unwitting subjects.

One ARTICHOKE experiment is documented in a CIA memorandum to the director dated July 14, 1952. The memo deals with the use of narco-hypnotic induction, sodium pentothal, and the stimulant desoxyn. The interrogation was conducted on Russian agents believed to be double agents.

According to the memo, "a psychiatric medical cover was used to bring the ARTICHOKE techniques into action. In the first case, light dosages of drugs coupled with hypnosis were used to induce a complete hypnotic trance. This trance was held for approximately one hour and forty minutes of interrogation with a subsequent total amnesia produced by posthypnotic suggestion. In the second case (an individual of much higher intelligence than the first), a deep hypnotic trance was reached after light medication. This was followed by an interrogation lasting for well over an hour. However, a partial amnesia only was obtained at this time, although a total amnesia was obtained for a major part of the test. Since further interrogation was desired, a second test was made on this individual in which the ARTICHOKE technique of using a straight medication was employed. On this test, highly successful results were obtained in that a full interrogation lasting two hours and fifteen minutes was produced, part of which included a remarkable regression. During this regression, the subject actually 'relived' certain past activities of his life, some dating back fifteen years while, in addition, the subject totally accepted Mr. [deleted, the case officer] as an old, trusted, and beloved personal friend whom the subject had known in years past in Georgia, USSR. Total amnesia was apparently achieved for the entire second test on this case."

The memo concluded, "For a matter of record, the case officers involved in both cases expressed themselves to the effect that the ARTICHOKE operations were entirely successful and team members felt that the tests demonstrated conclusively the effectiveness of the combined chemical-hypnotic technique in such cases. In both cases, the subjects talked clearly and at great length and furnished information which the case officers considered extremely valuable."

More insight into ARTICHOKE is provided by a conference summary, addressed to the Chief of Security, CIA, dated July 15, 1953:

"Mr. [deleted] then discussed the situation of a former Agency official who had become a chronic alcoholic and who, at the present time, was undergoing operative treatment in [deleted] for a possible brain tumor. This individual had called the Agency prior to the operation and warned that when given certain types of anesthetics (sodium pentothal), previously he had been known to talk coherently. The matter was taken care of by placing a representative in the operating room and by bringing the various personnel participating in the operation under the Secrecy Agreement. Mr. [deleted] stated that the subject did talk extensively under the influence of sodium pentothal and revealed internal problems of the Agency. Dr. [deleted] added that he was acquainted with the details in the case.

"[Deleted] then commented that this type of thing had been a source of great concern to himself and others in the operations work and stated that he hoped that the ARTICHOKE efforts to produce some method that would perhaps guarantee amnesia on the part of those knowing of Agency operations in vital spots would be successful. He stated that some individuals in the Agency had to know tremendous amounts of information and if any way could be found to produce amnesias for this type of information—for instance, after the individual had left the Agency—it would be a remarkable thing. Mr. [deleted] stated the need for amnesias was particularly great in operations work. Mr. [deleted] explained that work was continually being done in an effort to produce controlled amnesia by various means."

A CIA ARTICHOKE document, dated July 30, 1956, mentioned the use of the alkaloid bulbocapnine to induce catatonia or stupor. The document stated, "We desire to have certain psycho-chemical properties tested on man, using the bulbocapnine which we were fortunate to obtain from [deleted], a sample being enclosed herewith. More bulbocapnine is available if needed."

A request was included that subjects be tested for "loss of speech, loss of sensitivity to pain, loss of memory, and loss of will power." [4]

NOTES:

1. Lee and Shlain, *Acid Dreams*. (New York: Grove Press, 1985)
2. Marks, John, *The Search for the Manchurian Candidate: The CIA and Mind Control.* (New York: Times Books, 1979)
3. Bowart, Walter, *Operation Mind Control.* (New York: Dell Paperback, 1977); Halperin, Berman, Bororsage, and Marwick, *The Lawless State, The Crimes of the U.S. Intelligence Agencies.* (New York: Penguin Books, 1976); Hougan, Jim, *Secret Agenda.* (New York: Random House, 1984); Marks
4. Quoted in Bowart

Chapter 10:

COMING ON TO LSD

Members of the American intelligence agencies were not the first group to be interested in the use of psychedelic drugs for behavior modification. Early on, the main proponents of the use of psychoactive drugs in Western culture were the social planners and elite. Just before the new century, in 1898, medical man, literateur, and Fabian Socialist Havelock Ellis began experimentation with peyote.

Today Ellis is primarily known for his seven volume *Psychology of Sex*, but in the early part of this century he was a prime mover in literary and intellectual circles—particularly communist and anarchist groups. Ellis described his experiences with peyote in "Mezcal: A New Artificial Paradise," published in the January, 1898 issue of the *Contemporary Review*. [1]

Interest in peyote and the synthesized version of the alkaloid, mescaline, remained scant, outside of the occasional parlor peyote ritual conducted in a not-dissimilar way from the spiritualist fad of the same era, or the odd psychiatric monograph talking about how the drug seemed to reproduce schizophrenia.

But a far more potent brain-changer would soon appear on the scene. LSD was first synthesized in 1938 at Sandoz laboratories, in Basel, Switzerland, although the effects of the drug are said not to have been discovered by Dr. Albert Hofmann until 1943. Basle was the home of three huge chemical companies, Hoffman-LaRoche, Ciba-Geigy, and Sandoz, the latter owned by German chemical monolith I.G. Farben, the mainstay of the Third Reich's war. Although the connection is not often made, and is denied by Dr. Hofmann, I.G. Farben maintained a division researching psychoactive agents, and it is possible that Hofmann was employed in this capacity. It is also a world-class coincidence that S.S. and *Gestapo* doctors were doing mescaline experiments on prisoners at Dachau at the same time, less than

200 miles away.

Allen Dulles, who directed the CIA during the MKULTRA project, was station chief at Berne, Switzerland during the period of the LSD research, and had been an executive at I.G. Farben. His assistant was James Warburg, who later worked with acid-popularizer Aldous Huxley. [2]

Captain Al Hubbard, the spy who was termed "the Johnny Appleseed of LSD," told the story of the beginnings of LSD in a different form than the usual chronologies. He said that Hofmann had discovered LSD many years earlier, and that he had been a member of a secret group connected with Rudolf Steiner's mystical Anthroposophy group that had set out to manufacture a "peace pill" in the early 1930s. [3]

Early experiments with LSD were conducted by Werner Stoll, a psychiatrist affiliated with the University of Zurich. There were rumors that one of Stoll's female patients was given the drug without her knowledge, and had committed suicide, a foreshadowing of later CIA atrocities.

Although perhaps a marginally less potent drug than the television broadcasting that was launched at nearly the same time, the LSD infusion of America was to have a tremendous effect on the future of the country. When LSD arrived in America in 1949, psychiatry was booming, having experienced an approximate 12-fold increase since 1940. The character of psychiatry was, in many ways, an extension of wartime psychiatry, not surprising considering the fact that American "mental health" organizations were predominantly puppeteered from Tavistock. As per the "societry" engineered by that organization, after Brigadier General William Menninger was elected the head of American psychiatry an ambitious strategy was hammered out, namely the application of psychiatry to the man in the street. [4]

NOTES:

1. Stevens, Jay, *Storming Heaven*. (New York: Harper & Row, 1987)
2. Editors of the Executive Intelligence Review, *Dope, Inc.* (Washington, D.C.): *EIR*, 1992; Lee and Shlain, *Acid Dreams*. (Grove Press, New York, 1985); Lyttle, Thomas. "Blot Art," an interview conducted by Mark Westion. *Paranoia* magazine, winter 1995/1996; Stevens; Marks, John, *The Search for the Manchurian Candidate: The CIA and Mind Control*. (New York: Times Books, 1979)
3. Shlain, Martin. "The CIA, LSD and the Occult," an interview. *High Frontiers*, reprinted in *The Project*, Winter 1988/89, volume VI, number 1
4. Stevens

Chapter 11:

KULT OF MKULTRA

In September, 1950 Edward Hunter, a CIA employee working as a journalist, published information that the Chinese were using brainwashing techniques on American prisoners of war in Korea, forcing them to confess to crimes such as the use of germ warfare. In fact, the Americans were using germ warfare, but this provided the CIA with air cover: with their own mind control research they were simply attempting to catch up to advances by the Communists. This was not a true picture, as admitted by CIA deputy director Richard Helms in 1963, when he informed the Warren Commission that American mind control research had always been more advanced than that of the Communists.

CIA Director Allen Dulles was also out stumping for mind control.   Addressing the National Alumni Conference at Princeton University on April 10, 1953, he talked about "how sinister the battle for men's minds had become in Soviet hands." Three days later Dulles authorized MKULTRA, a greatly augmented series of mind control projects run by the Technical Services Staff of the CIA.

MKULTRA was the code name for a huge mind control project that was, according to CIA documents "an umbrella project for funding sensitive projects," run by the CIA and coordinated by British Intelligence, Scottish Rite Freemasons, and very-recently-reformed Nazis. The related MKDELTA "covered... policy and procedure for use of biochemicals in clandestine operations." [1]

MKULTRA was birthed when Richard Helms, the head of the CIA's Directorate of Operations (known as the "dirty tricks" department), recommended that the agency expand its work in both offensive and defensive brainwashing. No mere grunt in the CIA trenches, Helms was Eastern Establishment all the way, his grandfather the first director of the International Bank of Settlements, and a president of the Federal Reserve. Helms would be present at the death of MKULTRA when he ordered the destruction of the program's files in 1966.

The program was run by Dr. Sidney Gottlieb, "the brainstorming genius of MKULTRA", who until 1973 would supervise the CIA's research into mind control. Gottlieb was viewed with favor by Richard Helms, and would hang onto Helms' coattails as he climbed to higher and higher positions in the Agency. [2]

Dulles diverted an initial $300,000 for MKULTRA. According to Agency documents, the program was planned to operate outside of the normal channels without "the usual contractual arrangements" and was to be highly "compartmented." [3]

The primary front for funding MKULTRA operations was the Josiah Macy, Jr. Foundation, created in 1930 and staffed by Rockefeller-financed psychologists and eugenicists. The foundation was headed by Black Chamber alumnus General Marlborough Churchill. The Macy Foundation's medical director during 1954-55 was Frank Fremont-Smith, also a president of General Reese's World Federation of Mental Health. [4]

The recollections of an intelligence officer detailed in a CIA memorandum flesh out the scope of the MKULTRA project:

17 January 1975

MEMORANDUM FOR THE RECORD

SUBJECT: MKULTRA

1. The following represents the best of my unaided recollection regarding the MKULTRA program. I was first briefed on it in 1962. At that time it was in the process of a significant decrease in activity and funding. As Chief, Defense, and Espionage (C/D&E), I continued to decrease funds significantly each year until the program was phased out in the late 1960s.

2. MKULTRA was a group of projects most of which dealt with drug or counter-drug research and development. The Director Central Intelligence (DCI) and the Deputy Director of Plans (DDP) were kept informed on the program via annual briefings by Chief Technical Services Division (C/TSD) or his Deputy. Most of the research and development was externally contracted and dealt with various materials which were purported to have characteristics appealing for their covert or clandestine administration under operational conditions. The objectives were behavioral control, behavior anomaly production

and counter-measures for opposition application of similar substances. Work was performed at U.S. industrial, academic, and governmental research facilities. Funding was often through cut-out arrangements. Testing was usually done at such time as laboratory work was successfully completed and was often carried out at such facilities as the [deleted in original] and the [deleted in original]. In all cases that I am aware of, testing was done using volunteer inmates who were witting of the nature of the test program but not the ultimate sponsoring organization.

3. As the Soviet drug use scare (and the amount of significant progress in the MKULTRA program) decreased, the program activities were curtailed significantly as budgetary pressure and alternate priorities dictated.

4. Over my stated objections the MKULTRA files were destroyed by order of the DCI (Mr. Helms) shortly before his departure from office.

CI OFFICER
By Authority of 10272 [5]

A large network of doctors and facilities were employed in at least 149 subprojects, all of them relating to mind control. MKULTRA and MKDELTA researched the use of at least 139 different drugs, as well as radiation and electroshock, but also delved into more arcane social applications in sociology, anthropology, and psychiatry. What might those buzzterms have concealed? Eugenics experiments? Genetic manipulation? Tavistockian social engineering?

Within the first year of its operation, MKULTRA was taking it to the streets. Drugs that had shown promise in the lab were slipped to unwitting subjects in normal social situations; citizens were dosed with psychotropics without their knowledge. This portion of the project was supposedly terminated in 1963, although there are suggestions that this was not the case.

Early CIA LSD research by the CIA was conducted by Max Rinkel and Robert Hyde—reportedly the first American to take LSD—at Boston Psychopathic Hospital, Carl Pfieffer at the University of Illinois, Harold Hodge at the University of Rochester, Harold Abramson at Mt. Sinai Hospital and Columbia University in New York, Harris Isbell at the Addiction Research Center in Lexington, Kentucky, and Louis Jolyon West at the University of Oklahoma.

Other early experimentation in LSD research was done by Dr. Joel Elkes, who had concocted nerve gasses in Britain during

World War II. He performed experiments with LSD in England in 1949, later moving his base of operations to St. Elizabeth's Hospital in Washington, D.C. [6]

Dr. Harold Abramson, who had studied in Berlin prior to World War II, and was later employed in the Technical Division of the U.S. Army Chemical Warfare Service, received $85,000 for an LSD study. His proposal indicated that he "hoped" to give hospital patients "who are essentially normal from a psychiatric point of view... unwitting doses of the drug for psychotherapeutic purposes."

Abramson was directed to produce "operationally pertinent materials along the following lines:

"a. Disturbance of Memory; b. Discrediting Aberrent Behavior; c. Alteration of Sex patterns; d. Eliciting of Information; e. Suggestibility; f. Creation of Dependence."

Abramson performed his research at Columbia University and Cold Spring Harbor, Long Island, New York, the latter the location of both of the Dulles brothers' estates and ground zero for eugenics research in America since the turn of the century.

Abramson was responsible for giving LSD to Frank Fremont-Smith and British cultural anthropologist Gregory Bateson and his wife Margaret Mead, both of whom were involved with Tavistock and in MKULTRA projects. Bateson established an LSD research center at the Palo Alto Veterans Administration Hospital in California, and gave acid to Beat poet Allen Ginsburg, among many others. [7]

As CIA research into LSD continued, the intoxication was contagious. Dr. Sidney Gottlieb, the director of MKULTRA, and his staff were regularly partying with LSD, and spiking each other's drinks for a lark. At one bash in November 1953, Gottlieb slipped LSD into Dr. Frank Olson's Cointreau without his knowledge. Olson became deeply depressed and was taken to see Dr. Harold Abramson. After the first visit, Abramson came to see Olson at his hotel room carrying a bottle of bourbon and a bottle of Nembutal. As John Marks comments, "an unusual combination for a doctor to give someone with symptoms like Olson's."

Olson was scheduled to be taken to Chestnut Lodge, a Rockville, Maryland sanitarium where many of the psychiatrists had top secret CIA clearances. The night before he was to enter the sanitarium, he leaped—so it is reported—to his death through the closed window of the Statler Hilton in New York. [8]

The CIA immediately went into cover-up mode on the Olson death. Although his widow was given a government pension, the truth about the cause of the scientist's death would not be admitted for two decades. Alice, Frank Olson's wife, went on national television and read the following statement from the family at that time:

"We feel our family has been violated by the CIA in two ways. First, Frank Olson was experimented upon illegally and negligently. Second, the true nature of his death was concealed for twenty-two years... In telling our story, we are concerned that neither the personal pain this family has experienced nor the moral and political outrage we feel be slighted. Only in this way can Frank Olson's death become part of American memory and serve the purpose of political and ethical reform so urgently needed in our society."

For their complicity in Olson's death, Gottlieb and his team received a verbal reprimand that was not recorded in their personnel files.

The Olson story was not over. Forensic scientists investigating the case exhumed the man's body in 1994. They reported that they found skull fractures that suggested homicide, rather than an accident. One can only speculate about what really happened to Frank Olson. Was he threatening to blow the whistle on MKULTRA the night of his death? [9]

Freemason Dr. Paul Hoch was another person involved in investigating LSD for the CIA. Hoch was a member of the American Eugenics Society, and co-director, with former-Nazi eugenicist Franz Kallman, of research at Columbia University's New York State Psychiatric Institute. Hoch and Kallman worked under the direction of the Scottish Rite of Freemasonry's Field Representative of Research on Dementia Praecox, Dr. Nolan D.C. Lewis. Hoch was also appointed State Mental Hygiene Commissioner by New York Governor Averell Harriman, and was reappointed to the position by Governor Nelson Rockefeller.

Another MKULTRA mastermind was 33rd degree Freemason Robert Hanna Felix, director of psychiatric research for the Scottish Rite and NIMH director from 1949 to 1963. Using CIA funds, Felix personally oversaw the experiments of Dr. Harris Isbell, who gave black prison inmates LSD for 75 consecutive days, tripling and quadrupling the dosage when the inmates demonstrated drug tolerance, and where drug-induced sleep was periodically interrupted by electroshock.

According to the Senate subcommittee testimony of former inmate James Childs, volunteers for the Isbell project were paid off with heroin. Childs said, "You knock on this little door, and the guy would look out... and I would say, 'I want 15 milligrams.'

83

He would say, 'Where do you want it? In your arm, your skin or your vein?' Everybody that was on the research... got the payoff of the drug." [10]

In 1953, Los Angeles psychiatrist Dr. Nick Bercel was contacted by the CIA and asked to determine how much LSD it would take to send the entire population of the City of the Angels on a trip. Bercel's results were disappointing: he found that chlorine in the water supply neutralized the drug. The CIA, according to internal documents, went right to work on a version of LSD that would not be affected by chlorine. [11]

The CIA may have actually attempted the acid dosing of a town somewhat earlier. At Pont-Saint-Esprit, France, in 1951, the whole town suddenly went crazy.

Many persons died during the course of the unexplained hysteria, and hallucinogenic after-effects were felt by the townspeople for weeks. Although the incident is usually attributed to the effects of ergot contaminated rye flour, the date of the occurrence—near the beginning of CIA interest in LSD—is more than interesting.

A similar, although less deadly incident took place in the U.S. in 1989, when 600 junior and senior high school students were preparing for a music program in Santa Monica, California. A sudden rash of headaches, nausea, dizziness, and fainting affected about 250 students. Given the CIA and other intelligence agency's penchant for drug testing on civilians, it is not impossible that this was such another such case. [12]

In the mid-1950s Operation BIG CITY in New York used a 1953 Mercury automobile with a tailpipe extended 18 inches to emit a gas, probably LSD, into the streets. Another test in the same series tests were undertaken with battery powered emission equipment fitted into suitcases. The equipment was used to spray LSD in the New York subway system. An unnamed gas was released off of the Golden Gate Bridge about this time, although it is said to have dissipated in the wind without causing anyone any harm.

In 1957 CIA Inspector General Lyman issued the following internal memo, stating that "precautions must be taken not only to protect the operations from exposure to enemy forces, but also to conceal these activities from the American public in general. The knowledge that the Agency is engaging in unethical and illicit activities would have serious repercussions in political and diplomatic circles and would be detrimental to the accomplishment." [13]

From the beginning of the CIA's work with LSD there were

concerns about relying on the Swiss for their supply of the drug. While obtaining weekly supplies from Sandoz, the CIA was also funding the Eli Lilly company in the United States to synthesize the drug so as to ensure a steady supply. In 1954 Lilly announced that they had succeeded. A memo to Allen Dulles noted that with unlimited supplies, LSD could now be taken seriously as a chemical warfare agent, and that it could be bought in "tonnage quantities." [14]

The most infamous of MKULTRA doctors was Dr. Donald Ewen Cameron. In 1942 the Rockefeller Foundation founded the Allen Memorial Institute at McGill University, located at gothic Ravenscrag, in Montreal, Canada. Dr. Cameron was placed in charge of the psychiatric division, and began experimentation straight out of the Rocky Horror Show, but lacking the wit. The program was funded by the Canadian military, the Rockefeller Foundation, the OSS, and later, the CIA.

Cameron's training was at the Royal Mental Hospital in Glasgow, Scotland, under Sir David Henderson, a eugenicist. Cameron went on to found the World Federation of Mental Health's Canadian division, in association with his friend, Tavistock's Brigadier General John Rawlings Rees, and to become arguably the most influential psychiatrist on the planet. He became president of just about every psychiatric organization there was at the time; the Canadian, American, and World Psychiatric Organizations, the Quebec Psychiatric Association, the American Psychopathological Association, and the Society of Biological Psychiatry. Cameron was no rogue in the field of psychiatry, but instead one of its most influential leaders. [15]

Colonel L. Fletcher Prouty, a Pentagon liaison to the CIA at the time of Cameron's experiments, in 1992 stated: "If you get a hold of a directory for the American Psychiatric Association in around 1956 or 1957, you'll be surprised to find that an enormous percentage of the individuals listed are foreign-born. Mostly they came out of Germany and Eastern Europe in a big wave. They were all called 'technical specialists,' but really they were psychiatrists. They went into jobs at universities mostly—but many were working on these 'unconventional' mind control programs for U.S. intelligence... These would go to people like Dr. Cameron in Canada." [16]

In 1957 Cameron submitted a grant application to "the Society for the Investigation of Human Ecology," also known as the "Human Ecology Fund," a CIA front working out of the Cornell University Medical School in New York City. Cameron's application proposed the funding of experimentation involving:

"i. The breaking down of ongoing patterns of the patient's behavior by means of particularly intensive electroshocks (depatterning).

"ii. The intensive repetition (16 hours a day for 6 or 7 days) of the prearranged verbal signal.

"iii. During this period of intensive repetition the patient is kept in partial sensory isolation.

"iv. Repression of the driving period is carried out by putting the patient, after the conclusion of the period, into continuous sleep for 7-10 days."

After receiving the requested funding of $60,000, Cameron and his underlings employed these and a wide variety of other mind-blasting techniques on subjects who had in many cases not volunteered for experimentation. Those techniques, seemingly more suited for the torture of prisoners of war than for the rehabilitation of Canadian citizens, included the "sleep treatment" developed by Hassan Azima at the Institute, and the administering of Thorazine and barbiturates on a continuous basis so that patients would sleep 20 to 22 hours a day.

Using the British Page-Russell electroconvulsive technique, Cameron would put victims into drug induced coma for weeks, waking them to administer a one-second electroshock, followed by from five to nine additional jolts depending on the itchiness of his trigger finger. Cameron increased the voltage normally administered by practitioners of this technique, and the number of shock sessions from one to two or three per day. Predictably, patients given this kind of treatment were often reduced to a vegetables. [17]

Another of Cameron's strategies was to place his victims into sensory deprivation chambers for up to 65 days, devastating them with LSD, then using "psychic driving," in which a repetitive phrase taken from the emotionally charged material they had told to a psychiatrist would be played through a pillow with unremovable earphones. Cameron documented his researches in psychic driving, funded by the Department of Health and Welfare between 1961-64, in research papers titled "Study of Factors which Promote or Retard Personality Change in Individuals Exposed to Prolonged Repetition of Verbal Signals," and "The Effects upon Human Behavior of the Repetition of Verbal Signals". [18]

According to one psychiatrist, Cameron's theory was "the ways in which people behave are determined by some sort of nervous system arrangements in the brain. Since psychotherapy can change behavior, the neural arrangements must be reversible."

Cameron himself "wondered whether the behavior patterns of adults could be erased by a physiologic process that attacked neural patterns. Could adults be made theoretically patternless? Could they be returned to a state of neurologic and psychologic infancy for a short period, and then could new patterns of behavior be introduced?" Does one detect the flavor of Tavistock here?

By 1960 Cameron had developed his techniques, which he termed "ultra-conceptual communication," into something even more horrific. The period of psychic driving was increased to 16 hours a day for 20 to 30 days and patients were dosed with Sernyl to "block sensory input and produce underactivity." Sernyl is an extremely powerful drug used as an animal anesthetic. It produces "acute psychotic episodes and even the danger of chronic psychosis in humans." [19]

Although standards for medical experimentation had been clearly defined at Nuremberg almost ten years before Cameron's funding by the CIA, specifically requiring "informed consent" by subjects, subjects at the Allen Memorial Institute did not sign consent forms, nor did they in most cases have any idea of what they were getting into. This was the standard, rather than the exception, during most MKULTRA research, in fact.

Two of Cameron's assistants were Leonard Rubenstein, "an electrical whiz of Cockney descent who lacked medical bonafides," who effused about the possibilities of equipment "that will keep tabs on people without their knowing," and Dr. Walter Freeman, who had performed 4,000 frontal lobotomies in 20 years, reportedly on persons often suffering only from depression or paranoia. Freeman went on to become a highly successful brain specialist working for many years in San Francisco. [20]

In 1979 a public interest legal case was launched against the CIA for their activities during the MKULTRA period, with details of the lawsuit appearing in the Hamline Journal of Public Law and Policy. Dr. Paul Termansen appeared in court as an expert witness, and described what had happened to Robert Logie, one of Cameron's patients at Ravenscrag:

"Instead of a standard treatment, Mr. Logie underwent a series of experimental, highly controversial, procedures... Mr. Logie was not a suitable subject for any one of the experimental procedures he was subjected to, if, indeed, anyone would be suited for such procedures. Most certainly, no one would be suitable to the type of experimental procedures used at Allan

Memorial Institute at that time, unless they had volunteered to undergo those experimental procedures."

Dr. Termanson said that after being subjected to Cameron's experiments, "existence could best be termed marginal... He managed to function, work, and exist, but barely."

Another expert witness in the trial, Dr. Brian Doyle, provided information on the case of Rita Zimmerman, who was "depatterned" by Cameron with 30 electroshocks, had 56 days of drug-induced sleep, was subjected to 14 days of negative "psychic driving," and then was given 18 days of positive "psychic driving." Dr. Doyle said,

"Mrs. Zimmerman was not a candidate for electroshock therapy, much less the intensive 'depatterning' procedures that were so disruptive as to leave her incontinent as to bladder and bowel... The intensive electro-shocks that were used to 'depattern' Mrs. Zimmerman were clearly experimental, as was the entire 'depatterning' procedure that was carried to an extreme in her case. The nearly two months of drug-induced sleep and over one month of 'psychic driving' Mrs. Zimmerman underwent were equally extreme applications of clearly experimental procedures... The experimental 'depatterning,' prolonged drug induced sleep and 'psychic driving' procedures used on Mrs. Zimmerman would inevitably cause injury to her mental and physical health."

Doyle commented similarly on the case of Florence Langleben, who had received electroshocks and LSD, 43 days of drugged sleep, and 43 days of psychic driving:

"Mrs. Langleben was not a candidate for electroshock therapy, much less the intensive 'depatterning' procedures... The intensive electroshocks that were used to 'depattern' Mrs. Langleben were clearly experimental, as was the entire 'depatterning procedure. The six weeks of drug-induced sleep and six weeks of 'psychic driving' Mrs. Langleben underwent were equally extreme applications of clearly experimental procedures... The experimental 'depatterning,' prolonged drug induced sleep and 'psychic driving' procedures used on Mrs. Langleben would inevitably cause injury to her mental and physical health." [21]

Another of Cameron's many victims was Mary Morrow, whose background was in nursing. After completing a residency in neurology at the University of Michigan she approached Cameron for a fellowship at Allan Memorial. According to a legal document filed in Washington, D.C., "Because Cameron thought she appeared 'nervous,' he told Dr. Morrow that a medical examination would be required before her application could be considered. Dr. Morrow was then hospitalized at the Royal Victoria Hospital, a facility affiliated with McGill University and the Allan Memorial Institute. After she left the Royal Victoria Hospital, Dr. Morrow was admitted as a paying patient at the Allan Memorial Institute on May 6, 1960, and placed under Cameron's care. For an eleven day period from May 19, 1960, through May 29, 1960, Dr. Morrow was subjected to depatterning experiments employing Page-Russell electroconvulsive shock treatments and a variety of barbiturates, specifically thorazine and anectine. The combination of these drugs produced a condition of brain anoxia [insufficient oxygen reaching the brain] in Dr. Morrow and on June 17, 1960, she was transferred, at her family's insistence, to the medical department of the Royal Victoria Hospital, where she was diagnosed as suffering from acute laryngeal edema [a severe allergic reaction to the drugs]."

Similar experimentation was taking place elsewhere. Forty-two-year-old tennis professional Harold Blauer had been suffering from depression after a divorce. On December 5, 1952, he checked himself into a psychiatric hospital in Manhattan. Unbeknownst to Blauer, the hospital had contracted with the U.S. Army for a chemical warfare test with mescaline derivatives. Lacking any information as to whether the derivatives had ever been tested on humans, a doctor at the hospital injected Blauer five times with the concoction. Records show that for a while Blauer seemed to be experiencing some improvement, although it is questionable how mescaline might have contributed. Whatever the case, the experimentation on Blauer was continued until the fifth injection on January 8, 1953. That dosage was sixteen times the strength of the first injection. Blauer began to sweat and then went into convulsions, frothing at the mouth. The man lapsed into a coma and was pronounced dead two hours later.

The hospital did not inform Blauer's relatives that he had been the unwitting victim of a chemical warfare experiment, instead saying that he had died of an "overdose of a drug." When Blauer's family sued, the claim was settled for $18,000, half of it provided by the government through the hospital, on the condition that the the nature of the experimentation done on Blauer be kept secret by the hospital from the family and the world. [22]

Early on, the CIA had come to the conclusion that for truly realistic results it was necessary to test LSD outside of the lab, on persons in real-life situations. Harry Anslinger, head of the Federal Narcotics Bureau, supervised one such operation, run by George Hunter White, a narcotics officer who had organized a spy training school during World War II. Using CIA funding, White rented an apartment in Greenwich Village, and equipped it with surveillance equipment and two-way mirrors. White, posing alternately as a seaman and as an artist, lured unsuspecting persons back to his apartment and gave them LSD. The large number of adverse reactions to the acid—some requiring the subjects to have weeks of hospitalization—caused White to code name the drug "Stormy."

In 1955 White transferred his base of operation, and set up two experimental LSD launching pads in San Francisco. This was the period of Operation Midnight Climax, in which White paid prostitutes to bring customers to one of these unsafe-houses for unconventional action. The drinks of the unwitting participants were laced with LSD and their actions were observed by White, who sat behind a two-way mirror on a portable toilet with a drink in his hand. San Francisco Narco Bureau agents would also take advantage of Midnight Climax, sampling both the drugs and their purveyors.

White's activities continued until 1963, when CIA Inspector General John Earman found out about Midnight Climax during routine Technical Services inspections. Although an extended period of Agency soul-searching followed in the wake of revelations about safehouse experiments, the operations continued until at least 1966, when White retired from the Narcotics Bureau.

White reminisced about his CIA mission, in a quote made famous by chroniclers of the CIA and mind control: "I was a very minor missionary, actually a heretic, but I toiled wholeheartedly in the vineyards because it was fun, fun, fun. Where else could a red-blooded American boy lie, kill, cheat, steal, rape, and pillage with the sanction and blessing of the All-Highest?" [23]

One prominent victim of MKULTRA was Philip Graham, a graduate of the Army Intelligence School at Harrisburg, Pennsylvania, and the owner and publisher of the Washington Post and Newsweek magazine. Graham made the mistake of attacking the American news media in a speech to a meeting of publishers in January, 1963. Leslie Farber, a psychiatrist from the CIA's Chestnut Lodge, was dispatched to deal with Graham. Graham was drugged and flown to Maryland where after 10 days he was released, only to be returned to Chestnut Lodge in June. Released into the custody of his wife in August, he was found shot to death—allegedly a suicide. His will was declared void because of insanity, and Katherine Graham, his widow, inherited the *Washington Post* and *Newsweek*. [24]

Early in the research of mind control techniques, the "disposal problem" was encountered, i.e. how to get rid of persons who had been the subject of mind control programs. One way of dealing with these persons was to put them, according to an Agency document, "in maximum custody until either operations have progressed to the point where their knowledge is no longer highly sensitive, or the knowledge they possess in general will be of no use to the enemy." Other means of disposal were putting them into mental institutions, slipping them a lobotomy, or in certain cases "termination with extreme prejudice," killing them.

In two series of tests, in 1958 and in 1959-60, U.S. Army Intelligence, in conjunction with the Army Chemical Corps and the CIA, began a program of testing of LSD and other psychoactive compounds at the Medical Research Laboratories at Edgewood Arsenal. The focus of the testing was on "unwitting test reaction" with the intention to find out how an LSD-dosed soldier would fare during interrogation.

Groups of military personnel were given EA-1729, the Army's code designation for LSD, then filmed while interrogators tried to pry forth classified information from them. There were also "Memory Impairment Tests", evaluating the ability of the subjects to recall information that had been previously imparted, and drills in skills including tank driving, anti-aircraft tracking, and field maneuvers.

After the first phase of testing, a letter was sent from the Chief of the Clinical Division at Edgewood to the Commanding General of the Army Intelligence Center extolling the brilliant results of the acid tests. Also recommended was that "actual application of the material [LSD] be utilized in real situations on an experimental basis, if possible."

U.S. Army Intelligence encouraged Edgewood to go ahead with the field testing: "This headquarters has forwarded your letter to the Assistant Chief of Staff for Intelligence (ACSI), Department of the Army, concurring in your recommendation that actual application of the material be utilized in real situations on an experimental basis." In correspondence between the Director of Medical Research at Edgewood and the Commander, Chemical Warfare Labs, it was indicated that the plan was to use LSD outside of the U.S. or on foreign nationals.

On August 8, 1960, the Office of Assistant Chief of Staff

Intelligence Liaison Team flew to Europe to brief intelligence agencies on the joint project. At least two programs resulted, the first being Operation THIRD CHANCE, a 90-day European project involving the administering of LSD to foreign nationals and one American soldier who had allegedly stolen classified documents. Operation DERBY HAT was a similar project planned to take place in Hawaii, although accounts of it are contradictory. One source says that the project was aborted, while another states that an Army Special Purpose Team trained in LSD interrogations questioned seven alleged Japanese Communists, putting at least one of them into a coma.

Testing was apparently done on unknowing Americans citizens, as well. These experiments were reportedly reserved for small groups of individuals, although there were suggestions of larger scale testing taking place at some point in the future.

The Chemical Corps' Major General Creasy remembered, " I was attempting to put on, with a good cover story, to test to see what would happen in subways, for example, when a cloud was laid down on a city. It was denied on reasons that always seemed a little absurd to me." [25]

Records show that Chemical Corps officers were routinely given acid during their training at Fort McClellan, Alabama. Other tests of LSD on army personnel were conducted at the Aberdeen Proving Ground in Maryland; Dugway Proving Ground in Utah; Fort Leavenworth, Kansas; and Fort Benning, in Georgia. By the mid-1960s at least 1,500 army personnel are documented as having been used in Chemical Corps LSD experiments.

Other researchers that were funded by the military included Charles Savage at the Naval Medical Research Institute, Amedeo Marrazzi of the University of Minnesota and Missouri Institute of Psychiatry, James Dille of the University of Washington, Gerald Klee of the University of Maryland Medical School, Neil Burch of Baylor University, Henry Beecher of Harvard and Massachusetts General Hospital, and Paul Hoch and James Cattell of the New York State Psychiatric Institute. [26]

Soon the Army would go on to bigger, but not necessarily better things. Hoffmann-La Roche, a pharmaceutical company in Nutley, New Jersey, was the army's source for a new psychoactive compound, quinuclidinyl benzilate: BZ. This is a drug with even more profound effects than LSD, effects that last for about three days—but that have been known to last for six weeks. One army doctor noted of BZ that, "During the period of acute effects the person is completely out of touch with his environment." [27]

Dr. Van Sim, who was chief of the Clinical Research Division at Edgewood Arsenal, routinely tested on himself all of the new drugs that he would later give to recruits. Sim reported of BZ, "It zonked me for three days. I kept falling down and the people at the lab assigned someone to follow me around with a mattress."

Army testing of BZ began at Edgewood Arsenal in 1959, and continued until 1975. Dr. Solomon Snyder of Johns Hopkins University, who was involved in drug testing for the Chemical Corps, stated, "The army's testing of LSD was just a sideshow compared to its use of BZ."

An estimated 2,800 soldiers were given BZ, with some of them suffering drug-related disabilities to this day. BZ, deployed in the grenades, mortar shells, and missiles, was allegedly also used in combat in Vietnam. [28]

NOTES:

1. Bowart, Walter, *Operation Mind Control.* (Dell Paperback, New York, New York, 1977); Chaitkin, Anton. "British Psychiatry: From Eugenics to Assassination," *EIR,* October 7, 1994; Cannon, Martin, "The Controllers: A New Hypothesis of Alien Abductions", *MUFON UFO Journal,* Number 270, October, 1990

2. Constantine, Alex, *Psychic Dictatorship in the U.S.A.* (Portland, Oregon: Feral House, 1995); Marks, John, *The Search for the "Manchurian Candidate": The CIA and Mind Control,* (New York: Times Books, 1979); Chaitkin

3. Stevens, Jay, *Storming Heaven, LSD and the American Dream.* (New York: Harper & Row, 1987)

4. Chaitkin

5. Quoted in Bowart

6. White, Carol, *The New Dark Ages Conspiracy.* (New York: Benjamin Franklin House, 1984); Marks; Bowart

7. Chaitkin; White; Stevens; Hougan, Jim, *Secret Agenda.* New York: Random House, 1984; Marks

8. Chaitkin; Marks

9. Lee and Shlain, *Acid Dreams.* (New York: Grove Press, 1985); Marks; *The Modesto Bee,* July 26, 1994

10. Smith, Caulfield, Crook, and Gershman, *The Big Brother Book of Lists.* (Los Angeles: Price/Stern/Sloan, 1984); Chaitkin

11. Lee and Shlain

12. "Messing with the Mass Mind," *American Journal of Psychology,* 1989, otherwise undated clipping; Lee and Shlain

13. Unattributed segment in *Matrix III,* Val Valerian, ed., 1992

14. Stevens

15. Chaitkin; Weinstein, M.D. Harvey M., *Psychiatry and the CIA: Victims of Mind Control,* (Washington, D.C.: American Psychiatric Press, 1990)

16. Prouty, Colonel L. Fletcher. Cited in Constantine, Alex, *Psychic*

Dictatorship in the U.S.A. (Portland, Oregon: Feral House, Portland, 1995)

    17. Rauh and Turner, "Anatomy of a Public Interest Case Against the CIA," *Hamline Journal of Public Law and Policy,* Fall 1990; Chaitkin; Constantine, Alex, *Psychic Dictatorship in the U.S.A.* (Portland, Oregon: Feral House, 1995; Weinstein)

    18. Chaitkin; Anonymous untitled research paper, Stockholm: Mediaecco, 1993; Weinstein

    19. Weinstein

    20. Constantine

    21. Rauh and Turner

    22. Bresler, Fenton, *Who Killed John Lennon?* New York: St. Martin's Press, 1989

    23. Lee and Shlain

    24. Chaitkin; Constantine, Alex, "Operation Mockingbird: The CIA and the Media," *Prevailing Winds Magazine,* Number 3, 1997; Dr. John Coleman, *Conspirator's Hierarchy: The Story of the Committee of 300.* (Carson City, Nevada: America West Publishers, 1992)

    25. Lee and Shlain

    26. Marks

    27. Lee and Shlain; Victorian, Armen, "U.S. Army Intelligence Mind Control Experiments", *Lobster* magazine, number 23

    28. Lee and Shlain

Dr. Louis Jolyon "Jolly" West: Mind control programmer?

Chapter 12:

BRAVE NEW WORLD ORDER

Beginning about 1950, an ambitious project was launched by Tavistock for the massive LSD intoxication of the population of the United States. Aldous Huxley, who spearheaded the Tavistock LSD project, was the grandson of Thomas H. Huxley, one of the founders of the Rhodes Round Table group. Huxley had been tutored by H.G. Wells, that vocal proponent of the Open Conspiracy, and was a long term collaborator with Arnold Toynbee, a fifty-year member of the RIIA council, as well as the head of the British intelligence Research Division. To grasp Toynbee's politics, in 1971 he stated that a Bolshevik dictatorship of the world was necessary before a benevolent one world order could be instituted.

The new Tavistock project was intended to inject a euphoria-producing chemical on a widespread basis in America. Huxley's purposes in the dissemination of LSD in the United States may have been betrayed in the following statement:

"Now let us consider another kind of drug—still undiscovered, but probably just around the corner—a drug capable of making people happy in situations where they would normally feel miserable. Such a drug would be a blessing, but a blessing fraught with grave political dangers. By making a harmless chemical euphoric freely available, a dictator could reconcile an entire population to a state of affairs to which self-respecting human beings ought not to be reconciled..." [1]

Elsewhere, Huxley stated it more succinctly: "There will be in the next generation or so, a pharmacological method of making people love their servitude, and producing... a kind of painless concentration camp for entire societies." [2]

Finally, if there is any doubt about Huxley's beliefs, in *Brave New World Revisited* he stated,

"The twenty-first century... will be the era of the World Controllers... The older dictators fell because they could never supply their subjects with enough bread, enough circuses, enough miracles and mysteries. Under a scientific dictatorship education will really work—with the result that most men and women will grow up to love their servitude and will never dream of revolution. There seems to be no good reason why a thoroughly scientific dictatorship should ever be overthrown." [3]

The decadent Huxley had been a member of the Children of the Sun, a British drug and homosexuality cult whose roster of members illustrates a number of ideologies shared by British one-world elitists at that time and now. Among the other members of the group were the Nazi-sympathetic Prince of Wales, later to be Edward VIII; fascist Sir Oswald Mosely; the Mitford sisters (one the wife of Mosley, the other a bedmate of Hitler); George Orwell, British intelligence agent and the author of *1984*. (Orwell's *1984* is usually cited as a protest against totalitarian socialism, but in fact Orwell himself was a socialist who was protesting, as he said, certain excesses that had taken place in Russia).

Other members of the Children of the Sun included Huxley's homosexual lover, author D.H. Lawrence, and Guy Burgess, Soviet spy and member of the Apostles communist homosexual conclave at Cambridge (dubbed "a homosexual Freemasonry"), that spawned a Soviet spy cabal at the highest levels of British intelligence.

Another member of the Apostles was the famous Reilly, "Ace of Spies," a bisexual who—according to Reilly biographer Robin Bruce Lockhart—set up the Soviet spy group at Trinity College, Cambridge through which Western intelligence was massively compromised. Members of this group included spies Anthony Blunt, Burgess, Maclean, and others. Reilly's view may be gauged by a letter he wrote to Lockhart's father on the topic of "Bolshevism":

"I believe that... it is bound by a process of evolution to conquer the world, as Christianity and the ideas of the French Revolution have done before it... and that nothing—least of all violent reactionary forces—can stem its ever-rising tide... the much decried and so little understood 'Soviets' which are the outward expression of Bolshevism as applied to practical government, are the nearest approach I know of, to a real democracy based upon true social justice and that they may be destined to lead the world to the highest ideal of statesmanship—Internationalism." [4]

Huxley had earlier collaborated with Major John Rawlings Rees of the Tavistock Institute, and with cultural anthropologist

Bronislaw Malinowski in a project dubbed "Mass Observation." This was an anthropological survey of the British Isles, patterned after similar surveys of primitive cultures. [5]

Although Huxley had personally used drugs—there are rumors that he was initiated in the use of opium by Aleister Crowley in Berlin in the 1920s—he was introduced to the hallucinogen mescaline in 1952 by family friend and CIA-funded Dr. Humphrey Osmond. Huxley came to the U.S. accompanied by Osmond, who was immediately ushered into Dulles' MKULTRA. Huxley, Osmond, and the University of Chicago's Robert Hutchins immediately began planning for a mescaline project to be funded by the Ford Foundation, although this project was later called off due to objections from the head of the foundation. [6]

In 1953, one month after the creation of MKULTRA, Huxley was given LSD by Osmond. Huxley was overwhelmed by "the most extraordinary and significant experience this side of the Beatific Vision." Although Huxley was perhaps a sincere advocate of the mysticism-inducing properties of LSD, the sociopolitical implications of the drug did not escape him.

Huxley prepared the American population for LSD with articles like "The Doors of Perception," and sponsored a project at Stanford University where students were dosed with hallucinogenics. Two of Huxley's early acid collaborators were Alan Watts, who popularized his own brand of Zen *satori* based on a quart of gin a day, and Gregory Bateson, who had been an anthropologist with the OSS, and who started an LSD clinic at the Palo Alto Veterans Administration Hospital in California. Huxley was also in contact with MKULTRA heavyweight Dr. Louis Jolyon West. [7]

Huxley was to be the first director of the United Nations Economic, Social, and Cultural Organization (UNESCO), whose constitution was written by Bonesman Archibald McLeash. UNESCO has been a major phalanx in the New World Order program, advocating the "appropriate technology" of windmills and solar power rather than industry for the Third World, and mass sterilization drives implemented in those same countries.

Huxley collaborator Keith Ditman provided author Ken Kesey with an unlimited supply of LSD, and it was from this small group that arose Kesey's guerrilla theatrical Merry Pranksters and the Grateful Dead, a rock band that still commands a large cultic following after the demise of its leader. According to a 1968 FBI memorandum, Jerry Garcia, the leader of the Grateful Dead, was employed "to channel youth dissent and rebellion into more benign and non-threatening directions." [8]

A collaborator with Huxley in the acid infusion of the world was the spy, Captain Alfred M. Hubbard, who had given up American citizenship for Canadian prior to World War II. Characterized as a "mystery man" by those who knew him, and as a veritable "Johnny Appleseed of LSD" in most studies, his verified background is informative.

Hubbard was "a high-level OSS officer" who acted as a money conduit to a large number of European spy operations, and who directed the large scale smuggling of weapons to Great Britain prior to Pearl Harbor. He also worked for the Treasury Department, the Federal Narcotics bureau, and the Food and the Drug Administration. Hubbard is said to have worked with the Mafia—actually, sometimes the differentiation between these organizations is tenuous—being "able to ingratiate himself with both sides during Prohibition," according to one history of the period. At one time he became deputy chief of security for the Tropicana Hotel in Las Vegas.

Hubbard was the first large scale distributor of LSD to the world, reportedly amassing the world's largest stockpile of the drug outside of the CIA, and crossing and re-crossing the North American continent like a mysterious Rosicrucian of old, giving LSD to anyone and everyone who was willing to take it.

Osmond and Hubbard participated in a program to give political leaders in America LSD—without severing his connections and ongoing projects with various intelligence agencies. Although the details of this program are secret, an associate of Hubbard's has said that it "affected the thinking of the political leadership of North America." Participants in the program included a prime minister, UN representatives, members of British parliament, and assistants to heads of state.

Hubbard, oddly enough retaining a staunchly conservative bent throughout his proselytizing and distribution of LSD, led raids for the FDA on LSD labs characterized by his apologists as being run by "rebel chemists." Imagine, a rebel chemist having the audacity to make LSD.

One associate of Hubbard's was New World Order theorist Willis Harmon of the Stanford Research Institute. SRI had earlier received grants from the U.S. Army to research chemical incapacitants. When visited by a representative of the underground press at SRI in the early 1970s, Harmon told the man, "There's a war going on between your side and mine. And my side is not going to lose."

In 1968 Harmon invited Hubbard to join the Stanford

Research Institute as a "special investigative agent." According to Harmon, "Our investigations of some of the current social movements affecting education indicate that the drug usage prevalent among student members of the New Left is not entirely undesigned. Some of it appears to be present as a deliberate weapon aimed at political change. We are concerned with assessing the significance of this as it impacts on matters of long-range educational policy. In this connection it would be advantageous to have you considered in the capacity of a special investigative agent who might have access to relevant data which is not ordinarily available." Perhaps it is my cynicism that gives the above paragraph a decided tongue-in-cheek quality.

Hubbard took on the job for SRI, which lasted through the 70s, at $100 per day.

The most high profile of all LSD proponents was, of course, counterculture hero Timothy Leary. Leary met Aldous Huxley at Stanford University and became his protegé. While at the University of California from 1953-56, and employed by the U.S. Public Health Service from 1954-58, Leary received grants for his research from NIMH.

Leary subsequently was appointed as a lecturer at Harvard, where he was noticed by Dr. Harry Murray, who was in charge of the Personality Assessments department of the OSS during World War II. Although Leary and his biographers tiptoe around the matter, funding for his drug experiments while at Harvard came from the CIA, substantiated by the following quote from Walter Bowart, in the second edition of his *Operation Mind Control:*

"...At first he denied that any of his psychedelic research projects at Harvard were funded by the government. Yet when I finally sat with him face-to-face after *Operation Mind Control* had been published (1979), and naively asked him if he was 'witting' or 'unwitting' of his collaboration with the CIA, Leary answered with: 'Who would you work for, the Yankees or the Dodgers? I mean who was I supposed to work for, the KGB?'" [9]

Leary first administered LSD to prison inmates at the Massachusetts Correctional Institute, at Concord. Money for the project came from the Uris Brothers Foundation in New York City, and was doled out by Harvard to Leary. The results of Leary's Concord experiments were published in a 1962 paper titled, "How to Change Behavior."

The man who some have called Leary's "guru" and who Leary himself acknowledged as being a British intelligence agent was

Michael Hollingshead, a friend of Huxley's who had worked for the British Cultural Exchange and had acquired a gram of LSD, enough of the chemical for 10,000 trips. Hollingshead, dispatched by Huxley, was the man who turned Leary on to acid.

According to one account of the period, "Not knowing quite where to turn, he latched onto Hollingshead as his guru. Leary followed him around for days on end, treating the Englishman with awe. He was convinced that this pot-bellied, chain smoking prankster whose face was pink-veined from alcohol was a messenger from the Good Lord Himself."

Hollingshead later turned on most of the English rock music scene to acid. While in Wormswood Scrubs prison in England for 21 months for possession of hashish, Hollingshead made the acquaintance of George Blake, a convicted agent of the KGB. Hollingshead guided Blake in an LSD session, and a few weeks later the spy escaped from the prison and fled to Moscow. [10]

Leary and Richard Alpert (later, Baba Ram Dass, after that plain Ram Dass) were fired from Harvard in 1963—Alpert for giving acid to an undergraduate, Leary for missing a committee meeting—although the duo then carried on their research in Mexico. Expelled from Mexico, they moved their base of operations to Millbrook, New York, where Leary unveiled his acid guru persona to the millions in the hippie movement.

Mary Pinchot Meyer, a longtime friend of Leary, ex-wife of top CIA agent Cord Meyer, and a mistress of JFK, told Leary that, "dissident organizations in academia are... being controlled. The CIA creates the radical journals and student organizations and runs them with deep cover agents." Although this was difficult for Leary to believe, no doubt causing him to think that Meyer was a paranoid conspiracy freak, the statement was confirmed for him by an article in the February 1967 Ramparts magazine, detailing CIA funding and control of the National Student Association. [11]

A major Leary benefactor was stockbroker William Mellon Hitchcock, heir to the Gulf Oil fortune and nephew of Pittsburgh financier Andrew Mellon. Hitchcock turned over Millbrook, a 4,000 acre estate in Dutchess County, New York to Leary's International Federation for Internal Freedom. Aside from their ranking among the rich and famous, the Mellon family has many connections to the American intelligence community, and Mellon family foundations have frequently been used as conduits for CIA money. Several members of the family were members of the OSS, and Richard Helms was a frequent guest of the Mellons while he was CIA director. [12]

According to one account of the period, "Billy Hitchcock, the millionaire *padrone,* never really entered into the close camaraderie of the Millbrook circle," but still maintained close contact with his old friends, brokers and bankers and investors. Sympathetic accounts of the period are generally blind to the more arcane political underpinnings of the acid era, but in this one the authors wonder, "Was he simply a millionaire acid buff, a wayward son of the ruling class who dug Leary's trip? Or did he have something else up his sleeve?"

Hitchcock, by my lights, had plenty up his sleeve. He was an associate of Bernie Cornfeld and Seymour ("The Head") Lazare, directors of the Swiss-based Investors Overseas Services (IOS), a money laundry for the Mafia, Third World dictators, and the CIA. When a financial shortage was perceived at IOS, their assets were transferred to Robert Vesco, whose network of corporations are alleged to have been a CIA front by William Spector, a former CIA operative.

Hitchcock was also the single largest investor in the Meyer Lansky-linked Resorts International, which in 1970 evolved a private intelligence operation known as Intertel, sprung from the same FBI Division Five and British intelligence nexus as Permindex, the umbrella corporation that apparently ran the John F. Kennedy hit. These connections will be explored later in this book. [13]

Another of Hitchcock's associates was Ronald Hadley Stark, who appeared on the psychedelic scene in 1969 with yet another scheme to turn the entire world onto LSD. Stark was one more "mystery man," with a number of cover stories and a seemingly unending bankroll for travelling and maintaining an opulent lifestyle. He boasted that he worked for the CIA, and there is no reason to doubt him in this matter.

Stark financed a lab in Belgium that was the single largest underground manufacturing source for LSD at that time. He was seen at the student uprising in Paris in 1968, and was also present at the student demonstrations and labor strikes in Milan in 1969. In the 1970s he lived a posh lifestyle in Italy, hobnobbing with Sicilian *Mafiosi,* espionage agents of various coloration, and terrorists.

Stark was arrested by Italian police in Bologna in 1975, carrying what was suspected to be a vial of LSD, a key to a safe deposit box containing documents on the manufacture of acid, and friendly letters from a foreign service officer at the American embassy in London addressed to Stark's LSD lab in Belgium.

While in prison in Pisa, Stark arranged to inform on Renato Curcio of the Red Brigades, telling of a plot to assassinate Judge Francesco Coco of Genoa, who was going to preside over a trial of fifty Red Brigadesmen. In June of 1976 Judge Coco was murdered, as Stark had foretold. Another possible victim of the Red Brigades was Italian premier Aldo Moro. Information on Stark's involvement with this murder would later surface, as well as testimony linking Stark to a PLO plan to launch terrorist attacks on government embassies.

Transferred to a jail in Bologna, Stark was the recipient of regular visits from British and American consulates, members of the Italian secret service, and the Libyan diplomatic corps. Stark was also in close contact with General Vito Miceli, who at the time was on the CIA payroll. It is interesting that the American government never attempted to extradite Stark, who was wanted on drug charges in the United States.

In June 1978 a Bologna magistrate, Graziano Gori, was assigned to investigate Stark and his astounding web of associates. A few weeks later, Gori was killed in a car wreck. Later, Stark was charged with "armed banditry" for his connections to terrorist activities, but he was released from prison in April 1979 on the orders of Judge Giorgio Floridia. The reason for Floridia's order, according to the judge, was "an impressive series of scrupulously enumerated proofs" that Stark was CIA.

By the late 1960s the supply of ergotamine, one of the ingredients of LSD, had pretty well dried up. Synchronistically, in 1964 Dow Chemical Company provided samples of the vastly more potent STP to the US Army Chemical Corps at Edgewood Arsenal. According to one chronicle of the period, "In early 1967, for some inexplicable reason, the formula for STP was released to the scientific community at large... Shortly thereafter the drug was circulating in the hippie districts of San Francisco and New York." That "inexplicable reason" may have been hinted at in one of the thousands of CIA MKULTRA documents that were ordered shredded by CIA director Richard Helms, a classified manual titled "LSD: Some Un-Psychedelic Implications".

Another drug that "inexplicably" found its way to the dealers, suddenly appearing in quantity in hippie conclaves around the U.S., was PCP, touted as being synthetic marijuana, but which was in fact "Angel Dust." The army had tested PCP on soldiers at Edgewood Arsenal in the late 1950s, and Dr. Ewen Cameron had used the drug on his subjects in his MKULTRA torture garden. [14]

John Starr Cooke was another 60s notable who functioned as a guru to some influentials in the Haight Ashbury scene. Cooke is alleged to have been a leading Scientology operative and reportedly was close to Scientology founder L. Ron Hubbard in the early 50s. According to one account, Cooke was the first Scientology "Clear," although another man, John McMasters, was the person publicly touted in this role some years later—until he too had a falling out with "the fat boy" as he called Hubbard. Cooke's sister was married to Roger Kent, a leading light in the California Democratic Party, whose brother Sherman was head of the CIA's National Board of Estimates, and was CIA director Dulles' right hand man during the 50s. Cooke is said to have regularly hobnobbed with other CIA personnel.

From his digs in Cuernavaca, Mexico, Cooke sent forth members of a small group who called themselves the Psychedelic Rangers, imbued with the mission of turning on the world to acid. Among persons who visited Cooke in Cuernavaca were Andrija Puharich, who ran drug experiments for the military in the 1950s and was a publicist for the Israeli spoon-bending psychic Uri Geller; and the wealthy Seymour ("The Head") Lazare, an associate of William Mellon Hitchcock, and with Bernie Cornfeld, a director of the Swiss-based Investors Overseas Service (IOS). [15]

A CIA vampire hanging around the acid scene in the 60s was the omnipresent—in mind control programs—Louis Jolyon West, claimed to be the overall coordinator for all government mind control programs. West, like George Hunter White before him, rented a San Francisco safehouse to "study the hippies." One can only guess what kind of dirtywork he was up to.

West has been employed over the years as a hired gun to promote whatever position the CIA wants promoted. After the Kennedy assassination and the murder of Oswald by Jack Ruby, he was interviewed and not surprisingly dwelt on Ruby's "lone nut" characteristics. On the day of the Oklahoma City bombing, West went on the Larry King show to talk about alleged bomber Tim McVeigh, again characterizing him as one more "lone nut," i.e. not involved in a conspiracy. West again appears in an article in *Los Angeles* magazine, after the alleged murder by O.J. Simpson of Nicole Simpson, a case rife with inconsistencies and unexplained associated murders that have not been mentioned, much less explained, by the media. In the article West invokes the highly imaginative "Othello Syndrome," where black men kill their white spouses, due to their belief that "something must be wrong with their Caucasian mates for seeking love beyond the racial pale." [16]

In the acid-induced glow of the Flower Generation there were dissenting voices about the LSD experience, even famous ones. Some of the members of the earlier Beat Generation—who later became icons of the Flower Generation—had doubts about the usefulness of psychedelics, seeing early on that the drug could be used as for control as well as liberation. William Burroughs—at one time active in Scientology—was given acid by Leary in Tangiers in 1961. He wrote of his misgivings about the drug in his book *Nova Express,* published in 1964:

"At the immediate risk of finding myself the most unpopular character of all fiction—and history is fiction—I must say this:

"Bring together state of news—Inquire onward from state to doer—Who monopolized Immortality? Who monopolized Cosmic Consciousness? Who monopolized Love Sex and Dream? Who monopolized Time, Life and Fortune? Who took from you what is yours? ...Listen: Their Garden of Delights is a terminal sewer...Their Immortality Cosmic Consciousness and Love is second-run grade-B shit... Stay out of the Garden of Delights... Throw back their ersatz Immortality... Flush their drug kicks down the drain—they are poisoning and monopolizing the hallucinogenic drugs—learn to make it without any chemical corn."

The poet Allen Ginsberg's initial reactions to LSD, administered to him by Dr. Charles Savage, who had worked on hallucinogenic experiments for the U.S. Navy, were similar to those of Burroughs. Given acid in a clinical environment in Palo Alto, California, Ginsberg said, "I thought that I was trapped in a giant web or network of forces beyond my control that were perhaps experimenting with me or were perhaps from another planet or were from some super-government or cosmic military or science fiction Big Brother."

John Sinclair, of the White Panthers, was purged of his belief in the acid religion through experience: "It makes perfect sense to me. We thought at the time that as a result of our LSD-inspired activities great things would happen. And, of course, it didn't...They were up there moving that shit [i.e. LSD] around. Down on the street, nobody knew what was going on."

Quite so. But even now, the identity of "they" has not been clarified. "They" apparently, ultimately, was Tavistock.

NOTES:

1. Huxley, Aldous, "The Doors of Perception," *Collected Essays.* (New York: Harper and Brothers, 1958)

2. Cited in Smith, Caulfield, Crook, and Gershman, *The Big Brother Book of Lists.* (Los Angeles: Price/Stern, Sloan, 1984)

3. Huxley, Aldous, *Brave New World Revisited.* Cited in Epperson, Ralph A, *The New World Order.* (Tucson, Arizona, Publius Press, 1990)

4. *Executive Intelligence Review,* volume 14, number 23; Lockhart, Robin Bruce, *Reilly: The First Man.* (London, England: Penguin Books, 1987); Pincher, Chapman, *Too Secret, Too Long.* (New York: St. Martin's Press, 1984)

5. Editors of the Executive Intelligence Review, *Dope, Inc.* (Washington, D.C.: EIR, 1992)

6. Editors of the Executive Intelligence Review; Horowitz and Palmer, ed. Moksha: *Writings on Psychedelics and the Visionary Experience (1931-1963).* (New York: Stonehill Publishing Company, 1977)

7. Lee and Shlain, *Acid Dreams.* (New York: Grove Press, 1985); Krupey, Greg, "The High & the Mighty," *Steamshovel Press* magazine, number 10

8. White, Carol, *The New Dark Ages Conspiracy.* (New York: New Benjamin Franklin House, 1984); Hidell, Al, "Paranotes," *Paranoia* magazine, Winter 1995/1996

9. Lee and Shlain; White; Bowart, Walter, *Operation Mind Control.* (New York: Dell, 1977); Lee and Shlain; Bowart quote cited in "Honey, Did You Leave Your Brain Back at Langley Again? A Brief History of Modern Mind Control Technology," by Robert Guffey, *Paranoia* magazine, autumn 1997

10. Lee and Shlain; Krupey

11. Krupey

12. Lee and Shlain

13. Ibid; Editors of the Executive Intelligence Review

14. Ibid.

15. Ibid.

16. Guffey

Implantable Transponder

Product Description:

The Implantable Transponder is a passive radio-frequency identification tag, designed to work in conjunction with a compatible radio-frequency ID reading system. The transponder consists of an electromagnetic coil and microchip sealed in a tubular glass enclosure. The chip is preprogrammed with a unique ID code that cannot be altered; over 34 billion individual code numbers are available. When the transponder is activated by a low frequency radio signal, it transmits the ID code to the reading system. Independent testing has shown the transponder to be safe and easy to implant.

Although specifically designed for implanting in animals, this transponder can be used for other applications requiring a micro-sized identification tag.

Specifications:

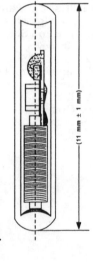

2.1 mm
Dia Max

(11 mm ± 1 mm)

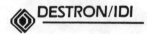

DESTRON/IDI

Chapter 13:

CHANGING IMAGES

The basic nature of the LSD infusion of the world was meant for, in a term that would only be publicized later, "Changing the Image of Man."

In May, 1974 a study was released by the Stanford Research Institute titled *Changing Images*, prepared by the SRI Center for the Study of Social Policy, Willis Harmon, Director. This 301-page report was authored by 14 researchers, supervised by 23 controllers, that included cultural anthropologist Margaret Mead, behaviorist B.F. Skinner, and Sir Geoffrey Vickers of the British armaments family and British intelligence.

The basic point of the study was the same old New World Order news: the self-image of mankind must be changed away from industrial growth to spiritual values. According to the study, "Many of our present images appear to have become dangerously obsolescent, however. An image may be appropriate for one phase in the development of a society, but once that stage is accomplished, the use of the image as a continuing guide to action will likely create more problems than it solves... Science, technology and economics have made possible really significant strides toward achieving such basic human goals as physical safety and security, material comfort and better health. But many of these successes have brought with them problems of being too successful—problems that themselves seem insoluble within the set of societal value-premises that led to their emergence... Our highly developed system of technology leads to higher vulnerability and breakdowns. Indeed the range and interconnected impact of societal problems that are now emerging pose a serious threat to our civilization... If [our] projections of the future prove correct, we can expect the associated problems of the trend to become more serious, more universal and to occur more rapidly."

According to the Stanford study, "Images and fundamental conceptions of human nature and potentialities can have enormous power in shaping the values and actions in a society. We have attempted in this study to:

"(1) Illuminate ways our present society, its citizens, and institutions have been shaped by the underlying myths and images of the past and present.

"(2) Explore with respect to contemporary societal problems the deficiencies of currently held images of mankind and to identify needed characteristics of future images.

"(3) Identify high-leverage activities that could facilitate the emergence of new images and new policy approaches to the resolution of key problems in society."

I believe that dumping LSD on the populace of the planet was seen as one of those high-leverage activities. It was a way of turning the masses away from a political activism that might net them a share of the world pie, and toward the life of ecstatic mystic peasantry.

The Tavistock-originated and CIA-funded Rand Corporation even sponsored studies reporting on the "changes in dogmatism" and political motivation of LSD users. According to one report, authored by Rand's William McGlothlin, "If some of the subjects are drawn from extreme right or leftwing organizations, it may be possible to obtain additional behavioral measure in terms of the number resigning or becoming inactive." [1]

Another group that closely tracked the Flower Generation was the Hudson Institute, founded by Herman Kahn, who had received funding from the Human Ecology Fund, a CIA cutout. Kahn visited Millbrook and other centers of psychedelic activity, although he was far from an advocate of the benefits of LSD. "He was primarily interested in social control," stated one Hudson Institute consultant.

It should be noted that some of the Tavistock-sponsored creators of the LSD culture, men like Tim Leary, may have felt that their motives were benign—LSD users tend to develop a messiah complex in which they see acid as the solution to all the world's problems, and try to turn everyone on to the drug—but the strategic underpinnings of those motives lay in the New World Order plans of the British elite. Leary and his court were either witting or unwitting agents of Tavistock.

Although the mass media vocally decry the idea that there could ever be a conspiracy of control functioning behind the scenes in society, the real members of the conspiracy are often quite straightforward in saying what is going on. Marilyn Ferguson, a protegé of Willis Harmon who derived her book *The Aquarian Conspiracy* from Harmon's *Changing Images,* talked about how the Tavistock restructuring of the world would take place. She called it the SPIN principle, Segmented Polycentric Integrated Networks. Although she suggests the idea is new, it is obvious that it has been the approach of the New World Order since the beginning:

"This is a source of power never before tapped in history: multiple self-sufficient social movements linked for a whole array of goals whose accomplishment would transform every aspect of contemporary life.

"Because SPINs are so qualitatively different in organization and impact from bureaucracies... most people don't see them—or think they are conspiracies. Often networks take similar actions without conferring with each other simply because they share so many assumptions. It might also be said that the shared assumptions are the collusion.

"The Aquarian Conspiracy is, in effect, a SPIN of SPINs, a network of many networks aimed at social transformation. The Aquarian Conspiracy is indeed loose, segmented, evolutionary, redundant. Its center is everywhere. Although many social movements and mutual-help groups are represented in its alliances, its life does not hinge on any of them."

The upshot of the Tavistock approach and where its SPIN of SPINs is heading is obvious. While a tiny percentage of the population will continue to exist within their plush Xanadus, the majority of the world will be reduced to subsistence standards of living, and denied the benefits of technology and industry, although furnished with all the drugs they desire. [2]

NOTES:

1. Lee and Shlain, *Acid Dreams.* (New York: Grove Press, 1985); Dr. John Coleman, *Conspirator's Hierarchy: The Story of the Committee of 300.* (Carson City, Nevada: America West Publishers, 1992)
2. Lee and Shlain

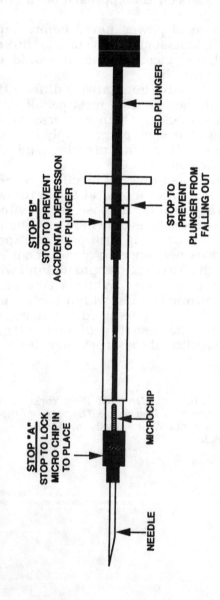

AVID

RED PLUNGER

STOP "B"
STOP TO PREVENT
ACCIDENTAL DEPRESSION
OF PLUNGER

STOP TO PREVENT
PLUNGER FROM
FALLING OUT

STOP "A"
STOP TO LOCK
MICRO CHIP IN
TO PLACE

MICROCHIP

NEEDLE

HOW TO USE THE AVID "SUDS"
(SINGLE USE DISPOSABLE SYRINGE)

Chapter 14:

CENTER FOR VIOLENCE

The dialectic at work.   Create violence through economic pressures, the media, mind control, agent provacateurs: thesis. Counter it with totalitarian measures, more mind control, police crackdown, surveillance, drugging of the population: antithesis. What ensues is Orwell's vision of *1984*, a society of total control: synthesis.

During the Nixon presidency, agents of the Law Enforcement Assistance Administration, an arm of the U.S. Justice Department, had a roundtable with Richard Nixon, Attorney General John Mitchell, H.R. Haldemann, John Erlichman, and other members of the White House staff, as well as Dr. Bertram Brown, director for the National Institute of Mental Health. Among other programs that the LEAA had evolved were the development of a National Population Surveillance Computer System, designed to monitor citizens of the U.S., as well as measures to create a national police force, including Operation Cable Splicer and Operation Garden Plot. [1]

At the meeting bonds were forged for the linkage of LEAA funding, police state goals, and the NIMH.   LEAA henceforth provided the cash for 350 NIMH projects related to "mental health" as it is so euphemistically called.   Among projects funded were dozens of mind control and behavior mod programs in hospitals, prisons, and schools.   These projects included a Department of Health, Education and Welfare program to screen all children on Medicaid for psychological problems; programs to treat prison inmates with psychoactive drugs; shock treatment for child molesters at the Somers Correctional Facility in Connecticut; psychosurgery programs on inmates in Michigan and California; the testing of a vomiting-inducing drug in prisoners who broke rules in Iowa; and the injection of the terror drug Anectine on prisoners in California.

The bond between the LEAA and NIMH reportedly was so tight that eventually the scientists of NIMH were under the direct control of LEAA. Eventually this collaboration changed the character of the LEAA itself, so that the organization was no longer fixated on martial law measures, but primarily involved in mind control funding for aversion therapy, psychosurgery, and behavior control through drugging. [2]

In November 1974 the U.S. Senate Subcommittee on Constitutional Rights, one of whose members was Congressman Leo Ryan who was murdered at Jonestown, began investigation into the federal funding of behavior modification programs. Senator Sam Erwin, who headed the subcommittee, interrogated Donald E. Santarelli, the head of the LEAA, about the kind of projects that were being funded, resulting in an announcement by the organization that they would discontinue providing cash for psychosurgery and other forms of mind control. Not that the pledge was heeded. At least 537 mind control programs, including operations involving psychosurgery continued to be funded. [3]

LEAA was still in the business of mind control when Dr. Louis Jolyon ("Jolly") West, chairman of the Department of Psychiatry at the University of California at Los Angeles and director of the Neuropsychiatric Institute, proposed to California Governor Ronald Reagan the creation of a Center for the Study and Reduction of Violence.

The original idea for violence research centers was birthed in the mind of CIA and FBI agent William Herrmann, employed by the Systems Development Corporation, and a counter-insurgency advisor to Governor Reagan. Herrman had worked at the Rand Corporation, the Hoover Center on Violence, and the Stanford Research Institute. During the Vietnam war Herrmann had worked in psy-ops in Vietnam and Cambodia, probably as a member of the Operation Phoenix assassination program, responsible for the death of thousands of Vietnamese. Herrman has also been identified as an international arms dealer who traded with Iran in 1980, and who may have been involved in the October Surprise. In 1995 Herrman was serving an eight-year prison term in England for an alleged CIA counterfeiting operation. His M.O., in short, reads as if he is a member of the Octopus as delineated by the murdered journalist Danny Casolaro. [4]

In 1970, Hermann is reported to have acted as control agent to Colston Westbrook, a Black CIA psychological warfare expert who had been involved in Operation Phoenix—quite a coincidence, that. Vietcong POWs are known to have been implanted with electronic transceivers during Operation

Phoenix. Westbrook had formed the Black Cultural Association at Vacaville Medical Facility, a euphemistically-named prison in California that was the site of a Maximum Psychiatric Diagnostic Unit (termed a maxi-maxi in prison parlance) where extensive drug behavior modification research had been done. It is alleged that there was a mind control assassination program at Vacaville, where men were programmed to murder prominent Blacks, including Oakland School Superintendent Marcus Foster, and Black Panthers Huey Newton and Bobby Seale. [5]

Donald DeFreeze, who between 1967 and 1969 had been employed by the L.A. Police Department's Public Disorder Unit, was the black organizer for the Black Cultural Association at Vacaville. Westbrook was the man who dubbed DeFreeze *"Cinque Mtume,"* meaning "fifth prophet," and who designed the seven-headed cobra logo for the group that Cinque later headed up: the Symbionese Liberation Army. [6]

Another Phoenix Program alumnus who backed the Violence Center in a big way was Dr. Earl Brian, Secretary of Health under Governor Reagan. Brian was involved in October Surprise, the illegalities and murders at the Cabazon Indian reservation in Indio, California, and the theft of the Inslaw PROMIS software, and was identified as a member of the "Octopus" international crime cabal by murdered journalist Danny Casolaro.

The head of the violence control center would be Louis Jolyon West. West's background in mind control-related research goes back to the antediluvian days of MKULTRA. A CIA memorandum entitled "Interrogation Techniques," from January 14, 1953, includes the following note:

"If the services of Major Louis J. West, USAF (MC), a trained hypnotist, can be obtained, and another man well grounded in conventional psychological interrogation and polygraph techniques, and the services of Lt. Col. [deleted], a well-balanced interrogation research center could be established in an especially selected location." [7]

Aldous Huxley, writing in 1957, also mentioned West, indicating that he had been doing research with hypnosis and mescaline. In 1961 Huxley commented that West had been experimenting with sense deprivation and noted his state of the art research facilities. West is also known to have directed a CIA-funded LSD research program in the 1960s at the University of Oklahoma, and to have run a safehouse of unspecified function in Haight Ashbury at the height of the hippie scene.

West was the psychiatrist who examined Jack Ruby, the

assassin of Lee Harvey Oswald, ordering that Ruby be treated for mental problems, quite possibly as a means to shut Ruby up in his claims that a conspiracy was responsible for the killing of John Kennedy. [8]

West was even involved recently in the "remote viewing" experiments of Project Grill Flame, conducted by Stanford Research Institute. Due to a certain amount of notoriety, one suspects, the man is currently going by the name "L.J. West," and can be seen acting as a hired gun promoting the government line on occasional television news programs.

After the announcement of the plans for the Violence Center, West dashed out a letter to then-California Director of Health, J.M. Stubblebine. It said:

"Dear Stub,

"I am in possession of confidential information that the Army is prepared to turn over Nike missile bases to state and local agencies for non-military purposes. They may look with special favor on health-related applications.

"Such a Nike missile base is located in the Santa Monica Mountains, within a half-hour's drive of the Neuropsychiatric Institute. It is accessible, but relatively remote. The site is securely fenced, and includes various buildings and improvements, making it suitable for prompt occupancy.

"If this site were made available to the Neuropsychiatric Institute as a research facility, perhaps initially as an adjunct to the new Center for the Prevention of Violence, we could put it to very good use. Comparative studies could be carried out there, in an isolated but convenient location, of experimental or model programs for the alteration of undesirable behavior.

"Such programs might include drug or alcohol abuse, modification of chronic anti-social or impulsive aggressiveness, etc. The site could also accommodate conferences or retreats for instruction of selected groups of mental-health related professionals and of others (e.g., law enforcement personnel, parole officers, special educators) for whom both demonstration and participation would be effective modes of instruction.

"My understanding is that a direct request by the Governor, or other appropriate officers of the State, to the Secretary of Defense (or, of course, the President) could be most likely to produce prompt results."

Among the programs that West foresaw as taking place at the Violence Center were genetic, neurophysiological, and biochemical studies of violent persons, studies on so-called "hyperkinetic" or "hyperactive" children, "hormonal aspects of passivity and aggressiveness in boys," and surveys of "norms of violence among various ethnic groups." Also proposed was "implanting tiny electrodes deep within the brain" for the monitoring and control of violent subjects. West had gotten tentative approval for a grant of $750,000 from the LEAA for the Violence Center, the money reportedly raised by alleged Octopoid Dr. Earl Brian. [9]

Reagan was so enthralled by the idea for the center that he included it in his January 11 State of the State address. Reagan said that the center "will explore all types of violent behavior, what causes it, how it may be detected, prevented, controlled, and treated." [10]

So far as we know, West's Violence Center was never activated, at least in the grandiose scale he proposed. Because of unwanted attention from civil liberties groups and, in particular, the Subcommittee on Constitutional Rights involved in investigating CIA mind control abuse, LEAA changed its policy to exclude funding "for psychosurgery, medical research, behavior modification—including aversion therapy—and chemotherapy." West was still seeking funding for the center in April 1974, but with Watergate in the news, the mood among politicians was such that they did not want to take any chances with potentially unpopular funding proposals. [11]

NOTES:

1. Pabst, Dr. William R., "A National Emergency: Total Takeover", Society for the Protection of Individual Rights and Liberties, undated article
2. Schrag, Peter, *Mind Control*. (New York: Pantheon Books, 1978); Krawczyk, Glenn, "The New Inquisition: Cult Awareness or the Cult of Intelligence?", *Nexus* magazine, December 1994/January 1995
3. Martin and Caul, "Mind Control", the *Napa Sentinal*, 1991
4. Krawczyk; Martin and Caul; Thomas and Keith, *The Octopus*. (Portland, Oregon: Feral House, 1996)
5. Krawczyk; Chorover, Stephan L., *From Genesis to Genocide: The Meaning of Human Nature and the Power of Behavior Control*, (Cambridge, Massachusetts: The MIT Press, 1979); Constantine, Alex, *Virtual Government*. (Venice, California: Feral House, 1997)
6. Krawczyk
7. Memorandum quoted in Krawczyk, Glenn, "Mind Control, Techniques and Tactics of the New World Order, *Nexus* magazine, December/January 1993
8. Krawczyk, "The New Inquisition"
9. Ibid.
10. Schrag; Krawczyk, "The New Inquisition"
11. Schrag; Colodny and Gettlin, *Silent Coup: The Removal of a President*. (New York: St. Martin's Paperbacks, 1992)

Senator Robert F. Kennedy lying dead on the floor of the hotel kitchen. The clip-on tie of his body-guard Thane Cesar can be seen near his right hand.

Sirhan Sirhan is taken into custody immediately after the shooting.

Chapter 15:

MIND CONTROLLED ASSASSINS

From the earliest days, a portion of the resources of the OSS and, later, the CIA were turned toward the creation of what has come to be called the Manchurian Candidate—taken from the fictional book by Richard Condon—otherwise known as the mind controlled assassin. As part of this research, Counterintelligence Director James Jesus Angleton defined three goals in hypnosis programs run by the CIA: (1) the speedy hypnotic induction of unwitting subjects. (2) the ability to create long-lasting amnesia. (3) the implanting of long-lasting, useful hypnotic suggestions. [1]

Dr. George Estabrooks, the chairman of the Department of Psychology at Colgate University, was involved in early OSS experiments in hypnosis. His boast was, "I can hypnotize a man without his knowledge or consent into committing treason against the United States."

Estabrooks informed a group of officials in Washington that 200 hypnotists with the right stuff could unleash an army of hypnotized agents in the U.S. during wartime. He laid out, in fact, a scenario in which the entire U.S. military could be taken over by a handful of mind controlled fifth columnists.

Hypnotizing volunteer soldiers of reported low rank and education, Estabrooks showed how they could be programmed to retain complex verbal information. In confirmation of Estabrooks' thesis, subsequent testing by J.G. Watkins on army volunteers showed that these men could be, contrary to popular wisdom on the topic, hypnotized to commit acts that violated their own moral codes, not to mention military codes.

One experiment that Watkins carried out involved hypnotizing army privates, and then telling them that an officer who was in the same room was an enemy infiltrator. Watkins told the hypnotized subjects that the officer would try to kill them. Without exception, on command the soldiers violently attacked the officer. In one case, the subject pulled out a knife and tried to stab the officer. [2]

In February, 1954 Morse Allen, the head of Project BLUEBIRD, continued this line of experimentation in creating a "disposable" assassin, to be activated with mind control and then "terminated with extreme prejudice." At about the same time the CIA funded research by Alden Sears at the University of Minnesota, and later at the University of Denver. Sears' focus was the installation of multiple personalities in his experimental subjects. [3]

Sheffield Edwards was the security officer for the CIA's Project ARTICHOKE. During this period the CIA collaborated with the Federal Bureau of Narcotics (FBN), one of whose members, Charles Sirgusa, was involved in setting up safehouses for later MKULTRA experiments. In 1960 Edwards contacted Siragusa for help in locating paid assassins for the murder of certain foreign leaders—whether hypnosis would be employed was not specifically indicated. Siragusa was not willing to take part in the recruitment, so Edwards turned to Robert Maheu, a top Howard Hughes aide and ex-FBI agent. Maheu contacted Mafia members Sam Giancana and John Roselli to assist him in obtaining hired hands for, in this case, the elimination of Fidel Castro.

The Castro assassination schemes were developed in the Technical Services Division (TSS) of the CIA, overseen by the head of MKULTRA, Dr. Sidney Gottlieb. In late 1961 the CIA's assassination programs, operating under the title ZR-RIFLE, were handed to William Harvey by Richard Helms, the man who had come up with the idea for MKULTRA in the first place. At the same time that TSS was involved in assassination and the recruitment of assassination squads, it was also involved in an expanded program of research into hypnosis. [4]

Lieutenant Commander Thomas Narut, a U.S. Navy psychologist stationed at the U.S. Regional Medical Center in Naples, Italy, in 1979 admitted to Navy programs to create mind controlled assassins. Narut made this apparent gaffe at the NATO conference for psychologists on "Dimensions of Stress and Anxiety" in Oslo, Norway.

The topic Narut spoke on at the conference was "The Use of a Symbolic Model and Verbal Intervention in Inducing and Reducing Stress," but his spiel was mostly about the benefits of doing research for the Navy. One thing he mentioned was that there was no shortage of enlisted men who could be studied, with psych profiles and background available on all subjects.

Afterwards, in a small group that included Peter Watson of the *London Sunday Times*, Narut was more candid about what the Navy was up to. He talked about his work with "combat readiness units," whose participants included commandos and undercover operatives at U.S. embassies worldwide, including "hit men and assassins." According to Narut, these men were desensitized by being strapped into a chair with their heads immobilized and eyelids clamped open, while they were forced to view violent true life splatter flicks, until finally the men were totally callous toward scenes of horrible carnage. Among the films shown were a brutal African circumcision, and a man having his fingers sawed off in a sawmill. Another technique of desensitization that was employed was propaganda aimed to make the customs and culture of another country appear as evil and less than human. Narut stated that successful programming of assassins took only a few weeks.

Candidates for assassination training were taken from submarine crews and paratroops, but included convicted murderers from military prisons. Another source of mind control fodder for the assassination programs was soldiers who had been awarded for bravery. Narut said that the men selected were programmed at the Navy neuropsychiatric lab in San Diego, California, and also at the Naples, Italy medical installation. Although Narut admitted that he did not have a high enough clearance to know where all of the programmed assassins were sent, he did know that some had been stationed in the Naples embassy—this would have provided for easy deployment throughout Europe. [5]

After Narut's admissions were printed in the *Sunday Times*, the Pentagon issued an official denial that the Navy had ever conducted "psychological training" or the training of assassins. Although admitting that Narut was on Naval staff in Naples, they reported that they had been unable to locate him in order to obtain a response to the allegations. A short time later Narut gave a press conference in which he stated that the information he had offered had only been theoretical—these were the kind of programs that the Navy might do in the future. Soon after, the U.S. Naval headquarters in London reported that Narut's rash statements had been made due to his "personal problems." This was almost certainly not true. Dr. Irwin Sarason, one of the organizers of the Oslo conference, admitted that a few years earlier he had been solicited by the Navy to participate in a project similar to the one Narut described. [6]

Daniel Sheehan of the Christic Institute public advocacy group also verifies this kind of research: "We have talked to half-a-dozen individuals who have told a startlingly similar story about how, at a very young age, usually between twenty and twenty-five, they were contacted, usually within the context of military training, and told: 'Look, we've got a special deal for you. You're going to come into the service under the normal designation of being an infantryman but you're going to leave the service after a while and you're going to have special training, and you're going to be brought into a special program. They're sent to special places where they are trained by mercenaries and then they're told: 'You're going to be called upon from time to time to do some things for us.'"

According to Sheehan, one young man was contacted at an army recruiting station and then turned over to an agent of the Bureau of Alcohol, Tobacco, and Firearms. His mission was to infiltrate a motorcycle gang and kill the leader of a rival gang, causing both of the gangs to fight and hopefully destroy each other. The man was also sent to a training camp in Hawaii, where training was being done for an assassination that was to take place in Central America. [7]

Another man, a 43-year-old German psychologist and doctor of economic and social sciences who chooses to remain anonymous, believes that he has been, since a child, the subject of mind control procedures. These include Cameron-style "depatterning" treatments using electroshock and psychic driving, drug hypnosis, ELF programming, and a drug capable of inducing near-death experiences.

One of the techniques he describes is aversive therapy using a "torture trouser," an electrical torture device that is "sort of a loin cloth made of leather and steel bonds by which an electrode is fastened to the genitals of the victim. For electric supply they use a cable or a battery so that you can freely move and if the torturer wants to torture you he sends an electric signal to the battery using a transmitter."

He states that, "In 1972, they tried to use me as an undercover zombie who should infiltrate German terrorist troops... Who were they? They said they were the *Mossad* and the *Shabak*. I was kidnapped and brought to an interrogation camp in a desert... I strongly believe that I was a victim of an international secret service and psychiatry cooperation headed by the Pentagon in the name of 'national security'...

"I clearly object to the suspicion that the organization behind this assault on human rights comes from outer space or has something to do with the Illuminati or another kind of conspiracy. I don't believe that aliens have visited our planet, but if aliens exist they are probably not so cruel as our human, all-too-human controllers...

"It is my strong belief that the basic ideas of mind control and human robot production stem from German KZs. I don't know who the Werner von Braun of KZ psychiatry was who was hired by the U.S. intelligence agencies after the war, but the modus operandi of mind control makes me believe that initially a potent Nazi brain was hidden behind it..." [8]

Another man apparently programmed as a mind controlled assassin was Colonel William Bishop, who made the following statement to researcher Gary Shaw in 1983:

"That was how, after the Korean War, I got involved with CIA. I have been subjected to every known type of drug. The medical doctors connected with the agency found that certain drugs work quite well in conjunction with hypnosis—hypnotic power of suggestion—with some subjects. It did with me. I speak with absolute certainty and knowledge and experience that this is not only possible, but did and is taking place today.

"I never understood why they selected me personally. There were any number of psychological or emotional factors involved in people's selection. Antisocial behavior patterns, paranoid or the rudiments of paranoia, and so on. But when they are successful with this programming—or, for lack of a better term, indoctrination—they could take John Doe and get this man to kill George and Jane Smith. He will be given all the pertinent information as to their location, daily habits, etc. Then there is a mental block put on this mission in his mind. He remembers nothing about it.

"Perhaps a month or a year later—rarely over a year, at least back in those days—the phone rings. A code word will be read to him in a voice that John Doe recognizes. That will trigger the action. John Doe will commit the assassination, return home, and remember absolutely nothing of it. It is totally a blank space.

"Now, there is a problem with this, and they never found a way that I know of to overcome it. From time to time—it happens to me now—I will see faces, names, places, gunfire, for which there is no rational explanation. I went back for deprogramming. In these sessions, they explain that this does happen from time to time, not to worry about it, just clear your mind and forget it.

"I know men who gradually lost their sight, or some of their hearing, or the use of their vocal cords. Some had chronic constipation. For entirely psychological reasons, not physical, because inadvertently these mental blocks developed. I myself became totally impotent. For obvious reasons, I don't care to go into this in any greater detail."

Bishop died of heart failure a few days after authorizing the release of a tape recording that included the above statement. [9]

NOTES:

1. Chaitkin, Anton, "British Psychiatry: From Eugenics to Assassination," *EIR,* October 7, 1994
2. Smith, Jerry, *HAARP: Ultimate Weapon of the Conspiracy,* (Kempton, Illinois: Adventures Unlimited Press, 1997)
3. Chaitkin
4. Russell, Dick, *The Man Who Knew Too Much.* New York: Carrol & Graf, 1992
5. Bowart, Walter, *Operation Mind Control.* (New York: Dell Paperback, 1977); Bresler, Fenton, *Who Killed John Lennon?* (New York: St. Martin's Press, 1989)
6. Bowart
7. Bresler
8. *Freethinking, The Newsletter of the Freedom of Thought Foundation,* Volume 1, number 4, March 1995. Letter sent to Walter Bowart
9. Russell

Model Candy Jones: Mind control victim or mind control hoax?

Chapter 16:

SO LIKE CANDY

The story of Candy Jones is ubiquitous in the literature of mind control, and has been repeated by virtually every researcher who has written a book on the subject. Here is Candy's story, related in a book authored by Donald Bain, *The Control of Candy Jones*: [1]

During World War II Candy had been one of the most popular pin-up girls in America. Touring the Pacific with the USO she caught undulant fever and malaria and was hospitalized in Manila. There she met a medical officer identified in Bain's book by a pseudonym, "Gil Jensen." He would later be one of her contacts in the world of CIA mind control.

In 1959 Candy started a modeling agency in the United States and, in regards to an office burglary, was contacted by an FBI man. Noting a microphone that she used for taping the voices of models, the FBI agent asked to borrow it, and Candy assented. Later the same FBI man convinced the woman to allow her modeling school to be used as an FBI mail drop. Candy Jones was later a courier for a piece of government mail that she took across the country. Shortly thereafter, she was recontacted by "Gil Jensen," the same man whom she had met in the Philippines. "Jensen" invited her to work for the CIA, and she accepted.

In 1973 Candy Jones married "Long John" Nebel, a popular radio talk show host who specialized in stories of UFOs and other *outré* subjects. On their wedding night, Nebel watched Candy go through a transformation into another person, this one cruel and cold; but the mood passed. The next evening, however, the cruel mood returned, then again faded away.

Jones was also plagued by insomnia, and Nebel hypnotized his wife, opening up a Pandora's box. Candy had apparently had an abusive childhood, and had developed an alter ego named Arlene. This was the "transformation" that Nebel had observed, Candy turning into Arlene.

During hypnosis Candy also revealed her contact with "Dr. Jensen," her regular hypnosis sessions with him, and the injections he had given her of what he had called "vitamins." She spoke of having to sign a government security oath, training in espionage work that she had undergone at a CIA camp, and her experiences as a split-personality courier, manipulated through hypnosis and drugs, and plying her twilight trade under a number of pseudonyms. She also recalled being tortured with electric shock by Chinese men in Taiwan over the contents of one of the messages she had delivered.

Candy Jones spoke of being one among several female CIA zombies who were tortured at CIA headquarters in Langley, Virginia. During the course of her deprogramming by Nebel, Candy revealed that she had been programmed to commit suicide on December 31, 1972 in Nassau, Bahamas, after her use to the CIA was over. Nebel's marriage had circumvented the trip and saved Candy's life. According to the book by Bains, Candy was still struggling with her alter-ego Arlene at the time of the writing of the book.

Investigators contacting the CIA seeking information on Candy Jones via the Freedom of Information Act have been turned out in the cold. Although the CIA does have a file on Jones, it will not release any portion of it.

If the mind control programming of Candy Jones is true, then it is powerful testimony for many of the mind control atrocity stories to follow, stories such as told by Cathy O'Brien in *Trance Formation of America*. The trouble is that although the story of Candy Jones is cited in virtually every book on mind control ever written, in all probability it is a hoax.

Author Paris Flammonde, who was a close friend of Long John Nebel, and who was the producer of Nebel's radio show for several years, is one of the persons who has said that Bains' *The Control of Candy Jones* is a hoax. In 1990 Flammonde wrote, "During a series of walks and lunches, John often spoke about, and we batted about ideas regarding a bizarre and commercial book about Candy. Briefly he toyed with consideration of my doing something along those lines (since I had ghosted a book for him earlier), but the thought was discarded for several reasons, the main one being that Candy did not especially care for me, contending to him that, even though I no longer had anything to do with the broadcast, he tended to let me 'influence' him.

"And I am happy to grant that the more I realized how 'far out' he wanted the 'fact book' to be, the more completely uninterested I became. In any event, the vast majority of the text is nonsense, and what little is true would be difficult to identify and impossible for the uninitiated—and profitless. The more vulgar, spiteful, and contemptible of the speculations are not worthy of comment—even by one who observed Candy to be a genuinely impossible individual at times, occasionally shudderingly coldblooded, and devoid of talkshow hosting talent." [2]

UFO investigator Jim Moseley knew both Nebel (who died of cancer in 1978) and Candy Jones (who also died of cancer, in 1989) for many years, and appeared on Nebel's WMCA radio show "hundreds of times" in relation to his research into UFOs. Moseley spoke out about his knowledge of the Candy Jones mind control case calling it "a crock of shit." He stated that his opinion had been confirmed by Sandy Teller, who had been Nebel's assistant for many years, and a friend of the man who had ghostwritten the Candy Jones volume. [3]

As such, the story of Candy Jones, cannot be considered to be proven factual.

NOTES:

1. The title of this chapter is taken from the Elvis Costello song of the same name

2. "Saucer Smear," ed. James Moseley, volume 37, number 4, 1990

3. Nanninga, Rob, "*The Control of Candy Jones*," Internet posting, February 10, 1994; Bowart, Walter, *Operation Mind Control*. (New York: Dell Paperback, 1977); Bain, Donald, *The Control of Candy Jones*. Chicago: Playboy Press, 1976); "Saucer Smear," ed. James W. Moseley, 1990, volume 37, number 2

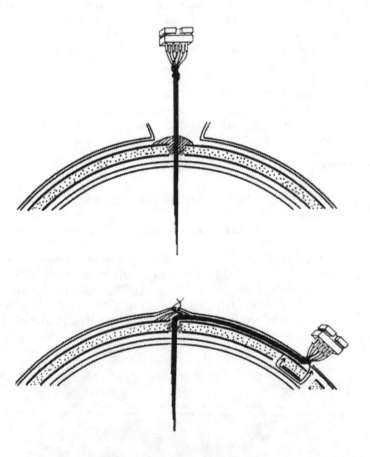

Above: Diagrams of implanting Delgado's "stimoceivers."

Chapter 17:

MIND CONTROL IMPLANTS

The first person we are aware of involved in research in direct brain stimulation was Swiss physiologist Walter Rudolf Hess, educated in Switzerland and Germany, and director of the Physiological Institute at Zurich from 1917 to 1951. His experiments included the insertion of fine electrically conductive wires into the brains of anaesthetized cats. To no-one's great surprise, given mild electrical stimulation the cats went berserk. [1]

Jose Delgado, funded by Yale University, the Office of Naval Intelligence, the U.S. Air Force 6571st Aeromedical Research Laboratory, and other institutions, and linked to Spanish fascist groups by researcher John Judge, carried Hess' research a great deal farther. Delgado was the first to specialize in the implantation of electronic devices directly into the brain. [2]

Delgado's early experiments in the 1950s involved rigidly locking the head of an animal or human in a metal clamp, and then plunging a long needle or needles into the brain. Once the needle was in place, electricity or chemicals were injected through it. Later experiments used what he termed "trans-dermal stimoceivers," tiny radio broadcasting/receiving units that were buried entirely into the brains of animals and humans, and carried electrical impulses to the brain, as well as broadcasting the subject's reactions back to a computer.

Delgado described the capabilities of such instrumentation in the early stages of his research:

"Microminiaturization of the instrument's electronic components permits control of all parameters of excitation for radio stimulation of three different points within the brain and also telemetric recording of three channels of intracerebral electrical activity. In animals, the stimoceiver may be anchored to the skull, and different members of a colony can be studied without disturbing their spontaneous relations within a group. Behavior such as aggression can be evoked or inhibited. In [human] patients, the stimoceiver may be strapped to the head bandage, permitting electrical stimulation and monitoring of intracerebral activity without disturbing spontaneous activities." [3]

Delgado stated further, "It is... already possible to induce a large variety of responses, from motor effects to emotional reactions and intellectual manifestations, by direct electrical stimulation of the brain. Also, several investigators have learned to identify patterns of electrical activity (which a computer could also recognize) localized in specific areas of the brain and related to determined phenomena such as perception of smells or visual perception of edges and movements. We are advancing rapidly in the pattern recognition of electrical correlates of behavior and in the methodology for two-way radio communication between brain and computers...

"The individual is defenseless against direct manipulation of the brain because he is deprived of his most intimate mechanisms of biological reactivity. In experiments, electrical stimulation of appropriate intensity always prevailed over free will; and, for example, flexion of the hand evoked by stimulation of the motor cortex cannot be voluntarily avoided. Destruction of the frontal lobes produced changes in effectiveness which are beyond any personal control."

But far from being an incredible invasion of the subject's life, Delgado reassured by stating that some subjects were more concerned about the cosmetics of the matter:

"Leaving wires inside of a thinking brain may appear unpleasant or dangerous, but actually the many patients who have undergone this experience have not been concerned about the fact of being wired, nor have they felt any discomfort due to the presence of conductors in their heads. Some women have shown their feminine adaptability to circumstances by wearing attractive hats or wigs to conceal their electrical headgear, and many people have been able to enjoy a normal life as outpatients, returning to the clinic periodically for examination and stimulation. In a few cases in which contacts were located in pleasurable areas, patients have had the opportunity to stimulate their own brains by pressing the button of a portable instrument, and this procedure is reported to have therapeutic benefits." [4]

Delgado admitted that not all subjects reacted with such equanimity: "During depth explorations, it was demonstrated that crises of assaultive behavior similar to the patient's spontaneous bursts of anger could be elicited by radio stimulation of contact 3 in the right amygdala. A 1.2 milliamperes excitation of this point was applied while she was playing the guitar and singing with enthusiasm and skill. At the seventh second of stimulation, she threw away the guitar and in a fit of rage launched an attack against the wall and then paced around the floor for several minutes, after which she gradually quieted down and resumed her usual cheerful behavior."

Delgado's experiments ultimately had very little to do with medicine and his touted "therapy". Delgado set up a one and one-half acre preserve on an island in the Bermudas, wherein the effects of stimoceivers could be tested in the manipulation of a gibbon colony and the interactions of their social hierarchies.

"The old dream of an individual overpowering the strength of a dictator by remote control has been fulfilled, at least in our monkey colonies," Delgado wrote, "by a combination of neurosurgery and electronics, demonstrating the possibility of intraspecies instrumental manipulation of hierarchical organization..." He speculates that, "in the near future the stimoceiver may provide the essential link from man to computer to man, with a reciprocal feedback between neurons and instruments which represents a new orientation for the medical control of neurophysiological functions." [5]

Social controller that he was, Delgado's main beef was with man's will, i.e. his freedom: "We may conclude that ESB [Electrical Stimulation of the Brain] can activate and influence some of the cerebral mechanisms involved in willful behavior. In this way we are able to investigate the neuronal functions related to the so-called will, and in the near future this experimental approach should permit clarification of such highly controversial subjects as 'freedom,' 'individuality,' and 'spontaneity' in factual terms rather than in elusive semantic discussions."

Delgado's revolution, what he calls a "master control of human behavior," is apparently not intended to be a democratic one: "The contention that an ideal society should be 'well behaved' may be disputed by many and in any case requires a clarification... In some old plantations slaves behaved very well, worked hard, were submissive to their masters, and were probably happier than some of the free blacks in modern ghettos. In several dictatorial countries the general population is skillful, productive, well behaved, and perhaps as happy as those in more democratic societies."

The open publication of Delgado's book *Physical Control of the Mind* met with a decidedly cool reaction from the public, and this may have warned other researchers in the field to keep quiet about the subject. To this day, Delgado's is the only popular book on the subject of implants and electrical stimulation of the brain (ESB). [6]

Although Delgado went on to, in his mind, better things, namely the use of direct electromagnetic irradiation of the brain, research into radio-controlled direct cerebral stimulation was not discontinued. Dr. Stuart Mackay, a colleague of Delgado and author of the book, *Bio-Medical Telemetry*, stated, "Among the many telemetry instruments being used today are miniature radio transmitters that can be swallowed, carried externally, or surgically implanted in man or animals. Recent developments include pressure transmitters, ultrasonic and radio units for free-swimming dolphins, units for tracking wild animals, and pill-sized transmitters of many designs and functions that can operate continuously for several years. The scope of observations that can be made is too broad to more than hint at with a few examples. Transmitters introduced through normal body openings in the human can sense pH in the stomach, the site of bleeding along the gastrointestinal tract, radiation intensity, the pressure changes in the bladder due to micturition, the pressure of teeth grinding together during sleep, vaginal temperature, and the like. Human and subhuman species have been studied, as have aquatic and terrestrial animals, cold- and warm-blooded animals, and so on. Some transmitters need only send their signal for an hour, whereas others are expected to transmit continuously for a year or more... It is hoped that these few preliminary words will give a feeling for the scope of this activity... The possibilities are limited only by the imagination of the investigator." [7]

During the latter days of MKULTRA research, a CIA memorandum, dated 22 November, 1961, announced, "Initial biological work on techniques and brain locations essential to providing conditioning and control of animals has been completed. The feasibility of remote control of activities in several species of animals has been demonstrated. The present investigations are directed toward improvement of techniques and will provide a precise mapping of the useful brain centers in selected species. The ultimate objective of this research is to provide an understanding of the mechanisms involved in the directional control of animals and to provide practical systems suitable for human application."

Did the mind control shrinks ever succeed in hardwiring anyone with their implants outside of helpless patients locked away in asylums by and for the insane? Absolutely.

The Los Angeles *Herald Examiner* for March 21, 1979

describes one such case. Leonard Kille was an electronics engineer and co-inventor of the Land camera. In 1966 Kille rightly came to believe that his wife was having an affair with another man, and his distress over the matter was interpreted by psychiatrists as a "personality pattern disturbance."

Kille was thought to be "dangerous" and was referred to CIA shrinks Vernon Mark and Frank Ervin. It is not known whether funding parameters played a part in their decision, but Mark and Ervin came to the conclusion that the best solution for Kille's problems was an electronic brain implant. Although Kille at first thought the solution excessive, his wife threatened divorce if he didn't take the cure. Predictably, after Kille got his brain wired she divorced him anyway and married the man she had been having an affair with.

Kille had four electrical strands implanted in his brain, each strand studded with about 20 electrode stimoceivers. The electrodes were used to diddle Kille's brain with current, adjusting his emotions at will. Dr. Peter Breggin of the Center to Study Psychiatry investigated Kille's case after he had been implanted, and found that the man alternated between a vegetative state and nightmares that he would again be operated on and be implanted with additional 'trodes.

In 1971 an attendant at the Veteran's Administration hospital happened upon Kille, who had placed a wastebasket on his head to "stop the microwaves." The Veterans Administration doctors had not been told that Kille had been implanted—a matter of national security, perhaps—and so assumed that he was stark raving. The VA doctors ordered additional "treatments" on Kille that left him paralyzed from the waist down. [8]

Robert Naeslund is another victim of Delgado's technology. He believes that in 1967, while undergoing surgery in Stockholm, Sweden, he was implanted with mind control devices. Naeslund reports that the implant was placed there by Dr. Curt Strand, injected through a nasal passage. Naeslund contacted the Swedish Board of Health and Welfare protesting the non-consensual experimentation, but when the doctors heard his story he was predictably declared mentally ill and locked away in a mental hospital.

After securing release from the hospital, Naeslund showed a number of Swedish doctors x-rays of his head that even to a layman plainly exhibit small unnatural objects in his head, but the doctors to a man declared the x-rays to be normal. It was not until 1983 that Professor P.A. Lindstrom, at the University of California in San Diego examined the x-rays and wrote, "I can only confirm that some foreign objects, most likely brain transmitters, have been implanted at the base of your frontal brain and in the skull. In my opinion, there is no excuse for such implantations. I fully agree with Lincoln Lawrence who, in his book [*Were We Controlled?*] on page 27, wrote, 'There are two particularly dreadful procedures which have been developed, those working and playing with them secretly call them R.H.I.C. and E.D.O.M.—Radio-Hypnotic Intracerebral Control and Electronic Dissolution of Memory.'"

After Lindstrom attested to the fact that there were foreign objects in Naeslund's head, ten other doctors came forward verifying their existence.

In 1985 Naeslund delivered a petition with 50 signatures to the Swedish Director of Public Prosecutions, informing him of the implanting of mind control devices in Sweden and demanding that the practice be stopped. Naeslund was also one of several persons responsible for placing an advertisement in 30 Swedish newspapers, exposing the situation of mind control. Apparently his activism brought Naeslund back to the attention of whomever was responsible for the implants. This time they had something different in store for the man.

Naeslund writes, "At about the same time the first advertisement was published, I noticed a radiation or frequency which seemed to rise up from below my flat. In the mornings it felt as though my face, shoulders and back had been sunburned. If I laid a sheet of paper on the floor, it would, after only a matter of hours, begin to roll itself up from both ends and all battery-operated equipment rapidly were quickly drained of power. The waves increased until I was forced to move out into a friend's flat.

"I hired another flat at *Kocksgatan* 38 in Stockholm where, for the first two weeks, everything was fine. By the first of May, however, the trouble started again. The effects were much the same; the feelings of burning heat and noticeable burns on the face after just an hour and the spreading of the sensation into the palate, throat and lungs. Paper rolled itself up whether hanging on the wall or lying on the floor—but now I also experienced how my blood circulation was being affected. I wrote of my last days in the flat: 'The radiation has increased for the last two weeks and now, the 29th of May, it is completely unthinkable to sleep here. It is possible to be in the flat for at most two hours, but after that one has to leave because the pain in the lungs, the dehydration, the dry cough, and general weakness.'

"Due to critical conditions caused by SAPO's [Swedish Secret Police] radiation, I was forced to abandon my efforts to expose their electromagnetic terrorism. It was to be five years before I resumed the fight."

Unable to locate a doctor in Sweden who was willing to remove the implants in his head, Naeslund travelled to Djakarta, Indonesia. "On August 4, 1987," he remembers, "I visited St. Carolus Hospital, Ji Salemba, Djakarta, and I met Professor Hendayo to whom I showed my x-rays, as well as reports from various doctors. He, obviously, could see the implanted foreign objects and more x-rays taken the same day confirmed the fact, so Dr. Hendayo agreed to operate. I stayed at the hospital until the following day. They took blood tests, etc., and informed me to come back on August 11th.

"On the morning of the 12th, I was shown to the operating room. Right outside of the door, I met Dr. Hendayo. He told me that something had happened which would cause the postponement of the operation. He would not say why. Considering how important this was to me, I insisted that he keep his part of the agreement and do the operation. His behavior and attitude that morning was much different than earlier. The complaisance and friendliness of the previous meeting were gone, replaced by irritation and stress. But he changed his mind and agreed to perform the operation. As soon as we entered the operating ward, two people entered from another room; they were Western middle-aged men. One of them had a syringe and gave me the sedative without a word or any preparation.

"In the middle of the operation I awoke with a horrible pain in my head. My arms and legs were secured with straps. One person held my head steady, while another held open the 5 cm. incision in my forehead with some sort of instrument. A third person held an object, resembling a branding iron used on animals, which he burned into my head. During the 45 seconds of the operation in which I was awake, I experienced the feeling that my head was being blown to bits. I screamed in pain and tried to free my arms and legs. I fell unconscious from the pain and shock. The next thing I knew, it was 2 a.m. and I could feel my brain on fire. This was 18 hours after the operation.

"The next morning I went to the hospital's radiology department and asked the doctor to x-ray my head. The picture showed the injury and that there was a foreign object in the damaged area. I went to the chief physician and told him what had happened. Afterward, I visited Dr. Hendayo and he told me,

"It wasn't my idea to do this... I had no choice... You should have listened to me and postponed the operation... Your country's secret police was involved..."

"The reason the operation turned out the way it did is quite clear. Prof. Hendayo was, at first, in favor of the operation. But the Swedish Secret Police (SAPO) followed me via mind control and they knew every step I took. When Dr. Hendayo promised to operate on me, SAPO also knew. In order to stop me, they informed their CIA colleagues in Indonesia, who forbade the doctor to help me, or they threatened to expose them. That was why the doctor could not say why he wanted to postpone the operation. SAPO/CIA had obviously wanted to warn me and show that there were other powers behind the decision. Now, five years later, I have physical pain in the area which was damaged. In addition, my mental and psychological abilities have been greatly altered. The difficulty in finding a doctor who will operate on me is the great secret behind the use of mind control telemetry and doctors' international solidarity with colleagues who use people for experiments. These transmitters have changed my life in many ways and torment me through their constant use."

In 1992 Naeslund contacted an activist organization, the International Network Against Mind Control, and participated in drafting a letter protesting such experimentation to British Prime Minister John Major. The day after the letter was sent, Naeslund believes that his apartment was again zapped:

"The first signs of radiation from electromagnetic weapons were noticed during the night of 11th October, the day after the letter was faxed worldwide. I was awakened at 3 a.m. by a blockage of the blood circulation in my hands, feet, forearms and parts of my legs, hands and feet swelled up and became numb. My face and back became sunburned as if I had been sunbathing on a hot summer's day. This was to be repeated night after night and it must be assumed that the electromagnetic waves were ultraviolet in nature, a radiation which affects the skin's pigmentation and which are known to cause cancer. The radiation continued during the following day and night and even though I tried to be at home as little as possible, it became quite clear that they still had the power to vary the spectrum and intensity of the radiation which they were using against me. From the first day, I experienced noticeable changes in my lungs and windpipe which resembled the symptoms following the radiation of 1985. The windpipe and respiratory passages became parched, my voice hoarse, and my lungs painful. I also suffered from acute amnesia whenever I crossed the threshold to my flat. By the third day, I considered it my safest move to leave my flat and so I went away for a week.

"On returning, I found myself in a radiation chamber of considerably greater power than the one I had left in which it was possible to generate a multitude of destructively painful symptoms by varying the spectrum and intensity. I was kept awake at nights and sent into a kind of trance during the days, but by far the most frightening effect was that on the lungs which even after the first night had been severely impaired. When, after two days, I also began to suffer from backache and an almost crippling immobility, and when even the shortest possible time in my flat began to be unbearable, I felt that it was time to desist risking my life and moved in with friends. Since I had to return occasionally to my flat, I was able to establish that the radiation continued to penetrate my flat and on one fortunate occasion I was able to identify its source. The deteriorating winter found me at home one evening taking in some flowers from my balcony when I noticed in the block opposite, in the window of the flat directly under my own, was some apparatus, partially visible between the angled slats of a venetian blind. It was directed up at my flat. It was emitting no light but its surface was lustrous.

"During the night I collected some infrared film and some binoculars so that I could study it more closely. As early as the previous summer, being more often out on the balcony, I had noticed that there was never any light in that flat, just as there is none nowadays. The day after, I called on the flat at *Verkstadsgatan* 22 and rung the doorbell above the name Broman. No one answered, not surprisingly since I heard from the neighbors that he had passed away some months back. The same day, I had the film developed; the picture I obtained revealed the apparatus with startling clarity.

"From here SAPO was terrorizing me and enfeebling my health with their destructive radiation, and so together with some friends I contrived to break into the flat and seize the apparatus. However, by 8 p.m. the same evening when I was home monitoring the situation, I noticed that the apparatus was gone. They had been there and removed it and with it the radiation. I was able to return home."

Naeslund continues to be active in exposing covert mind control worldwide. [9]

Another probable victim of mind control implants is Glen Nichols who in 1959 at the age of 12 was informed that he had a hearing problem and needed to have a hearing aid. Objections from friends and family prevented that from being done until 1962, when he was implanted with a miniaturized radio in his ear canal in the guise of receiving a hearing aid. "Then they would use very low volume subliminal messages to control me," Nichols protests. "They would give me post-hypnotic suggestions that I had ear infections and I must not clean inside my ear canals or I would suffer permanent hearing loss. Occasionally I would clean inside my ear canals and find a metal device that would be explained away by those around me."

Nichols believes that he also experienced periods of torture and mind erasure, and that in 1967 another Delgado-style electronic transceiver was implanted next to an eardrum. He was told that he had hurt his ear playing football. Nichols thinks that another implant was later inserted in his other ear, noting that he has several small scars above and behind both his ears. "For some reason," Nichols states, "in addition to the surgically implanted transceivers, at times additional miniature receivers were also inserted in my ear canals. I can recall having one found in my ear by a California State University, Northridge, health center medical doctor in 1971. I also found another one in my ear about 1988."

In another incident, "I can recall having an electrode inserted into my frontal brain through my nostril when I was about 33 in 1980. I experienced intense pain, confusion and disequilibrium. I was told I had a sinus infection. I explored the source of my pain and found a small bulb stuck to the roof of my nasal cavity. The doctors I contacted said it was an infection and not to touch it. I persisted and removed it myself with tweezers. It looked like a two-pronged electrode, with two sharp wires stuck up into my brain with the bulb hanging down."

By 1989 Nichols, living in Westlake Village, California, had completed his schooling and was a licensed counselor and psychotherapist, working with a large number of patients from the defense industry. Nichols had come to the realization that he was a victim of mind control, with memories of conditioning sessions and abuse returning to consciousness.

Nichols suspected that he was also experiencing electronic irradiation of some sort and obtained a radio frequency counter to check levels of emissions, which turned out to be extremely high around his apartment building. Nichols has also been vocal in decrying mind control experimentation, disseminating the account of his victimization over the Internet. [10]

Remy Chevalier is a journalist who writes on topics including alternative energy sources and political conspiracy. In correspondence with the author, he offers:

"I was abducted back in the late 60's by tall guys in full body white jump suits wearing big black goggles. For years I couldn't afford dental work until finally one of my teeth broke. I had no choice, I had to go. The dentist went to work and restored my mouth, taking out the old mercury fillings and replacing them with this new composite they use now that matches the color of your teeth. On the worse one, the one he had to grind down to fix a crown, he discovered something inside he'd never seen before. He and the assistant pondered for a few minutes wondering what the hell it was. I jokingly said, 'Maybe it's an alien implant,' and after I saw the look on his face, I added: 'Just kidding!' He had to pulverize the strange thing to keep working so we'll never know for sure. But since then I can stress my body much more than I ever could. Before I'd get these awful headaches if I lifted too much weight. Now I can go till muscle failure without my head killing me. I'd be in much better physical shape today if I could have worked out the way I do now ten years ago. Whether that was the mercury or an implant that hindered me physically, we'll never know, but at 45 it's a bit late for me now to cry over spilled milk. One thing's for sure, my head was messed with. When, for how long, and by whom, are still questions I don't have answers for." [11]

Another case of probable mind control is that of President Issayas Afeworki of the African country of Eritrea. Afeworki had conducted a victorious war against Israeli-supplied Ethiopia. Certainly this would have been adequate reason for the brain tinkers to take note of him. In the summer of 1993, according to one of his counselors, "he fell ill with a mysterious disease. Physicians called in from the U.S. said [Afeworki] had a rare 'brain fever' that could be treated only in a state-of-the-art Israeli clinic. Afeworki was rushed onto a military jet and flown to Israel.

According to the same counselor, "When he returned home a month later, he was a strangely changed man." Afeworki's policies toward Ethiopia, and for that matter, Israel changed into total cooperation.

According to an Algerian delegate, "We are told not to worry about this Eritrean flip-flop, but we do worry, and will worry more and more until we find out just what happened to President Afeworki in that Israeli neurology clinic where he became such a thoroughly changed man." [12]

Another case is that of James Petit, who in 1984 claimed to

the press that he was a drug and arms smuggler for the CIA, with his employment by the Agency confirmed by his attorney and an attorney representing a co-defendant in a drug trafficking case. After crashing his drug shipment plane in Columbia in 1982, Petit says that he was taken to the burn center at the U.S. Army Institute of Surgical Research, in San Antonio, Texas. His stay was confirmed by a spokesperson for the hospital. Petit believes that while he was a patient there, that electronic implants were injected into his neck, face, arms, and ears.

"After my release from the hospital," says Petit, "I was having such extreme pain it was unbelievable. It was directly due to the CIA transmitters." X-rays taken of Petit's head showed a bottle shaped object located behind his left ear. [13]

By 1994, the *London Times* estimated that in the previous decade there had been 15,000 cases of persons being implanted with electronic brain devices. It is impossible to know if the *Times* estimate is at all accurate, since it is unlikely that they would be privy to statistics of secret testing. Certainly, most anti-mind control activists would say that the figure was a gross underestimate.

NOTES:

1. Packard; "Hess, Walter Rudolf, *Encyclopedia Americana.* (New York: Americana Corporation, 1963); "Hess, Walter Rudolf; Funk & Wagnalls New Encyclopedia. New York: Funk & Wagnalls Inc., 1973
2. Delgado, Jose, *Physical Control of the Mind.* (New York: Harper & Row, 1969); Judge, John, "The Secret Government," *Dharma Combat* number 10
3. Delgado
4. Ibid.
5. Ibid.; Packard
6. Delgado
7. Mackay, Dr. Stuart, *Bio-Medical Telemetry*
8. Constantine
9. *An Open Letter to the Swedish Prime Minister Regarding Electromagnetic Terror By Robert Naeslund,* copy in the author's possession
10. Nichols, Glen, "The victims begin to speak out: 'I am a victim of mind control,'" *The Omega Report,* July and September/October 1994
11. Chevalier, Remy. Correspondence with the author, September, 1997
12. Mann, Martin, "African Leader as 'Manchurian Candidate'?," *The Spotlight,* February 17, 1997
13. *National Examiner,* April 30, 1984

Chapter 18:

FUTURE SHOCK
AND THE JFK HIT

If any event this century was calculated as a "future shock" programming of the American populace, it must be the assassination of John F. Kennedy. Although a majority of Americans believe that the murder of Kennedy was performed by a conspiracy, there are few who would suggest that it was an act of pure mind control.

The seminal research suggesting this interpretation of the assassination is that of "William Torbitt," reported to have been the pseudonym for deceased Texas lawyer David Copeland. Copeland was a prosecuting attorney in the early 1950s, later serving as a civil and criminal lawyer. He had been a close supporter of the Lyndon Johnson/Lloyd Bentsen political steamroller in Texas until 1963, when he severed his ties with the group for reasons that will become apparent. In 1970 Copeland wrote *Nomenclature of an Assassination Cabal*, circulated widely in photocopy, detailing information that he had gathered while investigating the murder of President John F. Kennedy. Nomenclature has only recently been brought out in paperback from Adventures Unlimited under the title *NASA, Nazis & JFK*, 27 years after the fact.

While revealing much of the information relating to the thesis of the present chapter, Copeland was not aware of certain facts that I believe would have allowed him to see the broader overall picture. According to Copeland, "The killing of President Kennedy was planned and supervised by Division Five of the Federal Bureau of Investigation... Actually, Division Five acted dually with the Defense Intelligence Agency which was acting on behalf of the Joint Chiefs of Staff in the Pentagon."

FBI Director and 33rd degree Freemason—the ranking Freemason in Washington, D.C. at the time—J. Edgar Hoover was according to Copeland, one of the conspirators. Vice President

Lyndon Johnson was another. Not surprisingly, William Sullivan, former assistant FBI director, has stated that Hoover and Johnson "mistrusted and disliked all three Kennedy brothers. President Johnson and Hoover had mutual fear and hatred for the Kennedys." [1]

According to Copeland, "L.M. Bloomfield, a Montreal, Canada lawyer bearing the reputation as a sex deviate, the direct supervisor of all contractual agents with J. Edgar Hoover's Division Five, was the top coordinator for the network planning the execution. A Swiss corporation, Permindex, was used to head five front organizations responsible for furnishing personnel and supervisors to carry out assigned duties."

Almost buried within the *Nomenclature* text is information that I consider among the most important revelations. He reports that prior to the assassination, in 1963, there was a top secret meeting at the Tryall Compound in Jamaica of Sir William Stephenson, Britain's top intelligence agent. At the meeting was Major Louis Mortimer Bloomfield of the British Special Operations Executive (SOE), an element of British intelligence allegedly created to infiltrate American intelligence; Colonel Clay Shaw, formerly of the OSS; Ferenc Nagy, who had been a cabinet minister in the pro-Nazi Horthy government of Hungary, and later the prime minister of that country; Georgio Mantello, a.k.a. George Mandel, former trade minister for Mussolini; and White Russian émigrées Jean de Menil and Paul Raigorodski. Shaw, Nagy, Montello, and Bloomfield were all officials of Permindex. According to Copeland, the matter discussed at the meeting was the assassination of JFK. [2]

The Kennedy family themselves were products of "The Conspiracy." During Prohibition "Papa Joe" Kennedy worked with Newark, New Jersey's Reinfeld Syndicate, half of which was owned by the Bronfman bootlegging gang of Canada. After the war, Kennedy was given a British distiller's license personally approved by Winston Churchill, with the Kennedy fortune administered by the the Lazard Brothers, Ltd., Rothschild affiliates and one of Europe's most influential families. As American ambassador to Great Britain, Kennedy attached himself to the pro-Nazi Cliveden set, where Round Tablers and Fabians congregated. Kathleen Kennedy, the sister of John, Edward, and Robert, married the Marquess of Hartington, son and heir to the Duke of Devonshire, the head of worldwide Freemasonry, and of course prominent among the British ruling elite. Harold Macmillan, who became British prime minister during the John Kennedy presidency, was a member of the Duke's family.

While in Britain Joseph Kennedy was inducted into the Most Venerable Order of St. John of Jerusalem. Joseph and John Kennedy were trained in the Fabian-founded London School of Economics under the personal tutorage of Harold Laski, a Fabian Society controller.

John Kennedy apparently crossed the conspiracy, and died because of it. Robert Kennedy's much touted war on the Mafia was in fact mostly a personal vendetta against Jimmy Hoffa, and a targeting of lower level operatives. Men like Meyer Lansky remained untouched. But in a number of foolhardy moves Kennedy began to buck the directives of the British, winding down U.S. presence in Southeast Asia, opening up a dtente with the Soviet Union, and putting out feelers for secret talks with Castro.

Although Copeland, in *Nomenclature,* implicates a complex weave of conspirators, including members of the Mafia, the fascist Solidarist movement, the FBI, NASA, and other groups, what he may have missed are what appear to me to be the highest levels of planning. Major Louis Mortimer Bloomfield had been recruited into the SOE in 1938, and while under commission in that organization, had been assigned to the American OSS, then detailed into the counterespionage Division Five of the FBI. At the time of John Kennedy's assassination, Bloomfield was still an officer in Division Five.

After the war, Bloomfield had resumed his career as an attorney in Montreal, Canada in the law firm of Phillips, Vinefield, Bloomfield, and Goodman. He was attorney and controller for the Bronfman family fortune who in these latter days affected an air of propriety for those who didn't know their beginnings.

The Bronfman family is the owner of Seagrams, the largest liquor company in North America. During Prohibition the Bronfmans made their fortune in bootlegging, furnishing the networks of men like Arthur Flegenheimer, a.k.a. Dutch Schultz, Arnold Rothstein, Meyer Lansky, Benjamin "Bugsy" Siegel, and Charles "Lucky" Luciano with their British-distilled product. After the repeal of Prohibition, the Bronfmans became street-legal, with members of the family being elected into the highest levels of the Most Venerable Order of St. John of Jerusalem and intermarrying with the Rothschilds. [3]

Bloomfield was also a high-ranking official in the United Nations, providing legal advice to that august body. He found his way into that position by being a representative of the Round

Table-established International Executive Board of the International Law Association, an offshoot formed in 1873 and charged with developing a one-world code of law. Bloomfield was also a high-ranking member of the Most Venerable Order of St. John of Jerusalem, and the annual chairman of the *Histadrut* campaign in Canada, that owns over one-third of the Gross National Product of Israel. Among his many positions, Bloomfield took on the role of consul-general in charge of the Western Hemisphere and Liberia, one of the largest centers in the world for the transfer of black market monies.

By 1958 Bloomfield had established Permindex, incorporated in Switzerland and purporting to be a trade exposition company, but in fact an international assassination bureau of the Special Operations Executive. All of the participants in the Kennedy plot at the Tryall Compound were officials and investors in Permindex.

One of the chief operatives of Permindex was Colonel Clay Shaw of the OSS. Shaw, like Bloomfield, was a homosexual—this mentioned to make the connection to the long term homosexual orientation of many premier operatives at the highest level of the conspiracy. Shaw himself has testified that he was the OSS liaison officer to the headquarters of British Prime Minister Winston Churchill. Shaw returned to the U.S. after the war and took over the directorship of the International House/World Trade Center, leaving it to found the International Trade Market in New Orleans. Later, Shaw would become a director of Permindex, and the ITM would become a subsidiary of Centro Mondiale Commerciale, an arm of that assassination bureau. In all probability, all of these companies were fronts for the Special Operations Executive, that had long adhered to a policy of working through commercial fronts.

At the time of this writing, there are over 50 World Trade Centers around the world, run from the World Trade Center Association of Clay Shaw, and connected by computer and satellite.

On March 16, 1967, Perry Raymond Russo testified before a criminal district court panel in New Orleans, that he had been present during a conversation between Claw Shaw, David Ferrie, and a person calling himself "Leon Oswald." Ferrie, an agent of Division Five, talked about the necessity of three shooters and a "triangulation of fire," and that a scapegoat could be used to enable the actual assassins to escape. According to Copeland, in *Nomenclature of an Assassination Cabal,* the person going by the name "Leon Oswald" was in fact William Seymour, an agent for a private detective agency called Double-Chek, reportedly used as a cut-out for Division Five and CIA operations.

According to *Nomenclature,* seven riflemen were used to shoot Kennedy, a Mexico-based assassination squad whose Oaxaca-based organization had been put together in 1943 by FBI Director J. Edgar Hoover and SOE Commander Sir William Stephenson.

Copeland seems to have intuited that there was a programming behind the assassination, although not apparently making the connect of who was responsible. He said, "It should be pointed out that during a few years following John Kennedy's murder, the crime rate in the United States more than doubled. Public opinion surveys during the time reflected about 80% of the people did not believe the Warren Commission report. The general public felt someone or some group had been behind the murder of John F. Kennedy and the guilty ones had not been punished. Such an attitude on the part of the public leads to a gradual breakdown of law, order and morals of society."

What Copeland did not see was that that breakdown was engineered by the very forces responsible for the mind control of America and the destruction of its way of life. The Kennedy assassination was a British intelligence—read Tavistock—hit, and its purpose was to shock the American consciousness into a near-comatose state for reprogramming, the standard Tavistock modus operandi.

Specific techniques of mind control may have also been employed in the Kennedy assassination at the microcosmic level. Lee Harvey Oswald in September, 1957, arrived at the Atsugi Naval Air Base to work as a radar operator with a security clearance, odd for a man so forthcoming about his pro-Communist views that he was dubbed "Oswaldovitch" by his fellow soldiers. Atsugi, aside from being the launch base for the top secret U-2 spy plane, also housed the Joint Technical Advisory Group, where MKULTRA LSD experimentation is said to have taken place. [4]

Once in Atsugi, Oswald engaged in more than radar monitoring. At a Tokyo nightclub called the Queen Bee, Oswald became intimate with a hostess who was believed to be a Russian spy, and contracted gonorrhea. Oswald's medical record states that the disease was contracted "in line of duty, not due to own misconduct." Obviously, Oswald was at the time functioning as an agent of the military, probably performing surveillance on the believed Russian spy at the Queen Bee. [5]

Kerry Thornley, perhaps Oswald's closest friend at the Atsugi base, in correspondence with the author recalls an attempt to recruit himself, Oswald, and a third man into a possible intelligence operation. Thornley writes,

"In the late 1970s I was contacted by David Bucknell, who said he was in Marine Air Control Squadron Nine with Oswald and me. When he mentioned that his nickname was 'Bucky Beaver,' I recalled Bucknell—a large man with buck teeth who wore his utility cap all the way down on his head, giving it a dome shape instead of the common stretched, flat-top shape.

"Bucknell asked me if I remembered an attempt to recruit us (Bucknell, Oswald, me) to military intelligence. I did not. Then he asked if I remembered approaching he and Oswald one day and being told by Oswald that 'This is a private conversation.' That I recalled clearly. Bucknell said it happened as we were on our way to the recruitment lecture.

"Indeed, I remembered the incident occurred as all three of us were walking in the same direction toward 'Mainside' on the base and away from the radar outpost. Bucknell said that minutes earlier, on the outpost, the names of Oswald, Bucknell and Thornley had been called over the P.A. system and that we were told to report to the squadron office. In the squadron office, we were ordered to report to base security over at 'Mainside' of L.T.A., the satellite of El Toro Marine Base where we were stationed.

"Bucknell said he and Oswald were running a loan sharking operation and their private conversation concerned whether or not they were now being called in for questioning about that. Oswald doubted it, because I had been called up at the same time and knew nothing about the operation.

"Bucknell says when we arrived at base security we were seated in a small auditorium or lecture room with a number of men from other outfits. Up in front, according to Bucknell, was a Marine captain and a Hispanic man in civilian clothes with a flat-top haircut. Bucknell was surprised to see that the Captain was acting as an 'errand boy' for this civilian, whom the Captain finally introduced as 'Mister B.'

"'Mister B.' said, 'We have reason to believe that Castro's new revolutionary government has been infiltrated by Soviet agents.' (This would have been in late May or early June of 1959, just after the New Year's Day Revolution, before Castro 'went Communist.' I recalled someone making that statement in a lecture I attended, but did not remember the context).

"We had all been called together, said Mr. B., because we were reputed to be admirers of Fidel Castro. As I understand it, and dimly recall it, the pitch was that Castro needed our help in getting rid of these agents. We were being asked to volunteer for a counter-espionage program!

"I'm sure I would have volunteered. To the best of my recollection, I was ostensibly turned down because I was already slated for a tour of duty in the Far East, to begin in June, and the training program was in the U.S.—But not before I signed some papers authorizing using me for intelligence purposes.

"Bucknell made detailed notes of this extraordinary event the day after it occurred, and when we met in San Francisco in the late 1970s he read me those notes.

"Volunteers were interviewed on a one-on-one basis after the recruitment lecture. Bucknell says he had a maternal grandfather named E.H. Hunt, who he listed on the recruitment form as a reference. Mister B. looked startled and said, 'Who is this E.H. Hunt?' Bucknell explained. Mister B. said, 'Oh!,' and laughed. (E. Howard Hunt was second in command under Nixon on the Bay of Pigs operation.)

"Bucknell was never contacted again in relation to this program. Neither was I.

"Bucknell says that the Marine Air Control Squadron's covert security was handled by Army Intelligence, and we now both suspect that Oswald may already have been an Army Intelligence agent pretending to be a Marxist at the time of Mr. B.'s recruitment attempt, which may have enhanced his qualifications for Mr. B.'s program.

"At about the time all this happened, I began having vivid audio hallucinations, usually just before falling asleep." [6]

Two weeks prior to Oswald's defection to the Soviet Union, Robert E. Webster, formerly with the Navy, renounced his American citizenship. Like Oswald, Webster would later do a turnabout and return to the United States—his return greased by "affidavits from Rand."

Webster had been at a trade exhibition in Moscow with the Rand Development Corporation. When Webster renounced his citizenship, he was accompanied by two Rand executives, Henry Rand and George Bookbinder, both of whom had been with the OSS. The Rand Corporation had been involved with American mind control research since at least 1949, when it issued a report on Soviet hypnosis experiments and proposed an American counter-offensive.

Although there is no direct evidence linking Webster or Oswald, who inquired about Webster at the time of his own return to the U.S., to Rand mind control experiments, it is plain that if Oswald and Webster had been American spies pretending to defect, then they probably would have received hypnotic programming to counter the inevitable interrogation in Moscow.

It is also fascinating to learn that the address of Webster's apartment building was in Marina Oswald's address book, and that she is known to have said that her husband defected after employment at an American exhibition that took place in Moscow. This was obviously not Oswald, but Webster. [7]

The pseudonymous "Lincoln Lawrence," in *Were We Controlled*, recalls a "deadly rumor" that Lee Harvey Oswald had been admitted to the Third Clinical Hospital's Ear, Nose, and Throat division in Minsk, Russia. Lawrence says that after Oswald was anaesthetized, a tiny radio receiver was implanted in Oswald's head that could trigger at will post-hypnotic suggestions that had already been induced. The same device could be used to erase his memory of events.

Whether or not Oswald was implanted, the "deadly rumor" seems to have reached the ears of CIA Director McCone, who penned a memo to Secret Service head James Rowley on March 3, 1964. McCone's memo stated that Oswald had possibly been "chemically or electronically 'controlled'... a sleeper agent. Subject spent 11 days hospitalized for a 'minor ailment' which should have required no more than three days hospitalization at best." [8]

One person who reacted with shock about Lincoln Lawrence's allegation that Oswald had been implanted with a control device was Marguerite Oswald, Lee's mother. She told Dallas assassination researcher Mary Ferrel, "I've got to find out who wrote this book, because he knew my son." Marguerite Oswald would not explain to Ferrell how she knew this, but Dick Russell, author of *The Man Who Knew Too Much*, speculates, "Marguerite would sometimes stand behind Lee's chair as he played some board game and rub his back and head. And she said the texture of his hair had changed, it wasn't soft like it used to be. Suddenly it came to me: What if, when she was doing that, she felt a little scar up inside the hairline."

Another person concerned about Oswald's appearance was his brother Robert. According to Epstein, in *Legend*, "The most marked change was his hair. Not only had it thinned almost to the point of baldness on top, but the texture had changed from soft to kinky. Struck by this loss of hair, Robert couldn't help wondering what happened to his brother during the intervening years in the Soviet Union... [and] later speculated that it might have been caused by medical or shock treatments." [9]

Herman Kimsey, an Army counter intelligence operative and CIA official who claimed an insider's knowledge of the Kennedy hit, was quoted in Hugh McDonald's *Appointment in Dallas* as saying, "Oswald was programmed to kill like a medium at a seance. Then the mechanism went on the blink and Oswald became a dangerous toy without direction." Three weeks after Kimsey offered these revelations to McDonald, he died of a heart attack, at age 55. [10]

One of CIA pilot and hypnotist David Ferrie's associates, in Bowart's *Operation Mind Control,* is quoted as having suggested that Oswald had been hypnotized by Ferrie to murder the president. Ferrie was a CIA contract agent and the high priest of a small religious group called the Apostolic Old Catholic Church of North America that, according to researcher Loren Coleman, engaged in animal sacrifice and the drinking of blood. Coleman states, "During Lee Harvey Oswald's last weeks in New Orleans, he attended many ritualistic parties in private homes and apartments with David Ferrie." [11]

If hypnotism was used to program Oswald, hypnotism may have been employed for his ultimate "deprogramming" through death by another assassin. On the scene immediately prior to the John F. Kennedy assassination was William Crowe, whose stage name was Bill DeMar. Crowe was employed as a stage hypnotist at Jack Ruby's Carousel Club on the week of the assassination. Jack Ruby, of course, was the man who shot Lee Harvey Oswald. [12]

Another mind-controlled assassin may have participated in the Kennedy hit. In 1967 the Phillipine National Bureau of Investigation (NBI) arrested 24-year-old Luis Angel Castillo on suspicion of planning to assassinate President Ferdinand Marcos in league with a group of Philippine guerrillas. Castillo's passport identified him as Antonio Reyes Eloriaga, a Philippine resident returning after expulsion from America for car theft and exceeding the time limit on his visa. The *Manila Times* reported that, while in America, Castillo had used at least five aliases.

At his request, Castillo was given truth serum and hypnotized. The hypnotist reported, "Initially, the subject indicated an admixture of desired susceptibility to hypnosynthesis but deep-seated resistance due to the presence of a posthypnotic block. This block appeared to have been connected with the presence—nightmarish—of a Mrs. Kreps. The total removal of this block may pave the way for maximum results." [13]

The hypnotist discovered that Castillo could be inducted to

four different levels of hypnosis, which he termed Zombie states I-IV, with each level possessing a different personality. Zombie I went by the name Antonio Loriaga, and he was involved in anti-American espionage. Zombie II was an unidentified CIA agent. Zombie III was an agent who was suicidal over having his cover revealed. Zombie IV may have been Castillo's true identity, Manuel Angel Ramirez, a 29-year-old native of the Bronx. Although he had little memory of his childhood, his later life had apparently been as an hypnotically-programmed operative for the Special Operations Group of the CIA.

Castillo revealed to the NBI that he had been contacted for training in espionage when he was a private in the Cuban militia, and received his initial training from Americans and Cubans near the Bay of Pigs.

Castillo also revealed that he had been programmed for another assassination, this one involving a man riding in an open car in Dallas, Texas, on November 22, 1963.

According to Castillo, the earlier-mentioned Mrs. Kreps, who had a German accent, was one of several persons who hypnotically programmed him in Dallas. He also recognized the names of several persons at the time being investigated for the assassination of John Kennedy by District Attorney Jim Garrison, and was able to provide a detailed account of his participation in the plot.

After the NBI contacted the FBI, the story was squelched. Castillo was returned to the U.S., and imprisoned for 37 months for robbery. After his release, Castillo apparently dropped off the face of the earth, and has not been located since. [14]

NOTES:

1. Sullivan, William, Quoted in "The Nazi Connection to the John F. Kennedy Assassination," by Mae Brussell, *The Rebel*, November 22, 1983
2. Brussell
3. Editors of the Executive Intelligence Review, *Dope, Inc.* (Washington, D.C.: EIR, 1992)
4. Krupey, G. J. "The High and The Mighty: JFK, MPM, LSD and the CIA", *Steamshovel Press* magazine, number 11, 1994
5. Krupey
6. Thornley, Kerry, correspondence with the author, August 30, 1997
7. Russell, Dick, *The Man Who Knew Too Much*. (New York, Carrol & Graf, 1992); Dickson, Paul, *Think Tanks*. (New York: Ballentine Books, 1971)
8. Lawrence, Lincoln, pseud., *Were We Controlled?* (New Hyde Park, New York: University Books, 1967); Russell
9. Cited in Russell
10. Constantine, Alex, *Psychic Dictatorship in the U.S.A.* (Portland, Oregon: Feral House, 1995); Russell

11.   Constantine; Coleman, Loren, "The Occult, MIB's, UFO's and Assassinations", *The Conspiracy Tracker,* December 1985

12. Russell

13.   Bowart, Walter, *Operation Mind Control.* (New York: Dell Paperback, 1977)

14. Ibid.

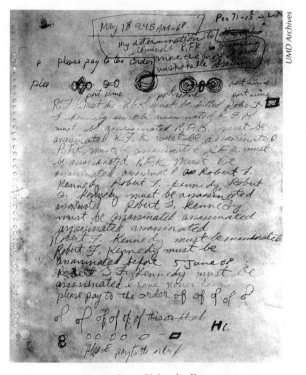

A page from Sirhan's diary.

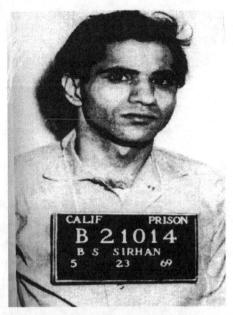

Mind control and the girl in the polka-dot dress: Sirhan Sirhan in prison. He doesn't remember anything.

David Chapman: John Lennon's mind control killer?

Chapter 19:

"RFK MUST DIE"

Another assassination that many experts believe was the product of a mind controlled "Manchurian candidate" was that of Robert F. Kennedy. Shortly before the murder of Kennedy, Sirhan Sirhan was seen in the Ambassador Hotel "staring fixedly" at the teletype machine. According to the teletype operator, "he came over to my machine and started staring at it. Just staring. I'll never forget his eyes. I asked him what he wanted. He didn't answer. He just kept staring. I asked him again. No answer. I said that if he wanted the latest figures on Senator Kennedy, he'd have to check the other machine. He still didn't answer. He just kept staring."

One eyewitness said that Sirhan was "enormously composed" during the commission of the crime. Reminding one of the stories of madmen exhibiting tremendous strength, another witness said that when people were attempting to subdue Sirhan during the shooting, "the little man's strength was fantastic."

After Sirhan was taken into custody, LAPD officers found out that he had the interesting ability to tell time—to the minute—without a clock. Again, this is reminiscent of the extended senses of the hypnotized or otherwise mind controlled subject. [1]

For his own part, Sirhan said that he did the shooting "without trying," and described his condition as being that of a "puppet." Sirhan has stated on several occasions that there are many aspects of the case that have not been revealed. He also has wondered whether he was mind controlled, suggesting one witness to the assassination in particular, who he thought could "Maybe... lead to someone who was playing with my mind."

When questioned by the public defender assigned to him in the case, Sirhan said, "I don't remember much about the shooting, sir, did I do it? Well, yes, I am told I did it. I remember being at the Ambassador [Hotel]. I am drinking Tom Collinses. I got dizzy. I went back to my car so I could go home. But I was too drunk to drive. I thought I'd better find some coffee. The next thing I remember I was being choked and a guy was twisting my knee." [2]

If Sirhan was in fact programmed, it could have been done in 1967 when he disappeared for three months, not informing his family where he was. After he had returned home, it was noted that he had become fascinated by the occult. [3]

And then there is the question of accomplices. Security guard Thane Cesar, in close proximity to Kennedy during the shooting, is believed by many researchers to have participated in the assassination. Cesar informed Ted Charach, co-producer of the movie *The Second Gun,* that he had attended "American-Nazi conclaves." Cesar was also employed at the CIA-connected Lockheed, and one retired engineer from the company said that Cesar worked in an area of the company run by the CIA.

Immediately after the Kennedy shooting a woman named Sandra Serrano saw a Caucasian woman in a white dress with black polka dots, and a young man, tentatively identified as Mexican-American, and wearing a white shirt and gold sweater, running down the stairs that provided exit from the hotel. The woman in the polka dots said, "We've shot him! We've shot him." Serrano asked, "Who did you shoot?", and the woman responded, "We shot Senator Kennedy."

Thomas Vincent DiPierro, the son of one of the maitre d's who was working at the Ambassador, said that he had seen Sirhan immediately before the shooting and that he had been in the company of a woman in a polka dot dress.

A third witness also saw Sirhan, an half hour before the murder of Kennedy, with a woman in a polka dot dress and a tall, thin man with dark hair. After Kennedy was shot, the witness saw the woman and the tall man running from the scene of the crime.

Another witness saw Sirhan on June 3, after a visit to the Ambassador Hotel, in the company of a woman and two other men.

Another witness said that she had seen a man who looked like Sirhan on June 3. The man was in a blue 1959 Ford. The car pulled to the curb and the Sirhan look-alike jumped out and began arguing with two other men in the front seat. The man's jacket flew open and the witness saw a gun in his waistband. Although the witness could not identify who was talking, she heard the words "Kennedy," and "Get in the car, we have to get him tonight," as well as "Don't want to," and "Afraid."

One of the busboys at the Ambassador told police about two men who had come to the hotel on the day before the shooting, attempting to obtain coats like those worn by the waiters, while a waitress in nearby Alhambra, California said that on the morning of June 4 she had seen a man she took to be Sirhan drawing a map—some kind of floor plan.

Reminding one of Lee Harvey Oswald's gun practice, in which he made himself conspicuous, Sirhan practiced shooting at a target range on June 4, where he signed in with his name and address. This in itself was odd, because the rangemaster did not usually monitor whether the shooters signed in or not. The rangemaster remembered that shortly after Sirhan had arrived, an attractive blonde in the company of a man had also arrived. Sirhan walked over to them and said, "Let me show you how to shoot." The woman's response was, "Get away from me, goddamnit, someone will recognize us." [4]

Sirhan was recognized buying bullets for the .22 caliber handgun he allegedly used to murder Kennedy. In his company, according to the clerk at the gunstore, were Sirhan's brother Munir and another man he was unable to identify.

A young man named Crispin Curiel Gonzalez was arrested in Juarez, Mexico, carrying notes showing that he knew Sirhan and that Sirhan had planned to murder Kennedy. Gonzalez was later found hanging in his cell in Juarez. Questioned about the incident by author Robert Blair Kaiser, Sirhan responded, "That kid didn't have to die. He didn't do anything."

Kaiser asked Sirhan, "Who would have wanted to get him out of the way?"

According to Kaiser, "Sirhan paused reflectively for a moment, then smiled. Then he changed the subject."

After the murder of Kennedy, police searched Sirhan's room and found a large amount of Rosicrucian (in this case AMORC, not the historical Rosicrucians) and other occult reading material. Sirhan is alleged to have also been acquainted with a member of The Process group, a Scientology offshoot, and to have attended parties at the home of Roman Polanski and Sharon Tate, who also may have been linked to The Process. Robert F. Kennedy dined at the Polanski mansion the day before he was assassinated. [5]

Sirhan left behind several notebooks filled with jottings indicating his strange state of mind prior to the shooting. A transcript of one page follows:

"May 18, 9:45 a.m. -68. My determination to eliminate RFK is becoming more the more of an unshakable obsession... RFK must die—RFK must be killed Robert F. Kennedy must be assassinated RFK must be assassination Ed RFK must be assassinated before 5 June 68 Robert F. Kennedy must be assassinated I have never heard please pay to the order of of of of of of of of of this or that please pay to the order of..."

Psychiatrist Dr. Bernard Diamond of UCLA, who examined Sirhan and would later examine Mark David Chapman, asked him about certain entries in his notebooks while he was hypnotically tranced.

Diamond asked, "Is this crazy writing?"

"YES YES YES," Sirhan responded in writing.

"Are you crazy?"

"NO NO."

"Well, why are you writing crazy?" Diamond continued.

"PRACTICE PRACTICE PRACTICE."

"Practice for what?"

"MIND CONTROL MIND CONTROL MIND CONTROL."

Seven years after the murder, Sirhan's voice during initial interviews with psychologists was analyzed using a Psychological Stress Evaluator (PSE), measuring micro tremors in the voice denoting stress. One of the originators of the PSE, Charles McQuiston, described by Walter Bowart as a "former high-ranking U.S. Intelligence Officer," stated that, "I'm convinced that Sirhan wasn't aware of what he was doing. He was in a hypnotic trance when he pulled the trigger and killed Senator Kennedy... Everything in the PSE charts tells me that someone else was involved in the assassination—and that Sirhan was programmed through hypnosis to kill RFK. What we have here is a real live 'Manchurian Candidate.'" [6]

Dr. John W. Heisse, Jr., president of the International Society of Stress Analysis, concurred with that appraisal: "Sirhan kept repeating certain phrases. This clearly revealed he had been programmed to put himself into a trance. This is something he couldn't have learned by himself. Someone had to show him and teach him how. I believe Sirhan was brainwashed under hypnosis by the constant repetition of words like 'You are nobody. You're nothing. The American dream is gone' until he actually believed them. At that stage someone implanted an idea, 'Kill RFK,' and under hypnosis the brainwashed Sirhan accepted it."

Another expert, Dr. Herbert Spiegel, a medical hypnotist, agreed: "It's very possible to distort and change somebody's mind through a number of hypnotic sessions. It can be described as brainwashing because the mind is cleared of its old emotions and values which are replaced by implanting other suggestions... This technique was probably used with Sirhan. From my own research, I think that Sirhan was subjected to

154

hypnotic treatment." [7]

NOTES:

1. Kaiser, Robert Blair, *"R.F.K. Must Die!"* (New York: Grove Press, 1970); Bresler, Fenton, *Who Killed John Lennon?* (New York: St. Martin's Press, 1989)
2. Ibid.
3. Constantine, Alex, *Psychic Dictatorship in the U.S.A.* (Venice, California: Feral House, 1995)
4. Kaiser
5. Terry, Maury, *The Ultimate Evil.* (New York: Bantam Books, 1987); Judge, John, "Poolside with John Judge", *Prevailing Winds,* undated
6. Bowart, Walter, *Operation Mind Control.* (New York: Dell Paperback, 1977); Bresler
7. Bresler

Top: Patty Hearst as Tania. Bottom: Colton
Westbrook: Did he create the SLA?

Chapter 20:

HAPPINESS IS
A WARM GUN

Mark David Chapman, the murderer of rock music star John Lennon, may have been a mind controlled assassin. Wielding a Charter Undercover .38 Special, Chapman fired five hollow point fragmenting bullets into Lennon's back as he walked into The Dakota apartment block in New York city.

There is much evidence to suggest that American intelligence agencies considered Lennon a menace, and this could have well provided a reason for his murder. John Lennon attracted the attention of the FBI for the first time in January 1969, when a Special Agent in Charge reported to J. Edgar Hoover on a demonstration in New Haven, Connecticut. The demonstration had been spurred by the suspension of the campus newspaper for the publication of nude photos of John and Yoko—reprints of the front and back covers of the "Two Virgins" record album, at that time available in record stores throughout the country.

In the years that followed, during Lennon's many shots at political activism, the FBI's file on the rock star-cum-culture hero would grow to at least 288 pages, although entire years of reports of surveillance on Lennon have never been released.

By 1972 the CIA was in on the act. Lennon had been very vocal in his disapproval of the war in Vietnam, and was seen as one of the most effective forces capable of rallying American youth in large-scale opposition to the war. On the 23rd of February of that year, a CIA agent filed the following report:

"Some American participants at the Soviet-controlled World Assembly for Peace and Independence of the Peoples of Indochina, held 11-13 February 1972 in Paris/Versailles, attempted unsuccessfully to include a call for international demonstrations to take place at the time of the Republican National Convention...

"John LENNON, a British subject, has provided financial support to Project 'YES' [an organization started by Yoko], which in turn paid the travel expenses to the World Assembly of a representative of leading anti-war activist (and Chicago Seven defendant) Rennie DAVIS... In Paris this representative in the World Assembly met at least once with officials of the Provisional Revolutionary Government of South Vietnam; it is not known if the Republican Convention was discussed."

Lennon believed, and with good reason, that by 1972 he was under constant surveillance. In late 1972, Lennon told Paul Krassner, "Listen, if anything happens to Yoko and me, it was not an accident."

Facing deportation from the U.S. ostensibly due to a marijuana conviction in Great Britain, Lennon fought back, claiming the deportation was really due to his politics and disapproval of the war in Vietnam.

On 21 April, 1972, E.L. Shackleford, a supervisor in the New York FBI office, sent a memo to one of his agents, one only partially available to us due to large blacked-out segments:

"In view of successful delaying tactics to date, there exists real possibility that subject [John Lennon] will not be deported from US in near future and possibly not prior to Republican National Convention. Subject's activities being closely followed and any information developed indicating violation of Federal laws will be immediately furnished to pertinent agencies in effort to neutralize any disruptive activities of subject."

As of May, 1972, Lennon had gotten the message, apparently from Leon Wilde, his immigration lawyer, that if he didn't want to be deported from the U.S., nor to jeopardize his position in his attempt to gain custody of Yoko's daughter Kyoko, that he would have to maintain a lower political profile. Lennon bowed to the pressure. In that month he went on the Dick Cavett television show and announced that he was canceling a planned "revolutionary road show" and pulling back in terms of political involvement. Lennon was reportedly "sick at heart" over the decision he was forced to make.

According to political activist John Sinclair, about whom Lennon wrote a song, "Cancelling the tour plan was wise. I know how much it meant for them to stay here—partially because of the thing with the kid. I understood perfectly."

In September of 1973 the U.S. Department of Justice admitted that Lennon's phone had been illegally tapped. The DOJ was not exactly clucking disapproval, only saying that the tap had happened and indicating the desire to obtain the transcripts.

After a lengthy retirement from the public eye, by 1980 Lennon seemed to be doing a turnabout. He had a new record album out, and was interested in returning to prominence, as well as getting back into political activism. Lennon had already bought the plane tickets to fly to San Francisco to support striking Japanese American workers. Lennon may have been seen as the only man in the world capable of re-igniting the militancy of the 60s. [1]

Lennon would soon encounter the penultimate nebbish with a gun: Mark David Chapman. Chapman was from Georgia, and began working for the YMCA in 1969, first as a full-time camp counselor and then as an assistant camp director. In CIA defector Philip Agee's book *Inside the Company: CIA Diary*, he indicates the YMCA as a CIA front organization. Curiously, Chapman's employment record is missing from the headquarters of the organization.

In 1971 Chapman had a religious conversion to Christianity. In 1975 he travelled to Beirut in the employ of the YMCA in their International Camp Counselor Program—his first choice being the Soviet Union, even though he was a vehement anti-communist. Chapman's visit to Beirut coincided with the period of time that Edwin Wilson and Frank Terpil were running a training school for assassins there. [2]

Returning from Beirut, he worked at a YMCA camp for Vietnamese refugees in Fort Chaffee, Arkansas. Chapman worked as an Area Coordinator, in charge of a seven-block area of the camp, with one American and fifteen Vietnamese assistants. One of the enigmas of Chapman's life is his longtime friend, known by the pseudonym "Gene Scott" in Fenton Bresler's account, who visited Chapman while working at Fort Chaffee.

One of Chapman's co-workers told journalist Craig Unger, "As soon as Gene arrived, Mark's behavior changed. Mark cleaned his nails for Gene, he put on his clean clothes for Gene, he made telephone calls for Gene. And there was Gene's gun. Mark was so non-violent. He hated guns. I still remember them sitting in the office of the YMCA center at Fort Chaffee, playing with this gun, looking at it, talking about it. It just wasn't like Mark. They started rough-housing, then Gene gave Mark this look. He froze."

In his account of Chapman, Fenton Bresler writes that, "several people to whom I have spoken in Decatur and elsewhere believe that the two men, who have known each other

159

since Columbia High School days, have complex undertones to their apparently still-continuing friendship. Certainly Mark idolized Gene, older by a few years and a handsome Rambo-like character who has never married: he is today a Georgia sheriff's officer." According to Bresler, "he was the man who gave Mark the hollow-point bullets, not knowing (as he said) that he would use them to shoot John Lennon."

In 1976 Chapman reportedly ended his job with the YMCA, and took a job as a security guard at the insistence of "Gene Scott." Chapman moved to Hawaii in 1977, and stayed in the YMCA hostel in Honolulu. Chapman also contacted the suicide hotline there, and went to the Waikiki Mental Health Clinic. Hawaii has been noted as the location of a mind control assassination training center in the account of several intelligence agency defectors.

In 1978 Chapman travelled around the world with a letter of introduction as a YMCA staff member, staying in YMCA hostels, the trip reportedly financed by a loan from the credit union of a hospital he worked at. This loan, to a relatively new employee, seems suspicious and follows in the tradition of many other "lone nut assassins" who, while non-employed or under-employed never lack for travel expenses.

Chapman returned to Hawaii. He was married in 1979 and shortly after, one in a string of obsessions, became fixated on the book *Catcher in the Rye*, identifying with the book's protagonist, Holden Caulfield. Some researchers have suggested that the book may have been used as a "trigger" for a programmed Chapman, although this is only speculation. In Honolulu Chapman purchased the gun that he would use to kill Lennon.

Travelling to New York, Chapman checked into the Waldorf-Astoria, then after a few days moved into a YMCA hostel. Chapman found that he could not buy bullets legally in New York. He travelled to Atlanta, where hollow points were furnished by his friend "Gene Scott" at Chapman's insistence that he needed to protect himself in the Big Apple. Chapman returned to New York only to be told by the doorman at The Dakota that Lennon and his wife were out of town. Chapman flew back to Hawaii, throwing away his copy of *Catcher in the Rye*.

In Hawaii, according to a psychiatrist, Chapman was receiving "command hallucinations" telling him to kill John Lennon. These could have been hypnotically programmed, or even broadcast electronically. Chapman called a different mental health clinic than the one he had dealt with before, and was turned away with a referral to still another clinic. Chapman's own account of the period describes an interior struggle lasting several months, "a struggle between good and evil and right and wrong. I just gave in. It was almost as if I was on some kind of special mission that I could not avoid."

A few weeks after his return from the mainland, Chapman returned to the States, again seemingly having money to burn. During his trips to the mainland Chapman carried large amounts of cash, although there has never been a satisfactory explanation of how he came by the money.

Chapman did not immediately fly to New York, but stopped off in Chicago for three days that are not accounted for. His plane ticket, according to Fenton Bresler, was later doctored to show that Chapman had flown non-stop to New York. This fact is substantiated by photocopies of two versions of the same ticket, one for Chicago, the other indicating a direct passage to New York. Who falsified the ticket remains an open question, but the existence of two versions of the ticket is compelling evidence for a conspiracy in the murder.

When Chapman did reach New York he went to the YMCA hostel located nearest to The Dakota. After checking at the hotel to find out that the Lennons were not in and that no one knew when to expect them back, Chapman that evening took a cab to west 62nd Street, where he went inside an apartment building for five minutes, and then to East 65th Street and 2nd Avenue, where he went into another apartment building for a few minutes. These visits have never been explained. Chapman was then dropped off in Greenwich Village. Chapman was carrying a satchel that has not been accounted for.

The next morning Chapman checked out of the YMCA hostel and booked himself into the more expensive Sheraton Center Hotel. In his hotel room he made a "shrine" on top of a bureau, with mementos of his life—a Bible, his expired passport, a Todd Rundgren audio tape, and other items—as well as a photo from the *Wizard of Oz* with Judy Garland.

Chapman hung around outside The Dakota for a full day without seeing Lennon, then returned the following day. As a gesture, he bought another copy of *Catcher in the Rye* and inscribed it "To Holden Caulfield from Holden Caulfield. This is my statement." When Lennon and his wife emerged from The Dakota around 5 p.m., Chapman got the star's autograph. The couple returned at 10:50 p.m. As Lennon walked toward the apartment building a reportedly "smirking" Chapman fired five bullets into his back. Then Chapman threw down his gun and began to read the paperback he had carried.

Chapman described the murder in this fashion:

"If you ever get the chance, go to The Dakota building. I just love that building... to think that's where it happened. There was no emotion, there was no anger, there was nothing, dead silence in the brain, dead cold quiet. He walked up, he looked at me, I tell you the man was going to be dead in less than five minutes and he looked at me, I looked at him. He walked past me and then I heard in my head said, 'Do it, do it, do it,' over and over again, saying "Do it, do it, do it, do it,' like that. I pulled the gun out of my pocket, I handed over to my left hand, I don't remember aiming. I must have done, but I don't remember drawing the bead or whatever you call it. And I just pulled the trigger steady five times."

One of the police officers who interrogated Chapman, Lieutenant Arthur O'Connor, described the apparent state of mind of the murderer: "I saw him within half an hour of his arrest. I was the first one to interrogate him. He was in a daze. He was composed yet not there. He gave me the impression he had done something: it was something he had to do and he'd done it."

Later O'Connor said, "It's possible Mark could have been used by somebody. I saw him the night of the murder. I studied him intensely. He looked as if he could have been programmed... That was the way he looked and that was the way he talked. It could have been drugs—and no, we did not test for drugs! It was not standard procedure. But looking back, he could have been either drugged or programmed—or a combination of both."

According to newspaper reports at the time, Chapman had in his possession at the time of the murder a cassette player and tapes with "about fourteen hours of Beatles tapes." Except that according to the arresting officer, Steve Spiro, Chapman did not have a cassette player or tapes on him when arrested. Either the cassette player was invented by an imaginative reporter, or it vanished—and if it vanished, might it have had something recorded other than Beatles' music?

After shooting Lennon, Chapman was in a "daze" for days. Chapman pleaded guilty to the murder in court after hearing "the voice of God" telling him to do so. Dr. Dorothy Lewis, who examined Chapman, said that "Mr. Chapman had been experiencing auditory hallucinations while at the hospital unit at Rikers Island and these experiences clearly influenced his decision to plead guilty... I question whether he was competent subsequently to plead guilty [since] it seemed to me that his fluctuating mental status made it impossible for him to understand the ramifications of such a decision or to assist his attorney in his own defense."

Chapman's guilty plea ended the investigation. The case was closed. As in the case of Sirhan Sirhan, James Earl Ray, Lee Harvey Oswald, David Berkowitz and others, there would be no trial. Not so messy that way. [3]

NOTES:

1. Bresler, Fenton, *Who Killed John Lennon?* (New York: St. Martin's Paperbacks, 1989)

2. Goulden, Joseph C., *The Death Merchant.* (New York: Simon and Schuster, 1984)

2. Bresler; Judge, John, "Poolside with John Judge", *Prevailing Winds,* undated interview

UNIVERSITY HOSPITAL
University of California
Medical Center, San Diego

PROGRESS RECORD

(Typewriter Copy)

Source   Request Date

Patient Identifica

TO WHOM IT MAY CONCERN:

Recently I reviewed a skull film marked: NASLUND, ROBERT and
dated 26-11, 1981. That film shows a couple of unusual
foreign bodies at the base of the skull, possibly some form
of brain transmitters.

However, I have not examined or talked to this patient and
do not know the pertinent history.

San Diego, CA
October 6, 1983

Ingmar Wickbom, M.D.
Professor of Radiology
U.C.S.D.

Chapter 21:

BOMBED

Timothy McVeigh, the man convicted of blowing up the Murrah Federal Building in Oklahoma City, Oklahoma, with its resultant toll in human lives, may have been another mind controlled murderer. This possibility is first noted in the statements of friends and acquaintances of McVeigh who say that his personality dramatically changed after a counseling session that took place after the Persian Gulf War, when he attempted to enter Special Forces. Turned down, McVeigh is said to have become disgruntled and left the army.

Still, "He didn't seem terribly depressed," fellow enlisted man William Dilly said of McVeigh's mental state at the time. Also, after McVeigh left the army, he joined the National Guard, hardly the action of a man disillusioned with the military.

Few make the connection that McVeigh's alleged accomplice, Terry Nichols, also left the army under mysterious circumstances. Lana Padilla, Nichols' ex-wife, questioned the family emergency that reportedly caused Nichols to drop out of the military: "I've always wondered just why he was released, less than a year after enlisting, and always been told it was because he had to take care of [his son] Josh. But this theory never washed with me because he'd had Josh with him all along..." [1]

Like Lee Harvey Oswald and John Hinckley, who shot Ronald Reagan, Timothy McVeigh may have had "doubles" of himself active prior to the bombing. This might have been to confuse his trail, but also possibly to incriminate him. According to the *Los Angeles Times,* "The investigators said authorities theorize that [McVeigh's companion] John Doe 2 could be two people, and that McVeigh and his alleged conspirators could have used different men to accompany him in order to serve as 'decoys' and confuse investigators trying to trace his movements." [2]

The *New York Times* noted, "Mr. McVeigh lived in the Kingman [Arizona] area for a year until he was evicted from a trailer park last June. The owner of the trailer park said Mr.

McVeigh had lived there from February to June 1994. Residents of the Canyon West Mobile Park drew a picture of an arrogant loner who worked as a security guard for a now-defunct trucking company, lived with his pregnant girlfriend, expressed deep anger against the federal government and often caused trouble for his neighbors."

Not in the headlines but only relegated to a tiny blurb on a back page of a few papers was the news that the owner of the trailer park later changed his mind. He said that the man had not been Timothy McVeigh after all. "They were the same height, the same age, they looked alike," he stated, also mentioning that both men had recently been released from the army. [3]

McVeigh complained that while in the army he had been implanted with a microchip in his buttocks. One acquaintance said that McVeigh believed he was being mind-controlled through the chip. After McVeigh was arrested, one of the few things that he complained about was the discomfort the chip was causing him.

After leaving the military, McVeigh soon had a job with Burns International Security Services, dispatched to the Calspan organization in Buffalo, New York. Calspan is engaged in a number of top secret projects, working in areas such as aeronautics, electronic warfare, microwave technology, and electronic telemetry. Monitoring by microchip is, by definition, electronic telemetry.

Additional possible substantiation of mind control comes from McVeigh's army acquaintance Todd A. Regier, who said he was "kind of cold. He wasn't enemies with anyone. He was kind of almost like a robot. He never had a date when I knew him in the army. I never saw him at a club. I never saw him drinking. He never had good friends. He was a robot. Everything was for a purpose." [4]

Walter "Mac" McCarty, a gun instructor who believed that McVeigh and Fortier were trying to involve him in a plot in Kingman, Arizona, also has strange things to say about the mindset of the men who allegedly did the Oklahoma City bombing: "He [McVeigh] was upset about things happening in this country to the point of being disoriented... I know brainwashing when I see it, those boys had really gotten a good case of it." [5]

Is it possible that like Lee Harvey Oswald, as many researchers believe, McVeigh left the army for the purpose of being recruited into a more secret military unit engaged in domestic work—particularly for the infiltration of the right-wing patriot underground?   This is substantiated by a letter that Timothy McVeigh sent to his sister Jennifer, claiming that he had been working in a military Special Forces group involved in criminal activity. The contents of that letter, to my knowledge, have never been mentioned in either the mainstream electronic or print media. [6]

Recall the words of Daniel Sheehan of the Christic Institute: "We have talked to half a dozen individuals who have told a startlingly similar story about how, at a very young age, usually between twenty and twenty-five, they were contacted, usually within the context of military training, and told: 'Look, we've got a special deal for you. You're going to come into the service under the normal designation of being an infantryman but you're going to leave the service after a while and you're going to have special training, and you're going to be brought into a special program. They're sent to special places where they are trained by mercenaries and then they're told: 'You're going to be called upon from time to time to do some things for us.'"

NOTES:

1. Padilla and Delpit, *By Blood Betrayed.* (New York: Harper Paperback, 1995)

2. "Feds charge Terry Nichols in bombing", *Los Angeles Times,* May 10, 1995

3. "Timothy James McVeigh: Tracing One Man's Complex Path to Extremism", *New York Times,* April 25, 1995; Kifner, John. "Arizona Trailer Park Owner Remembered the Wrong Man", *New York Times,* April 25, 1995

4. McFadden, Robert D., *New York Times,* May 14, 1995

5. Schaffer, Mark, "Gun class sheds new light on McVeigh", the *Arizona Republic,* May 28, 1995

6. Myers, Lawrence W., "OKC Bombing Grand Jurors Claim 'Cover-Up', *Media Bypass* magazine, November 1995

Charles Manson: Leader of a mind control cult?

Robert DeGrimston Moore, founder of The Process.

Chapter 22:

BERSERKERS

In recent years there have been an increasing number of instances of "berserkers," people who go crazy and commit murder. A common thread links many of these cases: their belief that they are mind-controlled.

—The *San Francisco Chronicle* for March 17, 1984, featured a story titled "Incident near White House: Gunman's bizarre claims," detailing the arrest of a man near the White House who claimed that he had been injected with a "crystalline implant" that broadcast messages telling him to kill the president. A far-fetched claim, until one remembers that the technology for such implants does exist, and has apparently been in use for decades. [1]

—Another case with a familiar ring to it is that of Emmanuel Tsegaye, a 33-year-old bank teller in Bethesda, Maryland, described as "rarely violent to others," who killed three fellow-employees at the Chevy Chase Federal Savings Bank. In the past he had been placed in psychiatric facilities, and had received undefined treatments at St. Elizabeth's Hospital, a facility infamous for CIA experimentation. Tsegaya said, in a letter to the judge who committed him, "I used to hear... voices both from space and as... exact repeated words... I used to hear a person speaking from [the] distance about the things I was speaking." Describing his state of mind after an attempted suicide, Tsegaye wrote, "I was depressed, mentally and physically weak... from the voices I used to hear and inadequate sleeps." [2]

—On May 5, 1991, Carl Campbell went to a bus stop in the parking lot of the Pentagon, and fired five gunshots into the chest and abdomen of Navy Commander Edward J. Higgins, who worked as an arms control specialist for the Department of Defense. Campbell was examined by psychologists who reported that Campbell had been haunted by voices, and believed he had been injected with a microchip by the CIA. Although Campbell was charged with first degree murder, he was ruled mentally incompetent to stand trial. [3]

—On December 2, 1993, Alan Winterbourne, a computer systems engineer, went on a killing rampage at a Ventura County, California, unemployment office. Winterbourne had been employed in classified scientific work, and had resigned after complaining of harassment by workers and that his phone was tapped. Winterbourne's problems had begun after he had written a letter to his congressman requesting a federal investigation of illegalities that he believed were taking place at Northrop. Before his murderous spree he had told his sister, "they're working on terrible things at Northrop that would kill millions of innocent people. Things you can't imagine." [4]

—William Tager, now in prison for killing an NBC stagehand outside the *Today* show studio in 1994, believed that messages were being broadcast directly to his brain from the media. In 1986 he is reported to have been one of two men who physically beat newsman Dan Rather, asking him repeatedly, "Kenneth, what's the frequency?" Tager—and his accomplice—apparently believed that Rather knew the electronic frequency of his believed mind control bombardment. [5]

—Shortly after 9 a.m. on December 14, 1995, 26-year-old Ralph Tortorici took hostage a history class at the State University at Albany, New York. Tortorici shot one student in the leg. After capture by the police, Tortorici yelled to bystanders "Stop government experimentation!" as he was being led away. Tortorici believes that the CIA has implanted a microchip in his brain. [6]

—The case of Robert Joe Moody is an unusual one in the annals of mind controlled murder. Moody was arrested for the murder of Michelle Malone, age 36, and Pat Magda, 56. Moody had been part of a sexual threesome with Malone and his girlfriend, Dora Lee, while Magda was his next-door neighbor, as well as being the wife of an Air Force officer.

Moody claimed, even before his arrest, that he was commanded by extraterrestrial aliens, or rather, what he calls "Extrasensory Biological Entities", to murder the two women so that he would accomplish his "ultimate mission," to be lethally injected and be resurrected by the alien entities. In an attempt to explain why he was representing himself in court in October 1995, Moody said, "I have never denied my participation in that... [but] it wasn't voluntary... I had no conscious control of what was going on."

Mind control researcher Walter Bowart, who has written

about the Moody case, believes that even though the man has been found competent to stand trial he is a Multiple Personality Disorder case, switching from personality to personality during interviews. During the jury trial, according to Bowart, Moody's various personalities fought with each other.

Of extreme interest is the fact that Moody was trained with the Navy Seals, had received a Top Secret clearance, and that during his time as a Seal, he had experienced "missing time." Moody also told the court that the EBEs had originally contacted him while he was serving as a weather observer for military aircraft. This took place, Moody says, shortly after he had read a top secret government document of the crash of a flying saucer craft with alien bodies. Might this have been the bogus MJ-12 document, and if so, who gave it to Moody?

According to Bowart, Moody may have been set up for execution earlier than his conviction. Bowart states, "There even was one uncomfortable moment when Prosecutor David White placed one of the murder weapons, a large butcher knife, in an opened bag on Moody's desk for his inspection.

"I could imagine Moody taking it, making a sudden menacing gesture before being shot down in the crossfire of the three deputies in the courtroom."

Prosecutor White focused on the EBE's in his closing statements, presumably concerned that Moody might receive an acquittal by reason of insanity. White asked, "Did the aliens need the money to buy plutonium to fuel their spaceships?" White's contention was that Moody was making up the aliens in order to feign insanity for the jury. "The aliens are innocent!" the prosecutor concluded. He may have been on to something.

As Walter Bowart said, "Many were disappointed that the aliens were not called to testify."

The jury found Moody guilty on two counts of first degree murder. [7]

NOTES:

1. Krawczyk, Glenn, "Mind Control & the New World Order," *Nexus* magazine, February/March 1993

2. Constantine; Alex, *Psychic Dictatorship in the U.S.A.* (Venice, California: Feral House, 1995); *The Washington Post,* February 17, 1989

3. Constantine

4. Ibid.

5. Hidell, Al, "Paranotes," "Dan Learns the Frequency," *Paranoia* magazine, Spring, 1997

6. "Hoffman II, Michael A., "The Invocation of Catastrophe: The Unabom Ritual in Alchemical Process," *Independent History and Research* newsletter, All Hallows Eve, 1995

7. Bowart, W.H.. "The Aliens are Innocent!: The Trial and Conviction of a 'EBE Possessed' Serial Killer," *MindNet Journal,* volume 1, issues 8a, 8b,8c, obtained on the Internet

Chapter 23:

CREATING CULTS

R.D. Laing, author of the popular *The Politics of Experience* and an associate of the Tavistock Institute, probably knew what he was talking about when he stated in an interview in *Omni* magazine,

"In the late 'sixties it became apparent to the elite with responsibilities for 'control of the population' that the old idea of putting people in the proverbial bin and keeping them there for life—warehousing people—wasn't cost-effective. The Reagan administration in California was one of the first to realize this. So they had to rethink just what the name of the game was. That has led to a schism between what is said to the general public and what is practiced by the executive in control of mental health. The same problem prevails across Europe and the Third World.

"To see what is happening, look at the textbook or manual called DSM-III: The Diagnostic and Statistical Manual on Mental Disorders (third edition, published by the American Psychiatric Association). Translated into economic and political terms, mental disorder means undesired mental states and behavior. The criteria for mental disorder in DSM-III include any unusual perceptual experience, magical thinking, clairvoyance, telepathy, sixth sense, sense of a person not actually present. You're allowed to sense the presence of a dead relative for three weeks after their death. After that it becomes a criterion of mental disorder to have those feelings.

"...these are not exceptional examples out of DSM-III. The overall drift is what contemporary modern psychiatry, epitomized by this DSM manual translated into eighteen languages, is imposing all over the world—a mandate to strip anyone of their civil liberties, of habeas corpus; and to apply involuntary incarceration, chemicalisation of a person, electric shocks, and non-injurious torture; to homogenize people who are out of line. Presented as a medical operation, it is an undercover operation." [1]

With increased scrutinization by Congress and the American people in the late 1970s the CIA and possibly other intelligence agencies moved their experimentation out of the laboratories and went underground. One of their strategies for experimentation as well as social manipulation was in the creation of mind control cults.

I do not maintain that all off-the-wall mystical or religious groups practicing mental manipulation were formed by intelligence agencies as test tubes for their projects. Examining various groups, however, solid connections to intelligence agencies are apparent in many of them. The apparency is that many of these groups have been formed in this way, while others have been infiltrated and influenced. A few examples:

—Charles Manson's leering face—with or without the homemade swastika tattoo on his forehead—is one of the defining images of the 1960s. It is perhaps one of the "*Changing Images of Man.*" Presented by the media as a madman holding his small band of followers under his sway in the desert, sallying forth to murder the rich and the famous, there is much to suggest that this is not the whole of the story.

Manson was released from a California prison in 1967, and under the stipulations of his parole reported to Roger Smith at the Haight Ashbury Medical Clinic in San Francisco, a facility sponsored by NIMH. The Haight Ashbury district itself was termed a "human guinea pig farm" by one CIA agent. Dr. Louis Jolyon West, for one, was running a mysterious safe house in the Haight in the Summer of Love.

While in prison Manson was connected to the AMORC Rosicrucians, the same group that Sirhan Sirhan had ties to. Manson was also in touch with members of The Process, an apocalyptic Scientology spinoff group, and he dubbed his own group the Final Church using Process terminology. In San Francisco Manson lived at 636 Cole Street while the Process group lived at number 407, close to the center of activity in the Haight. Manson's reported plan to unleash the apocalyptic "Helter Skelter" revolution also seems to have been copped straight from Process theology, but there is a familiar ring. The "process" of The Process is identical to that of Tavistock, the return of the blank slate, the *tabula rasa,* through violence.

David Berkowitz, convicted for the Son of Sam murders, later linked Manson to the L.A.-based wing of the satanic cult he was a member of, reportedly termed "the Children." Manson is also alleged to have been connected to Scientology, as well as to a coven in New Orleans whose members supposedly included Janis Joplin and the University of Texas tower sniper Charles Whitman. [2]

Manson's base of operation was at the Spahn Movie Ranch, later bought out by the owners of the ranch next door, the German Krupp family, who were key to the arming of the Third Reich. [3]

Manson—as well as alleged RFK assassin Sirhan Sirhan—are reported to have attended drug orgies at the Polanski/Tate mansion. Actress Sharon Tate was the daughter of an Army Intelligence officer, and her husband, Roman Polanski, directed the satanic-themed film *Rosemary's Baby.* Polanski later fled the United States after a statutory rape accusation. British warlock Alex Saunders claims that he personally initiated Sharon Tate into witchcraft. Jay Sebring, another of the victims, according to Sammy Davis Jr.'s biography, *Why Me?,* had acted as a high priest at a satanic simulated sacrifice. Sebring had visited the Spahn Ranch in the company of a woman in a wig identified as "Sharon."

Robert F. Kennedy is reported to have eaten dinner at the Polanski place the day before his assassination, a connection that may resonate with the Sirhan role in the murder.

The mansion where the five murders were committed on August 9, 1969, at 10050 Cielo Drive, was sublet by Roman Polanski from Terry Melcher, who was friends with Manson. Three days before the murder, a drug dealer was publicly whipped at Cielo. According to actor Dennis Hopper, "They had fallen into sadism and masochism and bestiality—and they recorded it all on videotape, too. The L.A. police told me this. I know that three days before they were killed twenty-five people were invited to that house for a mass whipping of a dealer from Sunset Strip who'd given them bad dope."

On August 5, shortly before the murders, Manson was at the Esalen Institute in Big Sur, California. Esalen, remarkably enough, is a New Age capitol assisted in its founding in 1962 by Aldous Huxley, and involved in sponsoring various kinds of meditational training and speakers. Process founder Robert DeGrimston is reported to have spoken at Esalen. One of the victims of the Tate murders was Abigail Folger, the coffee heiress. She had attended sessions at Esalen.

According to an Esalen newsletter, "Esalen started in the fall of 1962 as a forum to bring together a wide variety of approaches to enhancement of the human potential... including experiential sessions involving encounter groups, sensory awakening, gestalt awareness training, and related disciplines. Our latest step is to fan out into the community at large, running programs in cooperation with many different institutions, churches, schools, hospitals, and government." In other words, "society," to use the terminology of another organization.

At the murder site, Tate was hung upside down in the image of the Hanged Man Tarot card, a popular way for dispatching occultic traitors.

Were there puppeteers other than Charlie standing behind the Manson family murders? David Berkowitz, convicted for the Son of Sam killings, said that Manson "volunteered to do the killings" for someone else. One of the names that consistently comes up in investigations of the Manson family is The Process, but investigator Ed Sanders, who wrote a book on the Manson family, said, "There were so many investigations going on out there after the murders that I began to wonder if the Process was a front for some intelligence operation."

An ex-Processan provides more solid information: "You know, a lot of people say The Process is a fascist organization. It's actually half-true. It was founded by the German Democratic Party, a neo-Nazi group in Germany as a front to raise money over here in the States. But since that time it's grown more or less independent of the German group. I know a number of American Nazis and fascists who won't have anything to do with The Process. They say they don't want to be a part of a group that's run by Europeans."[4]

—An operation apparently sprung from the dragon's teeth of the CIA and the Louis Jolyon West Violence Center project was the Symbionese Liberation Army. Colston Westbrook was a Black CIA psychological warfare expert who had participated in Operation Phoenix in Vietnam, and was a part of Pacific Engineering Company, a subsidiary of Pacific Corporation, reportedly the largest CIA cut-out in the world. *Time Magazine* at the time simplified things by abbreviating his credentials to being simply a "linguist." Apparently based upon that job description, Westbrook got a job teaching "Black Lexicon" at UC Berkeley, then whipped up what was called the Black Cultural Association at the infamous Vacaville Medical Facility—actually a prison—in California. The program was organized by Donald DeFreeze, who had been a member of the Los Angeles Police Department's Public Disorder Unit between 1967-69.

DeFreeze, according to researcher Alex Constantine, "described his incarceration on the prison's third floor, where he was corralled by CIA agents who drugged him and said he would become the leader of a radical movement and kidnap a wealthy person. After his escape from Vacaville (an exit door was left unlocked for him), that's exactly what he did." Westbrook reportedly gave DeFreeze the handle "Cinque Mtume," and worked up the cobra logo for the SLA. The same logo was also used by alleged police agent Ron Karenga and his US Organization. [5]

After DeFreeze escaped from Vacaville he ended up on the doorsteps of the Vietnam Veterans Against the War and the Venceremos Brigade, offering his services as a hit man. This is a standard method of establishing an identity in underground cadres, by stepping forth as the "baddest of the bad."

Joseph Remiro and Nancy Ling Perry, members of the SLA, were political conservatives, according to researcher Mae Brussel, "with a kill-a-Commie-for-Christ background." Both were also drug addicts, a useful part of their profile. Bill and Emily Harris, also members, had no discernible background in radical politics, but came from the University of Indiana, a school used in the recruitment of the CIA. They had worked as a narc team for the Indiana State Police. The majority of individuals linked to the SLA by the police, in fact, had no earlier connection to radical politics, although several had worked with Colston Westbrook and Donald DeFreeze at Vacaville. [6]

On February 4, 1974, the SLA kidnapped Patricia Hearst, heir to the Hearst newspaper fortune. She was reportedly brainwashed and recruited as a member of the group, and was utilized in several very visible fund-raising events held at banks. She was arrested on September 18, 1975.

During the period that Hearst was eluding the police, there were one or more Hearst doubles in action. Researcher John Judge said in an interview, "There was a pick-up of somebody who said that she wasn't Patty Hearst but she looked exactly like her and she had gone to school up in Cleveland. A cop picked her up, and she had a scar in the same place, and everything was identical, but she wasn't Patty Hearst. Then an FBI agent supposedly came into the scene and said that if she ever got picked up again all she had to do was tell them to call this FBI agent and he would clear her—so it was a perfect way for Patty to move if there was an accidental pick-up—they had created a phony double." [7]

The media inflated stories of the SLA into what seemed to be the beginnings of a racial war—although it may have actually been planned that way. Then the cavalry arrived. On May 17, 1974, the headquarters of the SLA in Los Angeles was surrounded by 150 LAPD officers, 100 FBI, 100 Sheriff's Department officers, 15 highway patrolmen, and 25 motorcycle officers providing traffic control. The cops flamed the place, with six SLA members killed.

After the burning of the SLA headquarters, CIA-funded psychiatrists Martin Orne, Louis Jolyon West, and Robert Jay Lifton provided psychological pre-trial examinations of Patty Hearst. Another psychiatrist called upon to testify in the Hearst trial was Margaret Singer, who had studied returned Korean War prisoners at the Walter Reed Army Institute of Research in Maryland, worked with West at his Hashbury safe house, and who provided a book blurb on *Raven*, by Tim Reiterman and John Jacobs, a report on the Jim Jones' People's Temple that conveniently overlooked information linking the group to the CIA.

Orne and Singer later turned up as directors of the False Memory Syndrome Foundation, a group whose board is primarily made up of CIA and military doctors. The purpose of the group is to disprove claims of cult mind control. [8]

Here is Hearst's account of what happened after her arrest: "When the first of the psychiatrists came to see me on September 30, just eleven days after my arrest, I simply crumbled under his scrutiny. I cried, murmuring and mumbling out replies that were not answers to his questions. He thought I was refusing to cooperate with him. This was Dr. Louis Jolyon West, Chairman of the Department of Psychiatry at UCLA, Director of the Neuropsychiatric Institute, Psychiatrist-in-Chief of UCLA Hospitals, a licensed M.D., Chairman of the Council on Research and Development of the American Psychiatric Association, psychiatric consultant to the Air Force, author of books and studies on prisoners of war, an internationally recognized expert in his field. I thought he had a creepy hypnotic voice. A tall, heavy-set man who appeared to be kindly, I suspected 'Jolly' of being too smooth, too soothing to be trusted." [9]

Another of the shrinks to examine Hearst after her capture was Dr. Martin Orne, a CIA/Navy doctor involved during the 1960s in mind control experiments underwritten by the Human Ecology Fund and the Scientific Engineering Institute, both CIA fronts. At one point Orne boasted that he received routine briefing on all CIA behavior modification experiments. Orne is also one of the original members of the False Memory Syndrome Foundation, a group of psychiatrists, many of them with backgrounds linked to the CIA, whose mission is to prove that cult mind control and ritual child abuse does not exist. [10]

—The sound track for the '60s is of course provided by the Grateful Dead LSD and rock and roll organization. Until the death of leader Jerry Garcia, the Dead were arguably the most influential "cult" in operation. The first member of the Grateful Dead to take LSD, Robert Hunter, did so under the auspices of a "government sponsored" Stanford University drug study. An FBI internal memo from 1968 also mentions the employment of Jerry Garcia of the Grateful Dead as an avenue "to channel youth dissent and rebellion into more benign and non-threatening directions." It is obvious that with their "laid-back," non-politically involved stance, that the Grateful Dead have performed a vital service in distracting many young persons into drugs and mysticism, rather than politics. Whether they knew they were performing the service is a matter of argument. [11]

—Another repository of deadheads was Jonestown, the dystopic community established by evangelist Jim Jones in Guyana, South America. Most of us are familiar with the tragedy: nearly 1,000 members of the People's Temple are reported to have committed suicide there by drinking cyanide on the orders of Jones. But there is more to this apparent mass suicide than meets the eye in the triangle. Jonestown, without a doubt, was an MKULTRA project.

Suspicious associations of Jim Jones go back many years, to the man's boyhood, and his lifelong friendship with Dan Mitrione. Mitrione trained in the CIA-financed International Police Academy. He may have been the source of Jones' unexplained funding when in 1961 Jones travelled to Brazil. Mitrione, "working closely with the CIA at that point", accompanied him. At the time, Jones explained to his Brazilian neighbors that he was employed by Navy Intelligence, and both his food and the large house he and his small group lived in were provided by the U.S. Embassy. According to a local resident, Jones "lived like a king." At the time, Jones was making regular trips to Belo Horizonte, the headquarters of the CIA in Brazil. In 1963 Jones returned to the States, with an unexplained windfall of $10,000, sufficient to launch his next operation. [12]

In Ukiah, California, Jones established the first People's Temple. The Happy Havens Rest Home was also set up in the same location, guarded by electric fences, guard towers, dogs, and armed guards dressed in black. Persons attempting to leave the compound were sometimes forcibly restrained. There were at least 150 foster children living at the camp, along with elderly persons, prisoners, and psychiatric patients.

At that time the People's Temple linked up with the Mendocino State Mental Hospital, and members of the group were trained in medical techniques there. It is reported that in a short while the entire staff of the mental hospital were members of Jones' People's Temple.

California virtually handed the Mendocino State Mental Hospital to Jim Jones on a silver platter. According to researcher Michael Meiers, "The Mendocino Plan was a pilot program of the federal government designed to evaluate the feasibility of deinstitutionalizing the mentally ill. Dennis Denny, Mendocino's Director of Social Services, has speculated that the Mendocino Plan was the sole reason that Jim Jones moved to Ukiah." During the period that Jones was in Ukiah, Jones' group conducted behavior modification experiments on both the patients in the mental hospital, and on Jones' congregation. Jones used sensory deprivation on some of his congregation during this period, and it is said that Jones' expertise in the technique was passed on to Donald DeFreeze of the Symbionese Liberation Army, who would later use the method on Patty Hearst. [13]

In Ukiah, Jones is reported to have been in touch with CIA-connected World Vision, an evangelical anti-Communist church union that includes far-right church groups like Carl McIntyre's International Council of Christian Churches. World Vision is said to have employed Mark David Chapman, the murderer of John Lennon. John Hinckley, Sr., the father of the man who shot Ronald Reagan, is a friend of Reagan's Vice President George Bush—significant for the possible motive—and ran a World Vision mission in Denver, Colorado. Another of Hinckley Sr.'s sons was to have dinner with Neil Bush on the day of the attempted assassination.

Hinckley, Jr. was a prime candidate for mind control assassination programming. He was the recipient of mood-altering drugs from his hometown psychiatrist, and was on Valium when he shot Reagan. His "double," a man named Richardson, who followed Hinckley in Colorado and wrote love letters to Jody Foster, was a follower of Carl McIntyre. Hinckley also claimed to have met with David Berkowitz, the "Son of Sam" murderer, while in Colorado. [14]

In Ukiah Jim Jones hobnobbed with all the pillars of the community, and allied himself with Walter Heady, the leader of the local John Birch Society. Members of the People's Temple organized voting drives for Richard Nixon, worked with the Republican Party, and Jones was appointed chairman of the county grand jury.

A number of persons who would soon be influential in the People's Temple joined the group in Ukiah. According to researcher John Judge, "Most of the top lieutenants around Jones were from wealthy, educated backgrounds, many with connections to the military or intelligence agencies. These were the people who would set up the bank accounts, complex legal actions, and financial records that put people under the Temple's control." [15]

Among the most important of Jones' known supporters—who knows what scoundrels might have been lurking behind the scenes?—were the aristocratic Layton family, who financed Jones with large sums of money, and are related to wealthy British and German families. Dr. Lawrence Layton was Chief of Chemical and Ecological Warfare Research at the infamous Dugway Proving Grounds in Utah, working later at the Navy Propellant Division, as Director of Missile and Satellite Development. Layton's stockbroker father-in-law represented the German I.G. Farben monolith. The parents of George Philip Blakey, the husband of the former Debbie Layton, also had large holdings in Solvay Drugs, a division of I.G. Farben. Blakey is reported to have been a CIA operative and to have run mercenaries out of Jonestown, supplying forces to the CIA-backed UNITA in Angola. Blakey is reported to have made the original $650,000 deposit on the land in Guyana that was to become Jonestown. [16]

Another prominent alleged member of the People's Temple was Timothy Stoen, the Assistant District Attorney of San Francisco. Jones utilized his people to organize a voting drive for Mayor Moscone, and was rewarded by being put in charge of the San Francisco Housing Commission, a fact never mentioned in the mainstream press. Many of Jones' followers obtained jobs at the city Welfare Department, and were able to use those positions to gain recruits for the Temple.

Seven mysterious deaths connected to the People's Temple were reported in the local press, and increased scrutinization by the media and politicians apparently led Jones to pull up stakes and move his operation to Guyana. Guyana was not Jones' initial choice as a site for relocation. He had earlier decided on Grenada, and deposited $200,000 in the Grenada National Bank in 1977. After the Jonestown massacre, $76,000 remained in the bank.

The Jonestown location is a rich source of minerals and had earlier been the site of a Union Carbide bauxite and manganese mine. There had been earlier plans to bring in large numbers of workers to the area, going back as far as 1919. In current years, the area has been repopulated by 100,000 Laotian Hmong people. [17]

After the Guyanese location for the People's Temple was decided upon, it was prepared for habitation by members, with the cooperation of local officials and the U.S. Embassy. The Information Services Company states that "The U.S. Embassy in Georgetown Guyana housed the Georgetown CIA station. It now appears that the majority and perhaps all of the embassy officials were CIA officers operating under State Department covers."

Among embassy officials verified as being agents of the CIA are U.S. Ambassador John Burke, who attempted to stop Congressman Leo Ryan's investigation of Jonestown; Dan Webber, who was at the site of the massacre the following day; and Chief Consular Officer Richard McCoy, on loan from the Defense Department and reportedly "close" to Jones. [18]

The Jonestown compound in Guyana consisted of an hierarchical structure with an elite composed of all white male camp guards who received special privileges, and who were allowed to leave the camp freely and to carry money. Some of the white guards had been employed as mercenaries in Africa and elsewhere. The guards survived the Jonestown tragedy. The rest of the camp was 90% women, and 80% Black, and they existed under slave labor conditions, working 16 to 18 hours daily, with miserable rations. When Black members of the Temple arrived from the United States, they were bound and gagged before being taken to the compound. Once inside Jonestown, perceived infractions led to forced drugging, public rape, torture, and beatings. [19]

Jeannie Mills, a member of the People's Temple, reported that she had seen films taken inside a Chilean torture camp, either *Colonia Dignidad* or another located at Pisagua, while at Jonestown. These camps have documented connections to the CIA as well as to Fourth Reich Nazis, with visits reported from the negatively notable such as Dr. Josef Mengele and Martin Bormann.

The Jonestown mass suicide (or murder) was probably set off by the arrival in Guyana of Congressman Leo Ryan, who was perhaps the most active investigator in Washington of CIA abuses, and arguably number one with a bullet on the CIA's lengthy hate list. Among other accomplishments, Ryan had introduced the Hughes-Ryan Amendment to the National Assistance Act, transferring the overseeing of the CIA from the Armed Forces Committee—known for looking the other way in matters relating to the CIA—to the International Relations Committee of the House and Senate. [20]

Ryan had uncovered information linking the CIA to the creation of mind control cults, including the Unification Church of Reverend Sung Myung Moon, and the Symbionese Liberation Army. In response to stories of atrocities at Jonestown, Ryan decided to investigate for himself—and that determination sealed his fate.

After travelling to Jonestown and attempting to return to the States, Ryan, several reporters, and a Jonestown defector were killed on an airstrip at nearby Port Kaituma, with the mass Jonestown deaths taking place shortly afterward. Observers reported that Ryan's group was killed by armed men who acted like "zombies."

Cheering was heard 45 minutes after the mass death at Jonestown, and those persons have never been accounted for. For that matter, practically no one at Jonestown has been accounted for. Robert Pastor, an aide to Zbigniew Brzezinski, at the time national security advisor to Jimmy Carter, sent orders to the U.S. military to remove "all politically sensitive papers and forms of identification from the bodies." [21]

Dr. Mootoo, a Guyanese pathologist, was the first medical person on the scene, and the first to examine the bodies of the victims. Mootoo determined that there were fresh needle marks on the left shoulder blades of 80-90% of the bodies. Some of the victims had been shot or strangled. The gun that Jones had reportedly used to commit suicide lay 200 feet away from his body. Mootoo concluded to the Guyanese grand jury that all but three of the victims had not committed suicide, but were murdered. When autopsies were performed at Dover, Delaware, the forensic doctors were not informed of Dr. Mootoo's findings.

The body identified as Jim Jones did not have Jones' chest tattoos, and was so decomposed that it was not recognizable. Fingerprints on the body were checked twice, for no apparent reason—could it have been that they did not match Jones?—while his dental records were not consulted. [22]

The recovery of the bodies to the United States was botched, with all identification removed, and a delay of a week before they were transported. Rotting made autopsies impossible. Due to the decomposition only 17 of the bodies could be identified in

Delaware. Although the Guyanese had initially identified 174 bodies, that information was destroyed.

There were at least 200 survivors of Jonestown, and they were never contacted by the press. Jeannie and Al Mills, two survivors who were planning on writing a book about Jones and the cult, were murdered, while another survivor was murdered in Detroit, with the perpetrator never captured. According to John Judge, "Yet another was involved in a mass murder of school children in Los Angeles." The acknowledged survivors of Jonestown were represented legally in the U.S. by Joseph Blatchford, who had been accused of being involved in the CIA infiltration of the Peace Corps.

At the time of the Jonestown massacre, CIA agent Richard Dwyer, Deputy Chief of Mission for the U.S. Embassy in Guyana, was present. In a tape recording made immediately prior, Jones can be heard saying, "Get Dwyer out of here."

At the end, Jones had accumulated assets estimated to be between $26 million and $2 billion. The government receivership determined a figure of $10 million. Much of this money unaccountably disappeared.

Joe Holsinger, Congressman Leo Ryan's attorney and friend, said that a few hours after the murder of Ryan he had heard from a White House official that "we have a CIA report from the scene." Holsinger wrote, "The more I investigate the mysteries of Jonestown, the more I am convinced there is something sinister behind it all. There is no doubt in my mind that Jones had very close CIA connections. At the time of the tragedy, the Temple had three boats in the water off the coast. The boats disappeared shortly afterwards. Remember, Brazil is a country that Jones is very familiar with. He is supposed to have money there. And it is not too far from Guyana. My own feeling is that Jones was ambushed by CIA agents who then disappeared in the boats. But the whole story is so mind-boggling that I'm willing to concede he escaped with them." [23]

Not surprisingly, Louis Jolyon West wrote an article offering the sanitized version of Jonestown—sans conflicting evidence or CIA involvement. [24]

—Another cult with curious, somehow non-religious under-pinnings is the Unification Church of Reverend Sun Myung Moon, the power behind literally hundreds of fronts and businesses internationally. Among the acquisitions of the UC are the University of Bridgeport in Connecticut, which cost Moon a cool $50 million, and the *Washington Times* newspaper, which he admitted had set him back "close to one billion dollars."

Before its incorporation in the U.S., Moon was closely connected to the South Korean Central Intelligence Agency (KCIA), with four of Moon's followers in positions of prominence in the intelligence organization.

Bo Hi Pak—one of Moon's top aides—was a liaison to U.S. intelligence agencies for the KCIA. In 1962 he travelled to the U.S. where he met with CIA Director John McCone, Defense Secretary Robert McNamara, and Defense Intelligence Agency Director General Joseph Carroll. Pak was also known to make frequent trips to the National Security Agency at Fort Meade, Maryland.

Moon has received large contributions from right-wing politicians in Japan, and in 1970 Moon's Japanese organization hosted the rightist World Anti-Communist League annual conference. [25]

—The Church of Scientology is a group with incredible sway over the minds of its adherents. The founder of the group, L. Ron Hubbard, was reportedly a member of Naval Intelligence during World War II, as well as being a friend and participant in magickal workings with Jack Parsons, the head of the *California Ordo Templi Orientis* group of Aleister Crowley. In one of his recorded lectures, Hubbard describes Parsons as being the most brilliant man he ever met. Hubbard seems to have been a sincere Crowleyite, regardless of the protestations of the church hierarchy. According to his son, Ron DeWolf, "He was very interested in... the creation of what some people call the Moon Child. It was basically an attempt to create an immaculate conception, except by Satan rather than by God... getting a satanic or demonic spirit to inhabit the body of a fetus. This would come about as a result of black-magic rituals, which included the use of hypnosis, drugs, and other dangerous and destructive practice... He thought of himself as the Beast 666 incarnate... the Antichrist. Aleister Crowley thought of himself as such... When Crowley died in 1947, my father decided that he should wear the cloak of the beast and become the most powerful being in the universe." [26]

It is quite possible that Hubbard continued to be connected to U.S. intelligence after World War II. According to former CIA officer Miles Copeland, "arrangements" were made between the Agency and Scientology as well as the group Moral Re-Armament. The CIA's covert support for MRA is confirmed by the late CIA agent Jim Wilcott. Certainly there cannot have been too much animosity between the CIA and Scientology, judging from the Agency's Project Grill Flame remote viewing experiments, in which 14 Scientologists graded "Clear" and above participated.

According to a source quoted by Daniel Brandt, in the early 1960s Hubbard was given an award by the American Ordnance Association. According to this source, Hubbard "was on a friendly basis with top generals and admirals and their military-industrial associates." [27]

—The Finders group appears to be another cult created as a pet project of American so-called intelligence. Since 1987, the Finders have been on a roll, expanding their real estate holdings with properties estimated to be worth more than $2.2 million. The *Washington City Paper* reports that "the Finders constantly walk the streets, following people home and taking extensive notes and pictures."

Researcher Daniel Brandt was contacted by members of the Finders in 1984. They told him that they were members of the "Information Bank," and provided *gratis* a computer program that Brandt needed. One of the men who approached Brandt was later caught rifling the files of Washington, D.C. researcher Kris Jacobs. At that time he claimed he was from the National Journalism Center. In another encounter, the same person showed a business card with the legend "Hong Kong Business Today".

According to Brandt, who visited the warehouse headquarters of the Finders in Washington, D.C., "It was clear... that most group members were world-class travelers, which included travel to numerous Eastern Bloc countries. It was all a game to them. This was a small group—perhaps 40 adults—but they had no visible income to support their far-flung activities."

The founder of the group is retired USAF Master Sergeant Marion David Pettie. He reportedly started the outfit as early as the 1950s, originally calling the group the Seekers. His wife, Isabel, was a support secretary for the CIA in Frankfurt, Germany, from 1957-61. Pettie's son George, according to one report, "served in the CIA's drug activities in Air America during the Vietnam War."

"A three-page non-government memo of undetermined origin" cited by Daniel Brandt provides additional information about Pettie. According to the memo, Pettie began his career in contact with a number of OSS agents, and was the chauffeur to General Ira Eaker. He was a protegé of Charles Marsh, who ran a private intelligence agency, and received training in counterintelligence in Baltimore and Frankfurt, Germany. Pettie's control agent was Colonel Leonard N. Weigner of Air

Force intelligence and the CIA, and his case officer was Major George Varga, who passed on instructions from Weigner until Varga died in the 1970s. Pettie resigned—or should it be "resigned"?—from the military only to don bellbottoms and beads and plunge headlong into the counterculture.

One oft-cited incident involving the Finders took place in 1987, in Tallahassee, Florida, when the local police department was alerted to suspicious activities, and apprehended two men transporting six children. According to the report of the police officers,

"The police had received an anonymous telephone call relative to two well-dressed white men wearing suits and ties in Myers Park, [Tallahassee], apparently watching six dirty and unkept [sic] children in the playground area. A Mr. HOULIHAN and AMMERMAN were near a 1980 blue Dodge van bearing the Virginia license number XHW-557, the inside of which was later described as foul-smelling, filled with maps, books, letters, with a mattress situated to the rear of the van which appeared as if it were used as a bed. The overall appearance of the van gave the impression that all eight persons were living in it. The children were covered with insect bites, were very dirty and most of the children were not wearing underwear and all the children had not been bathed in many days."

One of the arresting officers voiced suspicions about the children being used in pornography in Mexico. A search warrant was issued for the Finders' Washington, D.C. headquarters, and police entered the building on February 5, 1987. Special Agents for the Department of the Treasury Ramon Martinez and Lynwood Rountree said in their report that, "During the course of the search warrants, numerous documents were discovered which appeared to be concerned with international trafficking in children, high tech transfers to the United Kingdom and international transfer of currency." The computer/cult connection will rear its head again.

The report continued, "Further inspection of the premises disclosed numerous files relating to activities of the organization in different parts of the world. Locations I observed are as follows: London, Germany, the Bahamas, Japan, Hong Kong, Malaysia, Africa, Costa Rica and Europe. There was also a file identified as Palestinian. Other files were identified by member name or 'project' name. The projects, appearing to be operated for commercial purposes under front names for the FINDERS. There was a file entitled 'Pentagon Break-In' and others which referred to members operating in foreign countries. Not observed by me but related by an MPD [Metropolitan Police Department] officer, were intelligence files on private families not related to the Finders. The process undertaken appears to have been a systematic response to local newspaper advertisements for baby-sitters, tutors, etc. A member of the Finders would respond and gather as much information as possible about the habits, identity, occupation, etc. of a family. The use to which this information was to be put is still unknown. There was also a large amount of data collected on various child care organizations.

"The warehouse contained a large library, two kitchens, a sauna, hot tub and a video room. The video room seemed to be set up as an indoctrination center. It also appeared that the organization had the capability to produce its own videos. There were what appeared to be training areas for children and what appeared to be an altar set up in a residential area of the warehouse. Many jars of urine and feces were located in this area."

According to researcher Wendell Minnick, the author of *Spies and Provocateurs: An Encyclopedia of Espionage and Covert Action,* a telex was found in the 1987 raid that ordered, "the purchase of two children from Hong Kong to be arranged through a contact in the Chinese embassy there." In substantiation, at the time of the raid a Chinese graduate in anatomy from Georgetown University, Wang Gen-xin, was living with the Finders.

A Washington, D.C. police detective named Bradley was contacted by one of the officers involved in the search of the Finders' headquarters, at which time it was agreed that the documents seized would be reviewed within a few days. An internal "Memo to File," dated April 13, 1987, and written by one of the Customs agents participating in the raid reported what ensued:

"On April 2, 1987, I arrived at MPD at approximately 9:00 AM. Detective Bradley was not available. I spoke to a third party who was willing to discuss the case with me on a strictly 'off the record' basis. I was advised that all the passport data had been turned over to the State Department for their investigation. The State Department in turn advised MPD that all travel and use of the passports by the holders of the passports was within the law and no action would be taken. This includes travel to Moscow, North Korea and North Vietnam from the late 1950s to mid 1970s."

The same memo also stated, "CIA made one contact and

admitted to owning the Finders organization... but that it had "gone bad.".....[I was advised] the investigation into the activity of the Finders had become a CIA internal matter. The MPD report has been classified Secret and was not available for review. I was advised that the FBI had withdrawn from the investigation several weeks prior and that the FBI Foreign Counterintelligence Division had directed MPD not to advise the FBI Washington Field Office of anything that had transpired. No further information will be available. No further action will be taken." [28]

—David Berkowitz, convicted of the "Son of Sam" New York murder series, was a "son of Uncle Sam" and, evidence suggests, the member of "the Children," an international satanic murder cult with links to the military. Terry Patterson, an army buddy of Berkowitz, stated that when Berkowitz joined the army he entered a special program reportedly for "profiled" candidates of an unspecified character, and was given hallucinogenic drugs, he admits, by the "brass."

Berkowitz may have known the source of his programming, as well. In the first handwritten missive he sent to the New York police he wrote, "I am the 'Son of Sam.' I am a little 'brat'," the possible implication being that he is an army brat. He also wrote, "I am on a different wave length than everybody else—programmed to kill." [29]

Berkowitz joined the New York Police auxiliary while in high school, and it is reported that he was tipped off from within the department when the police became aware that he was the—or one of the—Son of Sam murderers. Retired NYPD detective Sgt. Joseph Coffey has stated that he was ordered to destroy a letter that was sent to Berkowitz by Police Commissioner Michael Codd, and that he carried out the order. Berkowitz has said that three members of the Yonkers police department were members of the cult responsible for the Son of Sam murders. [30]

A letter from Berkowitz that was withheld from scrutiny for four years by the police states, "I David Berkowitz have been chosen since birth, to be one of the executioners of the cult." Berkowitz estimated the cult to have several thousand members. He linked the killing of Arlis Perry, butchered in a satanic ritual at Stanford University in California, to members of the group in Los Angeles. Perry had only moved to California from South Dakota a few weeks before, and the killing was reportedly done by the L.A. group as a favor to a chapter in Bismarck, North Dakota. The Los Angeles group supposedly counted Charles Manson as a member before his arrest.

John Carr, nicknamed "John 'Wheaties'", the Son of Sam (Carr), in one of the anonymous Son of Sam letters, associated with Berkowitz, and fits the description of one of the Son of Sam murderers. Berkowitz has confirmed the man's involvement in the crimes. Arlis Perry was murdered on Carr's birthday. Carr is alleged to have been involved in satanism since high school, and was in the Air Force until being discharged a few months before the beginning of the Son of Sam murders. He was a staff sergeant and stationed in Minot, North Dakota, with the headquarters of the satanic group he was associated with in Bismarck. He travelled back and forth between North Dakota and Yonkers, New York, where Berkowitz lived, with trips coinciding with several of the "Son of Sam" killings.

Berkowitz was also identified by a witness as being in North Dakota, and John Hinckley, who attempted to assassinate Ronald Reagan, has stated that he met Berkowitz in Colorado. John Carr was receiving psychiatric counseling during the period of the Sam murders. After the slayings, a body identified as Carr's was found at his home in South Dakota, allegedly murdered for "knowing too much," but identification on the corpse was questionable.

Carr's brother Michael was an executive in Scientology and had received therapy for a drug habit in New York. Berkowitz insisted that Michael Carr was a member of the New York cult, and involved in the murders. He also said that Michael and John were members of "an offshoot, fringe" group connected to Scientology. It is possible that this was The Process, the apocalyptic cult formed by disaffected Scientologists Robert DeGrimston and Mary Ann McLean DeGrimston. Charles Manson knew members of The Process, and may have been a member.

Michael Carr died in a car accident at the height of the Son of Sam investigation. The side window of Carr's sister's policeman husband John McCabe was shot out the next night, as it was driven by another officer taking McCabe's usual route. McCabe had phoned in sick so that he could identify Michael Carr's body. At almost the same time, two friends of John Carr were forced off the road in a car in Minot. A Yonkers mailman who had been threatened by the New York group committed suicide a month after Berkowitz' arrest. And there were other murders apparently linked to the coverup of the Son of Sam killings. Abundant evidence proves that there were several persons involved in the "Son of Sam" murders, apparently all of them linked to a single satanic cult, although no others than

Berkowitz were arrested for the crimes. [31]

—Maria Devi Khrystos claimed that she was the reincarnation of Christ, and predicted the end of the world on November 10, 1993. She planned to commit suicide with her estimated 12,000 followers in the White Brotherhood in St. Sophia's Square in Kiev, the city they called the New Jerusalem.

According to the *London Daily Mail*, "She is young and sexually attractive, with large, dark, kohl-smudged eyes and full lips. Her posters, in which she wears long white robes, holds a staff and has two fingers raised in a Christ-like gesture of peace, are plastered across Russia from Vladivostok to the western borders and throughout the other Slavic states, Ukraine, Byelorussia and Moldova."

Born Marina Tsvyguna in 1960 in the Ukraine, she worked as a newspaper and radio reporter, as well as an organizer for *Komsomol,* the Soviet youth organization. She abandoned her husband and son when she met Yuri Krigonogov, whom she later married. Krigonogov goes by the name Ioann Vamy ("John is with you") and is reported to resemble Rasputin in his facial features. He had formerly been a member of the *Hare Krishna* movement, but after being expelled from that group he formed the Center for Higher Yoga in Kiev in 1990. That group was turned into the White Brotherhood after he met Khrystos.

Suggesting that the CIA is not the only intelligence agency implicated in the creation of cults, Krigonogov worked for four years at the Kiev Institute for Cybernetics, in a secret KGB laboratory, researching drugs for psychological warfare. He is said to have learned hypnosis while working at the lab. According to the Associated Press, "There is little doubt that Khryvonohov [Krigonogov] writes the pastiche of prophecy, political ravings and instructions in civil disobedience that constitute the group's theology."

Alexander Naumov of the Ukrainian Ministry of the Interior, speaking of the recruits for the White Brotherhood, said "They are the top of the class, the gold medalists at school. They come from good families, they are intelligent and receptive to ideas, and at the same time used to behaving themselves and doing as they are told."

White Brotherhood members are reported to live in squats, or abandoned buildings, migrating from one location to another to escape detection. When apprehended the followers of Khrystos, some of them as young as four years old with many in their early teens, have gone on hunger strikes. The members, according to the reports of people in Kiev, all have glazed expressions with out-of-focus eyes, and a slight smile.

"What is frightening is that they are well trained to cope with hunger strikes," said Dr. Anatoly Gabriel of the Number One Hospital of Kiev. "They switch into well-rehearsed mass meditation to overcome their hunger pains."

Some psychiatric professionals in Kiev believe that there is a secret code composed of words or music that the followers of Khrystos are programmed to respond to, but they also confess they are unable to undo the programming.

When individuals join the group they go through a ceremony in which they are 'cleansed' with what is called 'Jordan Water.' Attempting to understand the makeup of the concoction, scientists in Kiev mixed red blood cells with the liquid and found that it caused mutations and the destruction of the cells' ability to create antibodies. They have speculated that Krigonogov was using his expertise in biowarfare to concoct a chemical that aided in brainwashing.

As Doomsday approached Khrystos and 60 followers were arrested by troops as they camped inside St. Sophia's Cathedral. "Today, Maria Devi has fulfilled her prophecy," said Khrystos. "Two years ago, I spoke of my final sermon at St. Sophia. Today you have captured God's house of worship, taking her as prisoner, arresting the living God."

Three leaders of the White Brotherhood were sentenced to prison terms on February 9, 1996, in Kiev. Members of the group wept openly in the courtroom as Khrystos received a four-year sentence for the seizure of public property—for invading the cathedral. Her husband received a seven-year sentence for the same charge and for inciting, causing public disorder, and resisting arrest. A third group leader, Vitaliy Kovalchuk, who terms himself Apostle Peter II, received six years on similar charges.

Khrystos and Kovalchuk were freed from prison on August 18, 1997, by presidential amnesty commemorating the first anniversary of the Ukraine constitution. There is no information on whether Khrystos has re-scheduled the end of the world at this time. [32]

—In the fall of 1994 in chalets in Granges, Switzerland, and Morin Heights, Quebec, Canada, 53 members of the Sovereign Order of the Solar Temple were found dead. Sixteen members are reported to have later committed suicide, in France in 1995.

The leader of the Solar Temple, Luc Jouret, was born in the Belgian Congo in 1947, leaving with his parents during decolonization. Jouret attended the Free University in Belgium, and is reported to have graduated in the mid-'70s with a degree in medicine, although his medical credentials were later challenged in Canada. While in school he reportedly attracted the interest of Belgian police for Maoist activities.

After leaving school, Jouret became interested in alternative medical therapies, including homeopathy. In 1976 he visited the Philippines to study the techniques of spiritualist healers, and in the early 1980s moved to the Lake Leman area between France and Switzerland to work as a homeopathic physician, reportedly gaining a wide following in Europe.

In the early 1980s Jouret began lecturing, catering to the New Age movement in France. He established an organization named Club Amenta (later the Club Atlanta), with branches in Switzerland, France, Canada, and Martinique. Jouret's "Club" was associated with the neo-Templarian tradition of Bernard-Raymond Fabre-Palaprat, who claimed during the French Revolution to be in possession of documents confirming the continuation of the historical Knights Templar. One of the organizational offshoots of Fabre-Palaprat's Templars was the Sovereign Order of the Solar Temple, founded by Jacques Breyer in 1952. That group generated another offshoot, the Renewed Order of the Temple, formed in 1968.

The Renewed Order was founded by rightwing political activist Julien Origas, and it was apparently Origas' Renewed Order that Luc Jouret joined in 1983. Jouret left the Renewed Order in 1984 to found Club Amenta.

According to documents mailed to the press before the mass deaths of the Solar Temple group, "the Grail, Excalibur, the Candalabra of the Seven Branches and the Ark of the Covenant were revealed to the living witnesses, the final and faithful Servants of the Eternal Rose+Croix. Following which false slanders and every kind of treason and scandal, judiciously orchestrated by different existing powers, sounded the knell for a last attempt to regenerate the Plans of Conscience."

In 1984 Jouret founded the Club Archedia, for the more dedicated members of his group, with another, a yet more rarified and secret level being the International Chivalric Organization, Solar Tradition (the French acronym being OICTS), also known as the Solar Tradition, and later, the Solar Temple.

Jouret is said to have been a friend of Third Position—European fascist—leader Claudio Mutti. Mutti was jailed in 1980 for a Bologna, Italy, railroad station bombing. A Sufi, Mutti is a proponent of the philosophy of the fascist/mystic

Baron Julius Evola.

Joseph Di Mambro, a leader in the Solar Temple, met Jouret in the 1980s, in Geneva, Switzerland. Di Mambro ran his own New Age group, called the Golden Way Foundation, as well as a more secretive inner order called "the Pyramid." Di Mambro is also said to have been an associate of an alleged organizer of the Nazi Black International, Francois Arnoud.

Through Di Mambro were allegedly developed links with the SAC private intelligence group in France and the P-2 Masonic order headquartered in Italy. According to French-Canadian journalist Pierre Tourangeau, Jouret's endeavors were financed in part by European and South American gun-running, with millions of dollars of profits laundered through the Bank of Credit and Commerce International.

At about the same time as his meeting with Di Mambro, Jouret also became associated with Julien Origas. Origas is alleged to have been a Nazi collaborator during World War II, was the French Grandmaster of the neo-Templar Renewed Order of the Temple, and an associate of Arnoud's Black International Nazi group. Origas was a confidante of Raymond Bellio, a friend of Francois Arnoud and a writer on qabalism. After the death of Origas in 1983 the membership of the Renewed Order of the Temple was transferred in the main to the Solar Temple.

In early 1986 Di Mambro made contact with an Australian Third Position leader in Geneva. In his first trip to Australia in 1986, Di Mambro is said to have held secret talks with "individuals known to be linked to extreme Nazi-Maoist activities in Australia." Over the next few years Di Mambro and Jouret would collectively make 11 trips to Australia, open several bank accounts, and start a book publishing company.

In 1993, Jouret and other members of the group in Canada were brought to trial on illegal weapons charges. Jouret pleaded guilty, then departed for France. According to one of the documents mailed to the press before the mass death, "...the year 1993 was marked in Quebec by the political-judicial scandal perpetrated against the Order of the Solar Temple and ARCHS. Amongst numerous members as well as the principal people in charge, Mr. Jean-Pierre Vinet and Dr. Luc Jouret were the victims of slander and false accusations of the most sordid kind for many months, such as: debauchery, individual or collective manipulation, swindling, illegal drug dealing, possession of weapons, etc...

"Let us remember that more than 80 agents of the Security Guard of Quebec were mobilized to launch a general investigation of the activities of the above-mentioned organizations. During this whole affair, the attitude of the Security Guard of Quebec was particularly questionable, ambiguous and cowardly. The investigation and the different police operations (the use of armored cars, machine guns, untimely arrests...) carried out with a great deal of publicity, have cost Quebec and Canadian taxpayers more than $6 million. If it were not for its tragic and pitiful aspect, one would want to laugh at the absurdity of the affair.

"Throughout the investigation, unscrupulous reporters excelled in perfidious manipulations consisting of misinforming the public. We specifically mention Mr. Pelchat, whose responsibilities were great during this somber and nauseating spectacle.

"Since no proof existed, government and police officials strove to fabricate an evil scenario of a 'plot of terrorists whose subversive activities were financed by dangerous sects...'"

After the mass death of the Solar Temple, variously claimed to be suicide or murder, the Swiss magazine *L'Hebdo* stated that between $127 million and $253 million had been deposited in Australian bank accounts by the Solar Temple. These funds were allegedly withdrawn from the accounts prior to the mass death, but are otherwise not accounted for. [33]

—In the well-to-do suburb of Rancho Santa Fe near San Diego, California, between March 23-25, 1997, 39 members of the Heaven's Gate UFO cult ate phenobarbital-laced pudding, chased it with vodka, put plastic bags over their heads, and died. The group was founded by Marshall Herff Applewhite, the son of a Presbyterian minister who became a family man while working as a music professor at the University of Alabama in the 1960s. Applewhite left his family and the college amid accusations of a homosexual affair, and migrated to the University of St. Thomas in Houston, Texas. Applewhite left there in 1970 due to "health problems of an emotional nature." Allegedly suffering from depression and hearing voices in his head, he checked into a hospital, asking for a cure for his homosexuality. According to Applewhite's sister he had experienced a heart attack and a near death experience at this time—some have suggested that, given his later career as a New Age messiah, this is the time that Applewhite may have been contacted by an unspecified intelligence agency and activated as a cult leader.

During this period Applewhite met Bonnie Lu Trusdale Nettles, a New Ager who left her husband and four children for Applewhite. They dubbed each other "Bo" and "Peep," but also called themselves The Two, from the *Book of Revelations.* They began recruiting followers for HIM, Human Individual Metamorphoses, promising inductees that they would be leaving on a UFO soon.

The philosophy was a typically byzantine New Age formulation: There are two universes, one governed by physical laws, space and time, the other referred to as the Non-Temporal Universe, the Next Level, God, the Spiritual Ground, and the Holodeck (from *Star Trek: The Next Generation*), where the Energy God Being (EGB) exists. The Next Level is structured like a massive Earth corporation, with a complex pyramidal organization chart. Beings on the Next Level do not eat, but take their nourishment straight from the EGB.

At a certain time in the past, Lucifer, a vice president of the Next Level, and some of his followers broke away and tried to form their own corporation. The Luciferians, according to the HIM philosophy, are the guys who pilot the UFOs we see in the sky, and are engaged in performing medical experiments and cloning on human beings. The master plan of the EGB is to harvest souls from the temporal universe every 2,000 years. Representatives act as recruiters, and then the enlistees are beamed to the Next Level.

The group forbade intoxicants and sex—some of the members even going so far as to be castrated to avoid carnal desires. Contact with families was discouraged, and the members were monitored closely, reportedly checking in with the leader every 12 minutes during waking hours.

When the promised UFO didn't show, most of the the HIM recruits defected, with the core of the group, about 50 members, staying together and moving from one place to another around the country.

Apparently Applewhite and Nettles changed their names every month or so to confuse the Luciferians who were hot on their trail. At some point The Two began calling themselves "Do" and "Ti," from the musical scale. In 1985 Ti died from liver cancer.

By 1993 the cult had taken on a more public face, and started calling themselves Heaven's Gate, announcing themselves with an ad in *USA Today* declaring, "UFO Cult Resurfaces with Final Offer." The ad promised "the last chance to advance beyond human."

In 1996 Heaven's Gate started a business designing Internet Web pages, called "Higher Source Contract Enterprises." They designed cut-rate Web pages for groups varying from a San Diego polo club to a Christian music group. Living in a $7,000-a-month mansion, the group is said to have become increasingly fearful of the government.

Learning about a UFO trailing the Hale-Bopp comet from the Art Bell radio show, the collective decided that was the sign that they were going to be taken up from Earth. As the comet approached the group prepared to shed their "earthly containers."

Curiously, some of the members talked about having a Chip of Recognition implanted in their skull, whereby they were able to recognize Luciferians when they came into contact with them. Whether this was a metaphor of 'spiritual sight,' or an actual physical implant has not been determined. It is unlikely that autopsies of the members of the group included skull x-rays.

A telling connection to Heaven's Gate was the murder of Ian Stuart Spiro, his wife, and three children, on November 1, 1992. His family were killed in their home in San Diego, while Spiro was later found dead in the desert. Spiro was extensively connected to the CIA and British intelligence, and is reported to have been involved in a wide range of spy-biz, including Iran-Contra and the October Surprise. At the time of his murder Spiro was assisting "Danger Man" Michael Riconisciuto in the collection of documents substantiating the Inslaw case, documented by myself and co-author Kenn Thomas in *The Octopus*. Spiro, who lived only a short distance away from the Heaven's Gate compound in San Diego, is alleged to have been a member of the group. [34]

NOTES:

1. Laing, R.D. cited in "The New Inquisition," Glenn Krawczyk, *Nexus* magazine, October/November 1994

2. Judge; Vankin, Jonathan, *Conspiracies, Cover-Ups & Crimes: From Dallas to Waco.* (Lilburn, Georgia: IllumiNet Press, 1996); Terry, Maury, *The Ultimate Evil.* (New York: Bantam Books, 1989)

3. Judge, John, "Poolside with John Judge," published by *Prevailing Winds*, undated; Terry, Maury, *The Ultimate Evil.* (New York: Bantam Books, 1989)

4. Austin, E. Edwin. "The Nazi-Cocaine Connection", *The Conspiracy Tracker*, issue 10; Raschke, Carl, *Painted Black.* (New York: Harper & Row, 1990); Judge; Blood, Linda, *The New Satanists.* (New York: Warner Books, 1994); The Editors of Executive Intelligence Review, *Dope, Inc.* (Washington, D.C. Executive Intelligence Review, 1992); Taylor, R.N. "The Process: A Personal Reminiscense", in *Apocalypse Culture.* Adam Parfrey, ed. (Venice, California: Feral House, 1990); Terry

5. Judge; Brussel, Mae. "Why Was Patty Hearst Kidnapped?," *Paranoid Women Collect Their Thoughts*, ed. Joan D'Arc, (Providence, Rhode Island:

Paranoia Publishing, 1996); "Strange Message from Patty", *Time Magazine*, April 15, 1974

6. Judge; Brussel

7. Judge, John

8. Constantine, Alex, "The False Memory Hoax," *Paranoia* magazine, Winter 1995/1996; Constantine, Alex, *Virtual Government*. (Venice, California: Feral House, California, 1997)

9. Krawczyk, Glenn. "The New Inquisition: Cult Awareness or the Cult of Intelligence?" *Nexus* magazine, December 1994/January 1995; Hearst, Patricia, *Every Secret Thing*, cited in Krawczyk

10. Constantine, Alex. "The False Memory Hoax"

11. Lee and Shlain, *Acid Dreams*. (New York: Grove Press, 1985); Hidell, Al. "Paranotes," *Paranoia* magazine, Winter 1995/1996

12. Meiers, Michael. *Was Jonestown a CIA Medical Experiment? A Review of the Evidence*. Cited in Krawczyk, "The New Inquisition"; Judge

13. Judge, John. "Evangelical Assassins?" *The Conspiracy Tracker*, issue 8, undated; Vankin

14. Judge

15. Ibid.; *Day 51: The True Story of Waco*, a video produced and directed by Richard Mosley

16. Judge

17. *Information Services Company*, July, 1980. Cited by Judge

18. Judge, John. "The Black Hole of Guyana," *Secret and Suppressed*, Jim Keith, ed. (Portland, Oregon: Feral House, 1993)

19. Judge; Krawczyk, Glenn. "The New Inquisition: Cult Awareness or the Cult of Intelligence?", Part 2, *Nexus* magazine, December 1994/January 1995

20. Brandt, Daniel. "Cults, Anti-Cultists, and the Cult of Intelligence", Namebase NewsLine, number 5, April-June 1994

21. Judge, "Poolside with John Judge"

22. Ibid.; Harris, William. "Jim Jones Still Alive in Brazil?", *The Globe*, 12 May 1981, cited in Krawczyk

23. Krawczyk

24. Judge, "Poolside with John Judge", published by *Prevailing Winds*, undated; Coleman, Loren. "The Occult, MIB's, UFO's and Assassinations," *The Conspiracy Tracker*, December 1985; Guffey

25. Brandt, Daniel, "Cults, Anti-Cultists, and the Cult of Intelligence," *NameBase NewsLine*, Number 5, April/June 1994

26. DeWolf, Ron. Cited in *The New Satanists* by Linda Blood (New York: Warner Books, 1994)

27. Brandt

28. Alexander, A.B.H. "Sex, Drugs, the CIA, Mind Control and Your Children," *The Probe*, volume 3, number 2, 1997; Brandt, Daniel. "Kooks or Spooks?," *NameBase Newsline*, April-June 1994; Minnick, Wendell. "The Finders: The CIA and the Cult of Marion David Pettie," undated article, available on the Internet

29. Hoffman III, Michael A., *Secret Societies and Psychological Warfare*. (Dresden, New York: Wiswell Ruffin House, 1992); Terry

30. Hoffman; Terry

31. Hoffman II, Michael A. "The Double Initial Murders", *The Conspiracy Tracker*, issue 9

32. "Worldwide Special: On the Apocalyptic Vision of the Leader of a

Bizarre Religious Cult as She Waits for the World to End", *London Daily Mail*, November 11, 1993; Kolomayets, Marta. "God in Kiev Jail Says World Ends Sunday", Associated Press, November 1993; Kolomayets, Marta. "White Brotherhood leaders sentenced", *Ukrainian Weekly*, February 18, 1996; Gutterman, Steve. "Leader of apocalyptic cult released, *Kiev Post*, August 20, 1997

33. Constantine, Alex, "The False Memory Hoax"; Douzet, Andre. "The Treasure Trove of the Knights Templars," *Nexus* magazine, volume 4, number 3, April/May 1997; Daugherty, James. "Solar Temple/Japanese Gassing/Nazi Link," posted to *alt.conspiracy* discussion group on the Internet; Introvigne and Melton. "The Solar Temple: A Preliminary Report on the Roots of a Tragedy," *Gnosis* magazine, Winter 1995

34. "Web of Death," *Newsweek* magazine, April 7, 1997; Vasil, Ruben, and Love. "Close Encounters with the Fourth Reich," *The Ever-Greener*, November 8, 1994

WARNING

Erection of these large cellular towers is currently being carried out under HIGH TONE and XENO in private business capacities under Black Ops cover. They emit cellular 800 MHZ waves. Due to the great proliferation of towers in key population areas, they will have a devastating effect. These towers may be associated with the very secretive Alaskan HAARP project.

Chapter 24:

DEATH RAYS

In the twentieth century a new technology has been developed that is startling in its power and implications. This is focused electromagnetic broadcasting, one application of which is in weaponry. These weapons are part of the new "non-lethal" arsenal—a misnomer, since this weaponry might just as well be called a death ray—touted by the military as a humane way for conducting war in the years to come. It may also be a way of conducting "peace"—of the *1984* and *Brave New World* mind-controlled variety.

Certainly this possibility has not been overlooked, as evidenced by the following quote from Zbigniew Brzezinski, in his *Between Two Ages: America's Role in the Technetronic Era:* "It may be possible—and tempting—to exploit for strategic-political purposes the fruits of research on the brain and on human behavior. Gordon J.F. MacDonald, a geophysicist specializing in problems of warfare, has written that artificially excited electronic strokes 'could lead to a pattern of oscillations that produce relatively high power levels over certain regions of the earth... In this way, one could develop a system that would seriously impair the brain performance of very large populations in selected regions over an extended period.' No matter how deeply disturbing the thought of using the environment to manipulate behavior for national advantages to some, the technology permitting such use will very probably develop within the next few decades." [1]

Early electromagnetic weapons experiments were conducted by the Japanese during World War II. Information on these "death rays" was revealed when Japanese scientists were interrogated. According to reports of the scientists the death ray was never used on humans, but was tested on animals. [2]

In 1960 there were rumors of a fantastic new Soviet super weapon employing Nikola Tesla electromagnetic technology. With subsequent revelations about Soviet research in these areas, it seems that these rumors were true. [3]

During the 1960s high levels of electromagnetic radiation were detected at the American embassy in Moscow. It was determined that the face of the embassy was being systematically swept with electromagnetic emissions by the Soviets. One guess was that a microwave beam was used to activate electronic equipment hidden within the building; another guess was more macabre: that the beam was being used to disrupt the nervous systems of American workers in the embassy. Giving weight to the latter supposition, many of the employees of the embassy became ill. Ambassador Walter Stoessel suffered a rare blood disease likened to leukemia, and experienced headaches and bleeding from the eyes. At least two other employees contracted cancer. According to researcher Alex Constantine, rather than informing embassy personnel of what was going on, the CIA chose to study the effects of the irradiation.

Dr. Milton Zaret, called in to investigate what was termed "the Moscow Signal," reported that the CIA wondered "whether I thought the electromagnetic radiation beamed at the brain from a distance could affect the way a person might act," and, "could microwaves be used to facilitate brainwashing or to break down prisoners under investigation." Zaret's conclusion about the Moscow Signal was that, "Whatever other reasons the Russians may have had, they believed the beam would modify the behavior of personnel." [4]

Author Len Bracken, who was present in Moscow at the time, has stated to the author in correspondence that the microwave radiation was beamed from a shack on a building across from the embassy. In 1977 the microwave shack caught fire and burned. Bracken says, "It was a Friday night and the Marine House Bar was playing 'Burn, Baby, Burn' [i.e. "Disco Inferno"]." Bracken also relates that "in '79 a strange box was installed in the wall in my room [in Moscow], supposedly relating to the heating system." [5]

Irradiation of the American embassy reportedly prompted a response from the Americans: the Defense Advanced Research Projects Agency's Project PANDORA, conducted at the Walter Reed Army Institute of Research from 1965 to 1970. One aspect of the project involved bombarding chimpanzees with microwave radiation. Referencing a reported statement by the head of the project, "the potential for exerting a degree of control on human behavior by low level microwave radiation seems to exist and he urged that the effects of microwaves be studied for possible weapons applications."

Within three years, Dr. Gordon J.F. McDonald, a scientific advisor to the president at the time, indicated that "Perturbation of the environment can produce changes in behavioral patterns." The perturbation that McDonald was alluding to was EM waves, and the changes in behavior were altered brain wave patterns. [6]

In 1965 the McFarlane Corporation in America came up with the Buck Rogers-sounding "modulated electron gun X-ray nuclear booster," a breakthrough in the "death ray" technology. Reports indicate that the device could also be used in communications, telemetry, and remote controlled guidance systems. McFarlane later claimed that the system was stolen from him by NASA, and that the principles of the acknowledged death ray were employed in MIROS, an orbital "communications system"; at least that is the way it was described by NASA. [7]

In 1972 the army admitted extensive research into the effects of irradiation on life forms, and the technology of electromagnetic weaponry. One of the byproducts of this research led to the invention of a powerful "electronic flame thrower." This may have been the weapon described in a study of the U.S. Army Mobility Equipment Research and Development Center, "Analysis of Microwaves for Barrier Warfare," describing the use of electromagnetic energy for an anti-personnel and vehicle weapon. The weapon discussed in this study was stated to be capable of producing third-degree burns on human skin. [8]

Dr. Dietrich Beischer, a German scientist employed by the American government, irradiated 7,000 naval crewmen with potentially harmful levels of microwave energy at the Naval Aerospace Research Laboratory in Pensacola, Florida, and talked about it at a symposium in 1973. Dr. Beischer disappeared soon after the experiment. According to PANDORA alumnus Robert O. Becker, he was to spend some time with Beischer but, "Just before the meeting, I got a call from him. With no preamble or explanation, he blurted out: 'I'm at a pay phone. I can't talk long. They are watching me. I can't come to the meeting or ever communicate with you again. I'm sorry. You've been a good friend. Goodby.' Soon afterward I called his office at Pensacola and was told, 'I'm sorry, there is no one here by that name,' just as in the movies. A guy who had done important research there for decades just disappeared." [9]

According to Eldon Byrd, of the Naval Surface Weapons Center in Silver Springs, Maryland, "Between 1981 and September 1982, the Navy commissioned me to investigate the potential of developing electromagnetic devices that could be used as non-lethal weapons by the Marine Corps for the purpose of 'riot control,' hostage removal, embassy and ship security, clandestine operations, and so on." Byrd wrote of experiments in irradiating animals with low level electromagnetic fields, mentioning changes in brain function, and stating that the animals "exhibited a drastic degradation of intelligence later in life... couldn't learn easy tasks... indicating a very definite and irreversible damage to the central nervous system of the fetus." The experiments went farther. Byrd wrote that, "At a certain frequency and power intensity, they could make the animal purr, lay down and roll over." [10]

By the early 1970s, according to Robert C. Beck, "Anecdotal data amassed suggesting that a pocket-sized transmitter at power levels of under 100 milliwatts could drastically alter the moods of unsuspecting persons, and that vast geographical areas could be surreptitiously mood manipulated by invisible and remote transmissions of EM [electromagnetic] energy." [11]

In the late 1970s Russian negotiators at the Strategic Arms Limitation talks (SALT II), proposed banning "a new generation of weapons of mass destruction" employing electromagnetic pulses. It has been suggested that the Russians, in proposing the ban, were attempting to feel out the Americans as to the current state of their electromagnetic weapons research. The Americans did not seem to have a clue as to what the Russians were talking about, and the proposal was tabled.

In fact, some Americans knew exactly what the Russians were talking about, although the Reds had a significant head start on several fronts. In 1959 Russian scientists Gaponov, Schneider, and Pantell had conceived of what was called a cyclotron resonance maser, essentially an industrial strength tunable ray gun. Beginning about 1966, the Russians launched into a heavily funded crash project to develop the gyrotron, another form of electromagnetic "gun," and in 1971 they were engaged in their first field tests with the gyrotron.

In 1975, physicists M.S. Rabinovich and A.A. Rukhadze and others active in Russian strategic defense at the Lebedev Physics Institute in Moscow announced that using a cyclotron resonance maser, they had produced microwave bursts that far outstripped anything the Americans were even theoretically proposing and that, according to the analysis of the American military, were powerful enough to be used in weapons applications.

A report from the American Rand Corporation at the time concluded that the Russian experiments were part of a larger Russian program designed for the production of electromagnetic weaponry, centered at the Institute of Applied Physics in Gor'kiy, Lebedev Physics Institute in Moscow, and another group of research institutes in Tomsk. By the 1980s, it was reported,

Russian gyrotron weapons had been reduced in size so that they would fit into a regular military truck, and had the capability of wiping out large military implacements or, at lower frequencies, irradiating whole towns. [12]

In 1982 the Air Force released a review of the use of electromagnetics on life forms, saying "Currently available data allow the projection that specially generated radio frequency radiation (RFR) fields may pose powerful and revolutionary antipersonnel military threats. Electroshock therapy indicates the ability of induced electric current to completely interrupt mental functioning for short periods of time, to obtain cognition for longer periods and to restructure emotional response over prolonged intervals.

"...impressed electromagnetic fields can be disruptive to purposeful behavior and may be capable of directing and/or interrogating such behavior. Further, the passage of approximately 100 milliamperes through the myocardium can lead to cardiac standstill and death, again pointing to a speed-of-light weapons effect. A rapidly scanning RFR system could provide an effective stun or kill capability over a large area." [13]

In 1984 the program researching the creation of pulsed microwaves was stepped up at Lawrence Livermore National Laboratories. [14]

According to the *Oregon Journal,* in March, 1978, in a story titled "Mysterious Radio Signals Causing Concern," the city of Eugene was irradiated by microwaves possibly beamed from a Navy transmitter, located several hundred miles away in California. According to an FCC report, "microwaves were the likely cause of several sudden illnesses among faculty researchers at Oregon State University." Numerous residents also complained of headaches, insomnia, fatigue, skin redness, and hearing clicks and buzzes in the head.

A study conducted by the Pacific Northwest Center for Non-Ionizing Radiation attributed the radiation instead to the Soviets, stating that it was "psychoactive" and "very strongly suggesting of achieving the objective of brain control." [15]

In September 1985, members of the Greenham Commons Women's Peace Camp in Great Britain, a global militarization protest camp located outside the U.S. Air Force Base at Greenham Commons, began experiencing a wide range of unpleasant physical symptoms including headache, depression, disorientation, memory loss, vertigo, and changes in their menstrual cycles. According to Dr. Rosalie Bertell and others who researched what was going on, the symptoms were of the type associated with exposure to radiation, and they began shortly after security at the base was switched from human guards to primarily electronic surveillance—this would have been a perfect opportunity to install electromagnetic broadcasting units disguised as surveillance equipment.

Dr. Bertell, former radar engineer Kim Besly, and others took readings of electromagnetic levels in the area, and found that they were as much as 100 times as strong as other nearby areas. [16]

That the electromagnetic arsenal is being used against citizenry in the new Russia is quite apparent from a statement published at the end of 1991 by *SovData DiaLine:*

"Psychological warfare is still being used by state security agents against people in Russia, even after the abortive August coup," said Emilia Chirkova, a Deputy of the Zelenograd Soviet and member of the Human Rights Commission. She recalls the scandal surrounding the alleged bugging equipment installed close to Boris Yeltsin's office. KGB agents admitted then that the directional aerial in the equipment was designed for transmission, not for reception. She believes it was part of an attempt to affect the health of the Russian president using high-frequency electromagnetic radiation. "The Human Rights Committee," Chirkova said, "had warned Yeltsin about such a possibility."

Substantiation for Chirkova's allegations is provided by Victor Sedleckij, design engineer-in-chief for the center Forma and vice president of the League of Independent Soviet Scientists. Sedleckij stated, "As an expert... I declare, in Kiev was launched a mass production of psychotronic biogenerators and their tests. I cannot assert that during the [Moscow] coup d'etat those used were the Kiev generators... All the same, that [psychotronic generators] were used is evident to me. What are the psychotronic generators? They are electronic equipment which produces the effect of guided control in human organisms. It affects especially the left and right hemisphere of the cortex. This is also the technology of the U.S. Project Zombie 5... I draw on my personal experience since I am myself the designer of such a generator." [17]

Emilia Chirkova cited several instances of the use of similar devices. Microwave equipment had been used in 1989 and 1990 in Vladivostok and Moscow prisons, in a mental hospital in Oryol, and in the Serbsky Institute in Moscow [also a mental hospital], she said. During his exile in Gorky, Andrei Sakharov noticed the presence of a high-tension electromagnetic field in his flat.   It was reported recently in the press that Ruslan Khasbulatov, Speaker of the Russian Parliament, had to move from his flat to another district of Moscow.   High-level electromagnetic radiation has been included among the possible causes of the discomfort he felt in his flat.

Purported victims of psychological warfare have written to the Russian paper.   From Voronezh: "They controlled my laughter, my thoughts, and caused pain in various parts of my body... It all started in October 1985, after I had openly criticized the first secretary of the City Committee of the Communist Party."

"Sometimes voices can be heard in the head from the effect of microwave pulse radiation which causes acoustic oscillations in the brain," explained Gennady Shchelkunov, a radio electronics researcher from the Istok Association.   In June 1991, a group of Zelenograd deputies sent an appeal signed by 150 people to President Yeltsin, demanding an investigation into the use of bio-electronic weapons.

An experiment conducted on Cable News Network in the mid-1980s demonstrated the reality of electronic devices that can project images into the mind from a distance. Physicist Dr. Elizabeth Rausher and electrical engineer Bill VanBise built a radio frequency "mind interference machine" using information in the open Soviet scientific literature. According to CNN, "The machine was inexpensive and easy to construct using parts from a consumer electronics store.   It emits a weak magnetic field pulsed at extremely low frequency."

The network commentator, a Mr. DeCaro, said, "As the subject of the test I was blindfolded and my ears were blocked to prevent inadvertent clues as to what was happening.   A magnetic probe was placed about 18 inches from my head.   As the experiment began, two signal generators produced waveform patterns that were transmitted by the magnetic probe at about one one-thousandth of the earth's magnetic field."

Here is a partial transcript of the exchange between VanBise, Rausher, and DeCaro during the experiment:

VanBise: Describe anything that you see.
DeCaro: I could see waveforms changing shape in my mind... A parabola just went by...
VanBise: Oh, yeah, I did. I just flipped the switch. Parabola?
Rausher: Uh-huh.
VanBise: All right, let's see. Check this out. That's what happened, I flipped the switch.

Rausher: Yeah!

DeCaro: OK, a spike right there!

Rausher: A spike there.

DeCaro: A tight spike.

VanBise: I dramatically changed the generator. I stepped it by ten right here, and the intermix from the two generators was right where you said that you saw a spike.

After the experiment, DeCaro interviewed VanBise, who said that the technology could "induce basically what would be considered hallucinations in people; direct them to do things against their so-called better judgment."

DeCaro wondered, "How easy would it be to assemble a weapon from existing off-the-shelf parts?"

"Three weeks," VanBise responded, "I could put together a weapon that would take care of a whole town." [18]

Portable electronic mind control weapons, small enough to be transported by truck, are now reported to be used routinely in offensive actions by the American military, and were employed in Grenada, Panama, and in the Gulf War. Although officially denied, it is reported that electromagnetic mind control weapons were used in Waco, Texas, in 1993, during the 51-day siege on David Koresh and his followers. Video footage taken during the siege by the British Broadcasting Company (BBC) shows the deployment of several advanced weapons systems, including a Soviet psychotronic weapon designed by Dr. Igor Smirnov of the Moscow Medical Academy.

Although it is denied that such weapons were used in the Waco massacre, the government does admit that Federal officials "considered" using Smirnov's acoustic psycho-correction projector on the Branch Davidians. It is also admitted that a series of closed meetings regarding the Branch Davidians took place beginning March 17, in northern Virginia between Smirnov and officials of the FBI, CIA, DIA, and DARPA.

According to one participant in the talks, "There was a strong interest among the intelligence agencies because they had been tracking Smirnov for years, and because we know there is evidence the Soviet Army's Special Forces used the technology during the conflict in Afghanistan."

An account of the meetings was issued in a memorandum of Psychotechnologies Corp of Richmond, Virginia. In the memo it was noted that unspecified attendees of the meeting wondered whether "psycho-correction detection, decoding and counter-measures programs should be undertaken by the U.S." [19]

A recent news release provides information on a new program by the National Institute of Justice, to develop "friendly force" electromagnetic weapons for use in the U.S. According to *Microwave News,* Oak Ridge National Laboratory is looking into the possibility of "thermal guns" that would disable an individual by causing his body to overheat, "seizure guns" that would induce epileptic fits, and "magnetosphere guns" that would cause a person to "see stars." [20]

In recent years, the heavy cost of research into electronic weaponry has been subsumed into the Strategic Defense Initiative, also known—to the chagrin of George Lucas—as the Star Wars program. In 1993, Aldric Saucier, a scientist with the Army's program of ballistic defense, spoke up to the House Government Operations Committee about Star Wars funds being channelled off into undocumented black operations. Saucier said that as much as half of the budget intended for SDI research, literally hundreds of millions of dollars, was unaccounted for.

NOTES:

1. Brzezinski, Zbigniew, *Between Two Ages: America's Role in the Technetronic Era.* (New York: The Viking Press, 1970)

2. *Strategic Bombing Survey,* Imperial War Museum, London. Cited in Wall, Judy, "Synthetic Telepathy," *Paranoid Women Collect Their Thoughts,* ed. Joan d'Arc. (Providence, Rhode Island: Paranoia Publishing, 1996)

3. "Krushchev Says Soviets Will Cut Forces a Third, Sees 'Fantastic Weapon,'" *New York Times,* Jan. 15, 1960, cited in Wall

4. Keeler, Anna, "Remote Mind Control Technology," *Secret and Suppressed,* Jim Keith, ed. (Portland, Oregon: Feral House, 1993); Brodeur, Paul, *The Zapping of America; Microwaves, Their Deadly Risk and the Cover-Up.* (Norton. New York: 1977), cited in Constantine, Alex, *Psychic Dictatorship in the U.S.A.* (Portland, Oregon: Feral House, 1995); Jameson, Donald F.B., *Robot Spies of the KGB,* undated clipping.

5. Bracken, Len, correspondence with the author, September 6, 1997

6. Wall; Constantine

7. Ibid.

8. Besly, Kim, *Electromagnetic Pollution,* cited in Wall

9. Becker, Robert O. and Selden, Gary, *The Body Electric: Electromagnetic and the Foundation of Life.* (New York: William Morrow, 1985)

10. Besly, Kim. Cited in Wall; Keeler

11. Beck, Robert C. "Extreme Low Frequency Magnetic Fields and EEG Entrainment: A Psychotronic Warfare Possibility?", *Bio-Medical Research Associates,* 1977

12. "The Russian lead in radio frequency weapons," *Executive Intelligence Review,* July 3, 1987

13. *Final Report on Biotechnology Research Requirements for Aeronautical Systems Through the Year 2000. AFOSR-TR-82-0643,* vols. 1 and 2, July 3, 1982, cited in Wall

14. "How Russia's radio frequency weapons can kill," *Executive Intelligence Review,* July 17, 1987

15. Smith, Jerry. *HAARP: Ultimate Weapon of the Conspiracy,* (1997: AUP, Kempton, Illinois.

16. Bolman, Betsy, and members of the Ad Hoc Committee on Electromagnetic Radiation, "The 'Zapping' of Greenham and Seneca," *Peace and Freedom,* January/February 1989

17. *Komsomolskaya Pravda,* August 27, 1991

18. CNN, "Special Assignment", undated transcript about 1985

19. Wall; Tapscott, Mark, "DOD, Intel Agencies Look at Russian Mind Control Technology, Claims FBI Considered Testing on Koresh", *Defense Electronics,* July 1993; Moore, Jim. *Operation Mind Control 1994: The History of Mind Control.* (Nashville, Tennessee: The Phoenix Foundation)

20. Schaefer, Paul, "The Politics of Control", *Exotic Research Report,* undated

Chapter 25:

IN YOUR HEAD

The Soviets reportedly began to delve into the biological effect of microwaves as early as 1953. A number of laboratories were set up across the Soviet Union and in Eastern Europe, including one at the Institute of Hygiene and Occupational Diseases, Academy of Medical Sciences. Although the Soviets reported on their experiments in the open literature, the parameters they defined were insufficient for duplicating the experiments, and some scientists in the United States questioned whether the whole matter was disinformation. It was not. [1]

Early CIA funding provided the wherewithal for a project launched at Honeywell, Inc. for "a method to penetrate inside a man's mind and control his brain waves over long distance."

At the National Institutes of Health, Dr. Maitland Baldwin, under CIA supervision, bombarded the brains of lobotomized monkeys with radio waves. According to researcher Alex Constantine, "His CIA monitors noted weird excesses: in one experiment, Baldwin decapitated a monkey and transplanted its head to the body of another, then attempted to restore it to life with radar saturation." [2]

In 1964, CIA Director Richard Helms sent a memo to the Warren Commission, mentioning "biological radio communication." Helms' theorizing about such methods was truly reminiscent of Orwell's *1984*. He said, "Cybernetics [or computer theory] can be used in the molding of a child's character, the inculcation of knowledge and techniques, the amassing of experience, the establishment of social behavior patterns... all functions which can be summarized as control of the growth processes of the individual." [3]

In 1977 Dr. Sam Koslov, the scientific assistant to the Secretary of the Navy, was briefed on a number of current research projects. One of them, in progress at Stanford Research Institute, was named "ELF and Mind Control." ELF is the acronym for extremely low frequency electromagnetic radiation. Koslov didn't like the sound of that project and ordered it cancelled, but according to the *Washington Post,* the funding was merely diverted into a different project heading and continued to go forward. [4]

The following report, although anonymous, provides a detailed first person encounter with what may be government electromagnetic testing. It was published in an underground magazine a few years ago. I do not maintain that reports such as these are absolute proof of government electromagnetic testing on citizenry, but well-reasoned accounts such as the following must be taken into consideration:

"The large black top of the Federal Building in San Francisco looks like a giant air-conditioning vent, 50 feet tall, comprising the entire top of the building. It is actually a radar, microwave, and radio transparent shield for an array of communications devices on the roof of the building. Such "blinds" on top of government buildings are nothing unusual, it isn't necessary to visually remind everybody that such buildings also are likenesses of Orwell's Ministry of Information (read, CIA). And as such are in need of systems of communications independent of civilian mediums. Which, anyway, would be purposely interrupted in any serious case of civil unrest.

"It is important to note three facts at this point, the purpose of which will come clear in the end: First, the Federal Building is located at the base of a broad hill. It is on the low rise of this hill where San Francisco's 'Skid Row' district, the 'Tenderloin,' uneasily rests. And so the Federal Building can be seen from virtually any place in the Tenderloin. And let us reverse this thought; virtually any place in the Tenderloin may be seen from the Federal Building. And it is this unimpeded view which brings to mind the second oddly coinciding factor; that Low Frequency Electromagnetic emissions like television broadcasts will not pass through earth (hills, or the horizon), nor do they even pass very well through buildings, and so require a fairly clear shot, unlike higher frequency emissions like radio. This is why you have to put TV antennas on the roof.

"Now fact three; Extremely Low Frequency transmissions, or ELFs, have been the focus of significant research by the military intelligence machines of several governments, including our own. ELF developments for military purposes is based on indications that ELFs at close range seem to cause aberrations in the thought processes of human beings, such as hallucinations, disordered thought, confusion, aggression, depression, anger, hopelessness. Not unlike television, a close companion to ELFs in the electromagnetic spectrum. It is not difficult to imagine the value of such a weapon to our secret government, so fond of the disruption of societies, the control and subjugation of individuals, and of war, 'the insane death dance of paranoid societies.'

"Now with these three things in mind, consider this fourth. Since I have had the fortune to live for three years in this ring of hell, the Tenderloin, I have noticed something very odd. At least 15 times I have noticed in the morning or early evening a pronounced buzzing or humming. Very low and hard to hear. Something like the sound which some can hear of a TV that is on in a room, but with the volume off. And on looking for the source of this sound, I found that it seemed to come from everywhere and nowhere. In other words it seemed to be coming from inside my head. I do not mean this figuratively. I mean that my head seemed to resonate with the vibration. And I felt that my thoughts were disrupted. The buzzing seemed to make thoughts fall apart just before forming, like sand on a vibrating metal plate, and I felt vaguely angry. On the third or fourth occurrence of this, I noticed that in the wake of the buzzing sound, an unusual number of fights could be heard breaking out all around me. From out on the streets, and from adjoining buildings, and apartments, came the shouts and threats of people overcome with anger. And I thought, though at first it seemed horrible to consider, 'Hadn't ELF subjects reported the feeling or sound of buzzing in their heads?' and 'what better section of the population could be chosen on which to conduct ELF experiments.' A large percentage of inner urban dwellers are already so close to the edge that he or she is highly likely to express any fluctuation of mood with a corresponding fluctuation of activity which might come to the attention of the police. In a neighborhood where aberrant behavior is common and expected, slight increases of such behavior would go completely unnoticed, but would be detectable by careful observation of incoming reports to the police department. It would be unlikely in the extreme that anyone would associate the strange buzzing sound with unaccountable accompanying emotional swings. Impossible that someone would suspect secret agents of systematically barraging the politically power-less with mood and consciousness ELF waves from atop the Federal Building. But even if such an impossibility came to pass, and allegations were made, would they not automatically be discredited by the general perception of the poor (i.e. Tenderloin inhabitants) as mentally unstable, alcoholic, drug

213

addicted, and of the government as an essentially well meaning parent, who would not really ever purposely harm her children?

"Tests of ELF effects could be precisely monitored by the existing police department recording system (at no extra cost), all recorded on the justice system's networked national computer system, containing exact times of complaints, record of outcome, location, identity, profile, and criminal history of all persons involved. Police department ignorance of the tests would actually be desirable. The entire operation could be run by as few as two people. ELF broadcast times would simply be correlated with any flux of reports to the police department. And the exact nature of the ELF effects on human emotion would be conveniently built into the data received from police reports. For example, an increase of domestic violence at 4%, and suicides 2%, perhaps one or two extra stabbings during your special hour-long broadcast of the latest ELF 'Top Ten.' A decrease in premeditated crimes might indicate a breakdown of thought process during the time of ELF transmission. Do you see? A double blind experiment (neither police nor populace have any idea) on a perfectly contained and monitored large population of control subjects, in a typical city, with an 'in place' monitoring system (police reports) with a plus or minus accuracy allowance of virtually 0% since the experiment can be performed an unlimited number of times over a period of years. Could such malignant experiments be pulled off in any other setting? If your aim were to induce murders, violence, psychosis, severe depression, or suicide, you couldn't really go calling on John Hopkins University now, could you? Anyway, the very point of such a thing would be its use on urban populations. Listen, you have a little country somewhere, you destabilize the populace with ELFs and conventional means and overwhelm the local law enforcement agencies, martial law is declared, the democratically elected government falls. You install a corrupt dictator. You say to the American people, 'We must send humanitarian aid.' A hundred million dollars is allocated to the small country. The corrupt dictator steals the goods and money, and deposits the laundered free and clear taxpayer dollars in an offshore American bank. Beginning to get the picture? Think of how perfectly foolproof this is, how elegant, how appealing, how logical, how insidious, how horrible, how possible, and all it costs is the suffering of thousands of people.

"Postscript; last week the buzzing happened again, so loud yet so easily dismissed against the background of city noise. How could I prove to myself that it was not simply just coming from my head, could I possibly have the rare hearing condition, tinnitus, which causes ringing in the ears? I remembered a Mr. Science experiment where the electromagnetic transparency of various substances was being demonstrated. A portable radio was placed into a wooden box. 'Hear that? The radio is still playing, which means? That's right, wood is electromagnetically transparent.' The radio was imprisoned in various other containers to see what would happen. Then finally it was wrapped in aluminum foil, and fell silent. I ran into the kitchen and grabbed the tin foil. Pulling a three foot strip of it, I wrapped it around my head, and the buzzing stopped." [5]

One of the strangest—and most ominous—episodes in the history of electromagnetic irradiation research is the construction of the network of Ground Wave Emergency Network (GWEN) towers, in the 1980s. The GWEN towers are almost 300 feet tall, and a 330-foot web of copper wiring extends out from them, broadcasting bursts of very low frequency (VLF) messages at 20 minute intervals or, from another source, hour intervals. These towers are spaced 200 miles apart from each other and describe a straight line across America. At this time there are 54 operational towers, although at least 29 more are scheduled to be constructed.

It is claimed that GWEN is part of the COG (Continuity of Government) program of the Federal Emergency Management Agency, designed to keep government functional in the case of disaster, including nuclear war. Some sources disagree that this is the purpose of the project, citing the statement of Colonel Paul Hanson, GWEN Program Director for the Air Force. Hanson has said, "The towers will not help wage a nuclear war because they would be destroyed in any protracted confrontation." Others note that since the GWEN hardware is transistor based, they are particularly vulnerable to the electromagnetic pulses of nuclear explosions. The location of the GWEN towers is also a matter of public record, meaning that they could easily be targeted in case of war or even terrorist threat. [6]

Robert O. Becker, M.D., in *Crosscurrents: The Perils of Electropollution,* says of GWEN: "GWEN is a superb system, in combination with cyclotron resonance, for producing behavioral alterations in the civilian population. The average strength of the steady geomagnetic field varies from place to place across the United States. Therefore, if one wished to resonate a specific ion in living things in a specific locality, one would require a specific frequency for that location. The spacing of GWEN transmitters 200 miles apart across the United States would allow such specific frequencies to be 'tailored' to the geomagnetic-field strength in each GWEN area."

A similar system is SECOM II, composed of five broadcasting towers in Idaho, New Mexico, Missouri, South Carolina, and Maryland. These towers were ostensibly constructed as communication links between a central monitoring station and vehicles carrying nuclear weapons and nuclear materials. SECOM II broadcasts in the 3-12 Mhz range, which, coincidentally or not, precisely blankets the resonant frequency of the human organism. [7]

Another group of towers is mentioned in an anonymous paper titled "Mind Control Operations/Aquarius Group Activities," that states, "With a general ignorance through arrogance of most public population in the U.S. the erection of large cellular towers being carried out under HIGH TONE and ZENO are largely going completely unnoticed. These projects are being carried out in private business capacities and therefore in Deep Black Operations cover. However, public populations would be wise to educate themselves in the construction of these seemingly innocent towers in large population areas. The cellular 800 MHZ waves are a constant wave. Due to the great proliferation of towers in key population areas, they will have a devastating effect."

An oft-heard allegation is that the CIA has developed a mind control technology they refer to as RHIC-EDOM. The acronym stands for "Radio Hypnotic Intracerebra Control—Electronic Dissolution of Memory," and refers to the ability to induce a hypnotic state from a remote location, impart hypnotic commands, and erase the memory of the programming and the period of time that it took place in. This technology allegedly includes electromagnetic broadcasting as well as intramuscular implants. The erasure of memory is reportedly accomplished by the electromagnetic stimulation of the chemical acetylcholine in the brain.

The first mention of RHIC-EDOM was in the 1969 book *Were We Controlled?* by the pseudonymous Lincoln Lawrence. Lawrence describes RHIC-EDOM in this manner:

"It is the ultra-sophisticated application of post-hypnotic suggestion triggered at will by radio transmission. It is a recurring hypnotic state, reinduced automatically at intervals by the same radio control. An individual is brought under hypnosis. This can be done either with his knowledge—or without it by use of narco-hypnosis, which can be brought into play under many guises. He is then programmed to perform certain actions and maintain certain attitudes upon radio signal."

Lawrence claimed that Lee Harvey Oswald had been manipulated through RHIC-EDOM, but not by the Russians or the CIA or its brethren. According to Lawrence, Oswald's controllers had been a worldwide cabal of commodities merchants who, through the assassination of the president, wanted to drive stock down and make a fortune. The idea is not entirely implausible.

The only other mention of RHIC-EDOM claiming insider knowledge of the technology is an article by James L. Moore, in a 1975 issue of *Modern People* magazine. In that article, Moore claimed that he possessed a 350-page manual originating from CIA sources on RHIC-EDOM. The manual had supposedly been prepared by the CIA shortly after the murder of John F. Kennedy.

Verifying RHIC-EDOM are the researches of the late L.L. Vasiliev, professor of physiology at the University of Leningrad, who described one experiment in remote hypnosis using undefined techniques of radio control:

"As a control of the subject's condition, when she was outside the laboratory in another set of experiments, a radio set was used. The results obtained indicate that the method of using radio signals substantially enhances the experimental possibilities. I.F. Tomaschevsky [a Russian physiologist] carried out the first experiments with this subject at a distance of one or two rooms, and under conditions that the participant would not know or suspect that she would be experimented with. In other cases, the sender was not in the same house, and someone else observed the subject's behavior. Subsequent experiments at considerable distances were successful. One such experiment was carried out in the park at a distance. Mental suggestions to go to sleep were complied with within a minute." [8]

Interesting in the context of RHIC-EDOM technology is a statement made almost ten years after the publication of *Were We Controlled?* Dr. Sidney Gottlieb, the MKULTRA heavyweight, during questioning by Senator Richard Schweicker in 1977 Senate hearings on CIA drug testing responded as follows:

SCHWEIKER: Some of the projects under MKULTRA involved hypnosis, is that correct?
GOTTLIEB: Yes.
SCHWEICKER: Did any of these projects involve something called radio hypnotic intracerebral control, which is a combination, as I understand it, in layman's terms, of radio

transmissions and hypnosis.

GOTTLIEB: My answer is "No."

SCHWEICKER: None whatsoever?

GOTTLIEB: Well, I am trying to be responsive to the terms you used. As I remember it, there was a current interest, running interest, all the time in what effects people's standing in the field of radio energy have, and it could easily have been that somewhere in many projects, someone was trying to see if you could hypnotize someone easier if he was standing in a radio beam. That would seem like a reasonable piece of research to do. [9]

Another statement was made by J.F. Schapitz who, working with the Department of Defense in 1974, filed the following research proposal:

"In this investigation it will be shown that the spoken word of the hypnotist may be conveyed by modulated electro-magnetic energy directly into the subconscious parts of the human brain—i.e., without employing any technical devices for receiving or transcoding the messages and without the person exposed to such influence having a chance to control the information input consciously."

Schapitz proposed an experiment wherein a subject would be subconsciously told to leave the laboratory, the command triggered by a word or action from the researcher. As in the tricks played by stage hypnotists, Schapitz was certain that the subject would rationalize the otherwise irrational desire to leave the lab. Records of Schapitz' research, beyond the initial proposal, have never been declassified. [10]

In a way, proof of the existence of RHIC-EDOM does not much matter. It is not vitally important if Lincoln Lawrence or James L. Moore were speaking from personal knowledge, or simply speculation that they wanted to render more believable. "RHIC-EDOM" is in essence just a name that describes a technology close to or identical to others that have been demonstrated to exist. [11]

A specific Russian mind control technology was outed by the *American Defense News* in 1993, termed "acoustic psycho-correction." According to the magazine, "The Russian capability, demonstrated in a series of laboratory experiments dating back to the mid-1970s, could be used to suppress riots, control dissidents, demoralize or disable opposing forces and enhance the performance of friendly special operations teams, sources say.

"Pioneered by the government-funded Department of Psycho-Correction at the Moscow Medical Academy, acoustic psycho-correction involves the transmission of specific commands via static or white noise bands into the human subconscious without upsetting other intellectual functions. Experts said that laboratory demonstrations have shown encouraging results after exposure of less than one minute."

Janet Morris, science fiction author and research director of the U.S. Global Strategy Council, a Washington, D.C. think tank, is one of the leading lights in the field of non-lethal weaponry which in practice is a nice euphemism that includes techniques of mind control. According to *Tactical Technology* magazine, "While visiting Russia in November 1991, Morris and other members of a team sent to investigate Russian technologies for commercial development were invited to a demonstration of a mind control technology. A volunteer from the U.S. team sat down in front of a computer screen as innocuous words flashed across the screen. The volunteer was only required to tell which words he liked and which words he disliked. At the end of the demonstration the Russian staff started revealing the sensitive, innermost thoughts of the volunteer—none of which had been previously discussed. The recorded message was mixed with what appeared to be white noise or static, so when played back it became undecipherable. Since there were no more volunteers in the U.S. group, the Russians volunteered to go upstairs and let the Americans choose a mental patient for a demonstration. The Americans declined the offer.

"The Russians told Morris of a demonstration in which a group of workers were outside the hospital working on the grounds. The staff sent an acoustic psycho-correction message via their machine to the workers telling them to put down their tools, knock on the door of the hospital and ask if there was anything else they could do. The workers did exactly that, the Russians said.

"The Russians admitted to using this technology for special operations team selection and performance enhancement and to aid their Olympic athletes and an Antarctic exploration team. Unlike lie detectors, this machine can determine when the truth is spoken, according to Morris.

"Being an infrasound, very low frequency-type transmission, the acoustic psycho-correction message is transmitted via bone conduction. This means that earplugs will not restrict the message. An entire body protection system would be required to stop reception. The message, according to the Russians,

219

bypasses the conscious level and is acted on almost immediately. The Russians say that the messages are acted upon with exposure times of under one minute.

"Morris envisions this technology will be miniaturized into a hand-held device. Presently, the International Healthline Corp. of Richmond, Va., is planning to bring a Russian team of specialists to the U.S. in the near future to further demonstrate the capability. International Healthline is a private corporation that is exploring Russian medical technologies for import to the U.S." [12]

A specific application of electronics in mind control is in the direct broadcasting of audible sounds, including voices, to the human brain. In 1961, biophysicist Allen Frey, working for the Defense Intelligence Agency (DIA), announced that human beings are capable of hearing microwave broadcasts, in the case of his experiments, what he described as buzzing or knocking sounds. Frey suggested "stimulating the nervous system without the damage caused by electrodes." [13]

In 1973, Dr. Joseph C. Sharp, at Walter Reed Hospital, while in a soundproof room heard spoken words broadcast by "pulsed microwave audiogram." Broadcast in a range between 300 MHz to 3GHz, Sharp was able to identify words that were broadcast without any form of electronic translation device—by direct transmission to the brain. [14]

A 1976 Defense Intelligence Agency report credited the Soviets with having made the same discovery as Sharp and Grove, although this was apparently disinformation in the interest of encouraging Congress to appropriate funding in order to play a pretended "catch up" with the Russians. [15]

One electromagnetic weapon that transmits at the frequency of the human nervous system is, according to researcher Harlan Girard, manufactured by Loral Electro-Optical Systems in Pasadena, California. In substantiation, it is reported that Loral had previously done research on electromagnetic weaponry for Lt. Gen. Leonard Peroots of the U.S. Air Force. Peroots is reported to have requested a weapon that would broadcast negative messages directly to the minds of the enemy—and positive messages to the minds of friendly troops. [16]

A study by A.W. Guy and others, released in 1975 by the DIA, reported on experiments to determine the particulars of the phenomenon of audible electromagnetics, and its relation to such things as pulse power, pulse shape, and frequency. Along with a number of details about the nature of electromagnetic interaction with humans and animals, Guy explained why the microwaves were audible: microscopic thermal expansion of brain tissues. Guy had even experimented with sending Morse code via microwaves.

Also reported on were Soviet capabilities: "Sounds and possibly even words which appear to be originating intercranially can be induced by signal modulations at very low power densities."

Dr. Robert O. Becker, in *The Body Electric*, commented on the technology: "Such a device has obvious applications in covert operations designed to drive a target crazy with 'voices' or deliver undetected instructions to a programmed assassin."

As with many other instances of claimed mind control, separating subjects experiencing hallucinatory voices from those broadcast electronically is a difficult task. One possible solution is suggested by Judy Wall, in her article "Synthetic Telepathy," published in 1996. Wall proposes that the effect of microwave voices could be detected with an electroencephalograph (EEG) machine. The main drawback to this technique is that if whatever agency was broadcasting the messages was aware of the use of monitoring equipment, the messages would undoubtedly stop. As Wall states, "While it is not a perfect solution, it is hopefully a start towards monitoring, validating, and correcting the problem of involuntary mind control experimentation and harassment of innocent victims."

NOTES:

1. Keeler
2. Constantine, Alex, *Psychic Dictatorship in the U.S.A.* (Venice, California: Feral House, 1995)
3. Bowart, Walter, *Operation Mind Control.* (New York: Dell, 1978)
4. Constantine, Alex, *Virtual Government.* (Venice, California: Feral House, 1997)
5. Anonymous, "ELF," *Off the Deep End* number 9, undated
6. *New York Times*, March 1, 1987
7. Schaefer, Paul, *Targeting Us... and Our Earth* newsletter, undated
8. Smith, Jerry, *HAARP: Ultimate Weapon of the Conspiracy*, AUP, Kempton, Illinois); Constantine, Alex, *Psychic Dictatorship in the U.S.A.* (Venice, California: Feral House, 1995)
9. Cited in Martin Cannon, "The Controllers: A New Hypothesis of Alien Abductions", *MUFON UFO Journal*, Number 270, October, 1990
10. Schapitz, J.F., cited in Cannon
11. Lawrence, Lincoln, pseud., *Were We Controlled?* (New Hyde Park, New York: University Books, 1967); Bowart; Cannon
12. Opall, Barbara, "U.S. Explores Russian Mind-Control Technology", *Defense News*, January 11-17, 1993; *Tactical Technology*, Feb. 3, 1993
13. Bowart; Constantine, *Psychic Dictatorship in the U.S.A.*
14. Smith

15. Wall, Judy, "Synthetic Telepathy," *Paranoid Women Collect Their Thoughts,* edited by Joan d'Arc. (Paranoia Publishing, Providence, 1996); Becker, Dr. Robert O., *The Body Electric: Electromagnetism and the Foundation of Life.* (New York: Wm. Morrow & Co., 1985)

16. Krawczyk, Glenn, "Mind Control & the New World Order," *Nexus* magazine, February/March, 1993

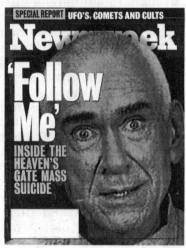

Heaven's Gate: Mind Control & UFOs.

Jim Jones: A CIA mind control project?

Chapter 26:

VICTIMIZED

Numerous persons claim to be victims of mind control by electromagnetic irradiation, implanted brain devices, or other means. I personally receive a great deal of mail of this sort. Are these persons actually the victims of mind control experiments by the government? Are they mentally disturbed individuals, attributing their dysfunction to the outside source of the government? I believe examples of both can be found. At the same time I am not the type of researcher, quite common in my experience, who believes that all such testimony is proof of government mind control. There is such a thing as delusion, and cases of claimed mind control should be carefully evaluated.

In favor of persons whose testimony about electromagnetic mind control seems irrational, it is obvious that persons undergoing this kind of harassment could be driven to madness. They should be given the benefit of the doubt in their testimony. Here are some examples of persons who credibly testify to their victimization by mind control:

—Marrti Koski, a Finnish national living in Canada, in the late 1970s began receiving irrational mental messages and experiencing an overall breakdown of his body. Koski wrote, " I began to lose control of most of my normal functions and emotions. It was as if someone or something could control my sleep, my sense of smell and taste. Food was, by turns, made to taste very salty or acidic. Sexual functions, urination, bowel movements and basic metabolism were all affected. Finally, I couldn't work. A welder by trade, I came to be unable to breathe in any air contaminated by carbon dioxide. It made me salivate excessively and foam at the mouth. By now the voices were with me 24 hours a day. I was being talked to every waking hour. I was allowed minimal sleep, about an hour every day. If I left my apartment I immediately became very drowsy, yet indoors I could not sleep. My heartbeat became erratic and finally uncontrollable."

In December, 1979, Koski experienced a heart attack, and was checked into the University of Alberta Hospital in Edmonton, Canada. Now the voice that had plagued Koski identified itself, saying that it was a spokesman for the Royal Canadian Mounted Police, and stating that Koski had been chosen to be a spy. The hospital would be where a portion of Koski's training would take place. During the period that Koski was in the hospital, he was constantly communicated to through the intercranial voice, told not to take medication, and ordered where to go and where not to go in the hospital.

Substantiating Koski's claims is the information that while in the hospital he was subjected to bizarre "testing" by the doctors, including electrical shock to his penis. Every time he would try to go to sleep, he would be jolted by severe headaches. Koski may have been the victim of the kind of "depatterning" that Ewen Cameron had conducted 30 years previously in Canada.

After Koski left the hospital, there was no abatement in the voices in his head, that had begun to call him the "Microwave Man." This is a telling detail, since microwave transmission would be the precise manner in which Koski would have been controlled if his implant was genuine, and it is not probable that he would have been aware of this, given only a layman's meager understanding of the techniques of mind control.

Koski relates that he was given meaningless assignments to perform, such as finding out the population of Toronto, broken down into the number of men and women. At one point, Koski believes that toxic gas was pumped into his apartment. Hoping to escape his harassment, Koski returned to Finland, but the voices did not stop. Now the content of the messages changed, with the voices identifying themselves as being from the star Sirius. Again, a telling detail (taken from Freemasonic lore) that is repeated again and again among mind control victims and alleged UFO contactees. Koski returned to Canada, still plagued by the voices and unable to sleep.

At home in Edmonton, Koski believes that he was gassed, and was subjected to elaborate "psychodrama" style experiments. Determining that his believed microwave bombardment was lessened in the open air, Koski was able to get sleep, and to experience a lessening of the voices.

Koski wonders, "Is there something special about me that singles me out for this kind of attack, or is it simply that "They" are out to get me? I believe that I happen to fit a set of characteristics that make me, or anybody with these characteristics, a likely subject. I am single. I live alone. My only relative in Canada lives thousands of miles from me. I do not belong to any fraternal groups, organizations or political parties. I have difficulty communicating with other Canadians because of my poor spoken English. In short, I am an ideal target because of my limited circle of acquaintances and contacts. I believe the preparation time, in my case four years, is designed to reinforce this isolation, to promote "strange" behavior which further discourages friendships or contacts." This parallels the rationale behind Dr. Cameron's usage of immigrants in his own mind control experiments in Canada in the 1950s. [1]

—Journalist Edward Kelly worked for an alternative news agency in Sweden in the mid-1980s. Part of his work involved investigating patients used in medical experimentation by Swedish hospitals. Kelly seems to have run afoul of the government when he contacted the *Socialstyrelsen* [Board of Health and Welfare] and other appendages of the state, trying to obtain records of hospital experimentation, and in letting them know the kind of research he was conducting. Within a week he became bedridden with an undefined sickness that left him unable to walk. More than that, there were strange indications that the sickness was not of natural origin. Papers that had been taped or stapled to his walls rolled up or fell off the walls. When visitors would spend time with Kelly, they also would become sick. The house cat, who had always favored Kelly's bed, would now not even enter the bedroom. Kelly was diagnosed with lumbago, but the illness worsened. Taken to the hospital, he was diagnosed with cancer. He died on the 28th of May 1985, at Karolinska Hospital. [2]

—Another indication that the Swedish Secret Police use citizens in mind control experimentation is that there are many complaints about a SAPO secret base, the *Tjadergarden* in Soraker just outside Sundsvall. Local residents claim that they have experienced harmful effects from electromagnetic radiation.

The following is a portion of a letter from *Tjadergarden* resident Ossian Andersson that is addressed to the Swedish government: "...owing to the terror, harrowing persecution and gross violations of human rights which I have been subjected to for the last eight years, I hereby request the government to allow me to resume a normal human existence. I am completely without legal protection while the security police and military researchers toy with me at their whim. My letters are to no effect, the authorities shirk any responsibility... I am being used as a guinea pig for weapons of ultrasonic, electromagnetic field, acoustic and death-ray type, and my central nervous system has been seized so that they can control my brain with micro-electronic technology and microcomputers... The symptoms of ultrasonic radiation are headaches, dizziness, disorientation and visual impairment. Other symptoms are a degeneration of intelligence with an additional effect on blood circulation and visceral pain... Acoustic weapons do not cause injury, rather they convey a nebulous disorientation which can shatter all one's organized activities. These weapons work by introducing chaos into one's life... The radiation penetrates all types of material which I have used for protection. For instance, I built a case with a 2 mm thick lead insulation, under which I lay at night, to no avail... Microchips are also part of the picture, since I became aware that they were able to control my entire rage of brain activity. These micro-devices must have been placed in my brain without my knowledge... It is cruel to force a pensioner such as myself to suffer day after day and to prevent him to sleep no more than an hour now and then."

According to researcher Robert Naeslund, himself a claimed victim of mind control, "Since I myself have been in Soraker and know Ossian well, I can affirm that what he describes is but a fragment of the truly frightening nature of his torment. He is now 82 years old, and the terror meted out to him is completely bereft of humanitarian norms. He is being seriously exploited in a harrowing experiment for periods of 22 hours during day and night in which he finds it impossible to snatch even a moment's sleep; and so it has been, with a persistent brutal intensity, for the last 20 years. Ossian has also undergone cranial radio-graphic examination from which the implantation of a foreign object with cerebral connections can be confirmed." [3]

—In November 1986, two alleged Arab terrorists were tried in West Berlin. When a guilty plea from pre-trial testimony was read to one of the defendants, called Salameh in the newspaper account, he said that at the time of his statement he was "not himself." The other defendant, Hasi, stood up and said, "In the name of Allah, commiseration, in the name of the Arab nation I would like to explain what I had to suffer here in the Federal Republic of Germany." Hasi said that he and his co-defendant were tortured using transmitted voices that "paralyzed their brains" and made them confess to crimes that they were not guilty of. [4]

—David Fratus entered the Utah State Prison in May 1986.

His crime was second degree burglary. Fratus, in a letter dated October 18, 1988, said that after 11 months in the prison he "ran afoul of prison officials as a result of a minor altercation with other inmates and what was then deemed to be a poor attitude on my part." Among other repercussions, according to Fratus, was that his food was tampered with, he was threatened with carcinogens and disease organisms, and was told that his parents would be murdered if he didn't remain silent about his treatment in prison.

Fratus was put in solitary confinement. "Once isolated," he reports, "some extremely peculiar things began to occur. I became disoriented to the extent that my cell and surrounding area would take on a surrealistic appearance as though I were under the influence of a hallucinogenic drug, and I was plagued by severe headaches and insomnia for weeks at a time. I had absolutely no inkling what was happening, and after a couple months of having some fantastically cruel games played with my mind ultimately reducing me to a state of anxiety, the psychiatric squad was called in to play their roles in this colossal 'set up' and I was declared to be suffering from a mental illness after undergoing a farcical and cursory interview in duration of no more than 15 minutes. Delusional persecution and paranoia was, I believe, how they so conveniently labeled me. It was obviously a deliberate and prearranged plan, and throughout these actions the staff would make malicious comments as to, 'How are you enjoying your headaches?', 'Need some aspirin?', and, 'Are you sleeping well, Mr. Fratus?'"

Fratus indicates, "I began to receive, or hear, high frequency tones in my ears. Like the test pattern on a TV set. The volume or intensity of frequencies is adjustable and some are so high and piercing that they've literally had me climbing the walls. When I plug my ears with cotton or fingertips, the tones are still inside and become amplified. It's as if they had become electrified echo chambers with the sounds coming from the inside out. When I complained or acted out, I was beaten and thrown into a strip cell with no clothes, mattress, toilet paper or drinking water. Nothing—and the intensity of these frequency transmissions would be crescendoed to maddening levels. Much mental distress! This is still being done to me three shifts, 24 hours a day, and the combination of these demoralizing mental torments and sleep deprivation for weeks on end has exacted a heavy toll on me."

Fratus describes inner torment so fine-tuned as to be unbelievable, but in terms that makes one wonder: "They are

227

going into my subconscious, or memory bank, bringing forth unpleasant memories long forgotten, and I am being punished for past as well as present indiscretions. I can think of anything from the past—a friend or situation from 30 years ago, for instance, and the voice will provide names and particulars. I have repeatedly tested and attempted to trick them on this. No way. They have better access to what's in my head with this nefarious invention than I do. I can converse with my antagonists merely by thinking what I wish to say... And I welcome you to the Twilight Zone!! How the hell is this being done?? They are using those frequency impulses to perpetrate some very vicious maltreatment on me. With the apparent ease of manipulating a keyboard they can, with the flick of a switch, strip me of all energy and motivation to where I'm forced to lie on my bunk and stare at the wall like a zombie. I've been left in this state for weeks at a time—literally chained to my bed without the actual use of physical restraints, having not the energy to walk back and forth in my cell even a few times. For almost the entire eleven months I have continuously been made to feel low down and chronically depressed."

Fratus talks about "the most powerful of these frequency impulses" that were used on him. He says it is "jokingly referred to as the 'Death Ray' by guards, and is so potent it causes an intense physical sensation of having an electrical, or magnetic force field combined with a vibrating tuning fork in my head. Different parts of my brain are targeted by this thing, causing a variety of mental and physical reactions. Sometimes I can feel it at the base of my brain where it joins the spinal cord, other times up in the frontal lobes, and it is in fact comparable to a lobotomy, as it causes my brain to lock up and malfunction to where I cannot concentrate or spell simple words... They have, at times, assailed me with this 'Death Ray' in bursts ranging from seconds to minutes, causing me to psychologically bounce up and down like a human yo-yo."

Perhaps there is a lack of proof of what David Fratus has said. But given our knowledge of mind control technology, there is reason to believe the man's account. [5]

—A report documented by the Association of National Security Alumni in February, 1992, concerns a Dayton, Ohio, woman whose husband worked at Wright-Patterson Air Force Base as an electronics engineer on a "transitional technologies" project. While her husband was at the Industrial College of the Armed Forces at Fort McNair, Virginia, in the mid-1980s, college faculty requested that the woman obtain a psychological examination, using the justification that the information obtained would be beneficial, given the stressful nature of her husband's job. After the psychological evaluation the woman "became the target of massive electronic harassment and may have been drugged on recurrent occasions." Immediately after contacting the Electronic Surveillance Project in Silver Spring, Maryland, associated with the National Security Alumni, the woman's husband had her forcibly committed to a psychiatric facility at Good Samaritan hospital, claiming that she was suicidal. Although she was released from the hospital, according to the woman the electronic harassment continues.

—One of the finest of current writers and researchers on the topic of mind control is Alex Constantine, the author of *Psychic Dictatorship in the U.S.A.* and *Virtual Government,* both published by Feral House. Constantine believes that he personally has been the subject of mind control programs. The following is the text of a letter he authored and sent to the magazine *Mondo 2000* in December, 1994:

"For five years I have been the victim of a formal torture program at the hands of the CIA. The torture is electromagnetic and difficult to trace, retaliation for my political research linking certain cliques in the military and federal government to cult formation (the firm has, since the early '60s, used cults to cover for mind control experimentation, including People's Temple, the SLA and the Finders), drug distribution and the like.

"All of this is to say that your article on the Pentagon's electronic weapons arsenal... was appreciated by someone who knows first-hand their insidious potential. I hope the effect of the article is not merely tittilation of violence-prone addicts, but alerts your readers to the awesome threat that EM [electromagnetic] weapons pose to human rights and political opposition to CIA-DoD [Department of Defense] chaos and disinformation.

"I have been subjected to a gruelling daily regimen of torture rendered from a remote source. I have been burned by microwaves, kept awake for days at a stretch by shrieking noises in my ears, the effect of pulsed audiograms. One evening I was hit by an infra-sound attack (the diagnosis comes from the Association of National Security Alumni's Electronics Surveillance Project) on my spine, the most painful experience of my life. I was left crawling and screaming across the floor. I could go on cataloging the tortures I've endured. My example should serve to demonstrate that fascists do not need concentration camps to silence political dissent. One's own home can be transformed into a torture chamber.

"For die-hard skeptics, I can offer this proof: Two of the leading child psychologists in the country once witnessed magnets repelled from my cranium. When I wrote a letter to Amnesty International about my plight (it was ignored), friends of mine were subjected to microwave attack.

"Public interest groups monitoring federal abuses of mind control technology tell me that there are scores of others under assault. 'Alien' abductions have long served as a cover for the development of electronic weaponry. Addressing the reality of the government's mind control experimentation may lead to public outcry against this carefully concealed attack on human rights.

"So far the disinformationists (proponents of false memory) have had a field day selling the rest of us out. Please continue to expose the national disgrace of EM weapons and their sadistic use on unwitting human targets." [6]

—The letter that follows was sent to a foreign consulate in Houston, Texas, on December 4, 1995:

"To Whom It May Concern:

"With this letter I am requesting political asylum from your government as an American citizen and victim of mind control carried out presumably by the CIA. I am taking such drastic measures because I am in fear of my life and safety and because I have exhausted every legal and other means available to me. I have received no assistance from the President of the United States, the FBI, the CIA, the Attorney General, my Congressman, to mention just a few. The fact that this technology exists and is being used against private citizens and innocent people like myself no one in any position of responsibility in government will officially acknowledge.

"I hope this is an acceptable condition for political asylum. If need be I am willing to relinquish my citizenship and be declared stateless as a means to this end. This is a well thought-out decision on my part and I am aware of all the ramifications that could occur. Naturally it is not a decision that I have taken easily, but under the circumstances it is likely that it is the only one that will prolong my life or give me any quality of life.

"I would like to provide a chronology giving the events leading up to this decision.

"As a university student I spent a year abroad in France and Germany and in Paris. I met a German university graduate whom I later married. We eventually returned to Germany to live after we finished our studies in the U.S. (I did my B.A. and he did a postgraduate degree in international business). A few years later we were divorced in Munich, Germany. I then became a graduate student and teacher, and resided for almost ten years in what was then West Berlin, Germany. There was nothing unusual in my life until the year 1983. At that time I co-taught a parapsychology course in the Community College system of West Berlin. A friend attended this class and brought a guest. The guest whom I will call 'C.L.' and I became friends later. Through these people I got to know some other new acquaintances and whether these people are incidental to, or pivotal figures in what later transpired is something that can only be speculated about. However, a certain pattern would appear to emerge from this.

"One of the persons I got to know casually was Peggy Woolsey who had worked as secretary to Richard Helms, former head of the CIA in Iran (He was there during the coup). Peggy would often tell me about her life in Iran. Once when I was in her apartment having a drink I discovered at least an inch of sediment on the bottom of my drink. I commented on this and was told it was the 'Berlin water'. Another time I went to East Berlin in her car with diplomatic plates and felt a strange mood of paranoia almost as if I was hallucinating. I remember Peggy asking me where the Russian embassy was. I remember thinking, 'How should I know?' In fact, I was at that time so naive I had not realized there was a Russian embassy in West Berlin. I had crossed the border previously primarily to go to the opera or theater or to buy books (German literature classics in cheap editions). I had the impression that something strange was transpiring. It was during this time that I was on three occasions, at three different locations, talked to during my sleep by people I was acquainted with. On these occasions I had awakened abruptly during my sleep and became aware of what was transpiring. I went to the U.S. Consulate and named names. After this I was harassed by a man in a white car who would drive by my apartment and when in close proximity, would zap me with an electrical field of some sort. He was very brazen. I would find my body pulsating during my sleep especially at the base of my spine, but my whole body would vibrate as well and I would see flashing lights on my wall. I had to go to the U.S. Consulate several times and they expressed disbelief in what I was saying, rudely stating: Who would be interested in you—you have no important political or military contacts. Ultimately I decided to return to the U.S. where I did not know what would be in store for me when I returned to a living hell and unbelievable torture, abuse, and experimentation.

"In retrospect the only conclusion that makes reasonable sense is that I must have exposed a CIA operation. I was then classified as a 'write-off' or expendable as a human being. By some unfortunate decision I was designated for a constant monitoring, inhuman method of electronic incarceration utilizing intracerebral microwave induction of voices. This is one of several sadistic approaches they have used to destroy my life. So for 13 years now I have never known one moment of privacy, or peace. My entire life has been stolen from me. My apartment serves them as the cage of a guinea pig.

"What they attempted to do with very crude, unsophisticated human input (not to say criminal and immoral) coupled with an electronic technology totally unknown to the public was to set up some artificial controls (or 'handlers') utilizing the voice and emotive responses of some individuals recognizable to me and get them to 'control' my behavior by the use of positive and negative reinforcement. These were not 'voices' talking to me live but were a whole catalog of reactions that were activated in my brain by some means. For example if I did something they did not like they would use the voice characteristics of 'C.' crying or whining or expressing despair. Thus the same expression would be played over and over again like canned laughter on a TV quiz program. I might hear the same emotive phrase played over five times in one day however absurd that may seem. When they realized that I was not being hoodwinked or deceived into thinking that this was a real person (and naturally they selected the voices of former lovers) they did not attempt to project this artifice but instead would harass me with the voices. Often I was interrupted at what I was doing at the rate of once a minute throughout the day. At other times it was once every four minutes. At other times every time I made a decision, drew a conclusion from something, or followed instructions it was reinforced. The implication being that these swine were in charge of my behavior and thinking. This reaches the point of fanatic absurdity on their part. And it still continues even as I type this. They are constantly trying to reinforce or keep in place their repulsive 'program'.

"Here are some examples: Through a business contact I got to know 'S.' and every time I met with her it was euphorically reinforced. This was something I could not fathom. I would think why are not my friendships with 'V.', 'E.J.', or others reinforced like this. It did not make sense to me as S. was a rather unsophisticated but warm-hearted Iranian hairdresser.

Later I discovered that under the Shah, S. had been married to a judge, connected in high places, had hidden people in her home and had had to flee when her husband was arrested.

"I think that one of the things they had planned to use was to start relationships with certain targeted individuals. They kept up a rabid campaign to get me to re-establish a contact with a foreign national who reputedly had intelligence contacts. I refused but they never stopped harassing me. They tried to establish a whole associational network of things supposedly characteristic of this person to constantly keep him in my mind which was revolting to the extreme. So I frequently formed the impression that I was constantly dealing with people who were my intellectual inferiors, ignorant provincials who were in a mad rush to use their high-tech equipment on any designated victim. The irony of all this pain and suffering was that the same things could have been achieved by very conventional and mundane methods. But this high-tech equipment was being used by individuals very unlike myself where I had the feeling I was being corrupted by the association, that I was being polluted by the contact and as a result I feel I have lost or had murdered my spirituality, my refinement, my dignity and privacy as a woman, my idealism, my joy in living, my sexuality, my feelings of freedom, my comfort zone, i.e. all that had once been the essential ingredients of my life.

"Their sadism knows no bounds. They will talk with you and make it a point of letting you know that they are watching you while you are on the toilet, for example.

"Needless to say, I attempted suicide but was stopped in the woods by another motorist.

"I would be more than happy to reveal their whole mind control program but there is not enough time now.

"What happened to precipitate this decision to seek asylum is that I discovered that there were other victims on whom the same or similar technology was being used and began networking with them and sharing information with plans of going public and getting organized. I was also able to upgrade and expand my technical knowledge and met victims of the CIA's Project Monarch and MKULTRA.

"I then started to get heart palpitations of a severe nature and my thyroid would be microwaved so that it would pulsate. I would awaken with a field directly to my stomach and intestines (the genital stimulation during sleep was by now old-hat) so that my midriff would be sore. When I would cover my thyroid with my hands to shield it I would later have arthritic-similar pains in my hands. I woke up two days ago with pain in my left armpit and both groin lymph nodes. I am afraid I am being 'taken out.' One of the deprogrammers and most knowledgeable persons on the CIA's codes, techniques and tactics has been suddenly diagnosed with terminal cancer that apparently appeared out of nowhere.

"I fear for my safety. I have gone to extremes to protect myself—trying to set up improvised Faraday cages, sleeping on the bathroom floor, wrapping myself in copper, aluminum, and the ringing is terrible—the program that gets activated during my REM sleep especially. And last night for the first time they actually used some equipment that lifted my body out of the galvanized aluminum shields I had erected. I was actually knocked backwards. I then tried to write this letter at home but my electric typewriter malfunctioned—when I would hit the 'n' key I would get 'q' for example.

"Your speedy attention to this urgent matter would certainly be appreciated.

"Sincerely, C.P. Austin, Texas" [7]

—In an open letter titled "Modern Human Experimentation/Torture" Dave Bader describes his believed victimization by mind control:

"I have been the unwitting subject of a painful and inhumane mind manipulation project for nearly three years now without a clue how to combat it because it is invisible and, for the first year, beyond my comprehension. After applying for a security clearance for my job as a LAN administrator for a D.O.D. contractor in California (Titan Research and Technology), I was mentally invaded by unknown to me members of this government. I have no idea what the goal of this torture treatment is, it makes no sense at all other than to drive me crazy and lose all faith in my fellow man and our so called democratic society...

"My real life nightmare began in mid-January 1993 about six months after applying for a security clearance for my job at a defense contractor in Northridge, California and less than a month after a major dental procedure by a dentist referred to me by the company (Dr. Pasternak). One day in January 1993 I began hearing voices talking to me in my mind (although I was not aware where they originated from at first) and a high pitched tone in my ears like a very high frequency radio wave that pulses. I cannot remember the exact date and time because it was the most traumatic experience I've had in my life, and my concern was not to document times and dates at the moment.

234

The voices were at a high enough volume to sound like it was a person in the room with me. At first I believed someone had tampered with my stereo equipment or put speakers in my walls. This was proven false when I went for a walk to escape and I continued to hear the voices. I proved this by plugging my ears, the sound comes from the center of my head. Learning this took me from fright to near psychosis because of their constant attack and my mind not accepting the unacceptable truth...

"As the days/weeks/months/years went by at an accelerated rate due to the traumatic stress, I did seek an answer by getting an x-ray of my head (I suspected some kind of device had been implanted in me because I had been to a dentist for an extraction just prior to the invasion). Also the night prior I was driving back from Van Nuys [California], (being severely tortured by the voices) when I stopped for a light, I looked at the car next to me and the man had his head tilted up and was pointing to a spot in his neck which later turned out to be the exact location of the object. Who this was, I will never know. I got the x-ray from a general practice doctor claiming that I felt pain in my throat and wanted to see if everything was OK. The x-ray showed a small metal object below my jaw directly under where my tooth was extracted. I asked the doctor if it could have accidentally fallen there due to the procedure, he replied that it was nearly impossible because it was located below the jaw in the soft tissue of my neck and it would require drilling through the jaw bone. I then spilled the beans and told him the truth, thinking stupidly that he would understand and be on my side with the evidence we just found. I asked him to refer me to someone who could remove it and I made an appointment for an ear/nose/throat doctor (the first ear/nose/throat I have seen), but the GP strongly suggested that I see a psychiatrist first. I assured him that I knew the correct course of action to solve my problem. I went to the ENT doctor and he gave me a bullshit examination then he asked what I wanted. I said that I wanted the metal object that showed on the x-rays removed. He said that it was like searching for a needle in a haystack and that it should not be removed. I protested and said I would sign a waver. He said that he wouldn't do it without a clearance from a psychiatrist (obviously the two doctors had spoken). I went to a psychiatrist and told him my situation, he responded as expected, he told me that I was suffering from a mental illness and could offer me his costly time and drugs but wouldn't sign anything related to removal of my foreign object. I went to another ear/nose/throat doctor and got more x-rays showing the same thing, but this time I didn't mention anything about my situation and stuck to the story about pain in my throat. He sent me to get a CAT scan, I did so and his final judgment was it would be like searching for a needle in a haystack and didn't want to do it. Since then I moved to Washington and changed jobs (trying to escape). I have been to two more doctors and got the same results.

"The voices started mildly like they were announcing their presence (on a Friday, I think). They spoke to me like they were friends but would evade all questions as to who they were and how they were doing it. This was maddening, but at the same time I couldn't imagine it lasting more than a few days as some kind of a sick joke. Monday came after a weekend that could fill a book (they played up every fear I could come up with to explain their existence, like a torture chamber where your worst nightmares come true). At this time I was speaking to them verbally as I expected they were talking to me by some means (maybe having everywhere I go bugged and speakered. Which was much more acceptable to my mind than the fact that my own mind was bugged)."

Bader details other aspects of his torment, and says, "The most notable effect on my life is that they turned me into an alcoholic to cope with the psychological pain and to get to sleep (they did not stop when I decided I should sleep, nor did they stop while I was sleeping, for that matter). They woke me up at two hour intervals making real sleep impossible. This sleep deprivation left me in a zombie-like state and less able to handle their audio attacks..."

"After a few weeks they became violent, meaning they didn't pretend they were my friends and used the pitch and volume of their usually synthesized voices as a weapon. I woke up to a screeching psychopathic woman's voice uttering high-pitched nonsense. Background noise severely worsens the effects of their electronic/verbal attack, for instance, being near machinery that whines or hums makes their voices unbearable. On the other hand being in complete silence is just as bad because the voices have a sickening electronic sound that you are completely aware is coming from between your ears. Basically every waking moment is a painful thing that is to be coped with in one way or another..."

"During the most violent period the voices were synthesized to sound like "monsters," low and ultra high-pitched that made my ear drums pulse. What they said was either painful nonsense (repetition of words or sentences: 'I'm in your mind, I'm in your mind, I'm in your mind,' a synthesized male voice that went in circles like a tape in an endless loop). The goal seemed to be to weaken me mentally, which worked but also drove me into furious rage with no one to confront. Can you imagine how maddening it is to be mentally tortured with no way to fight back?...

"Voices are not the extent of my torture. In the second year of my electronic harassment I have been electrically shocked, had involuntary limb movement (the muscles in my left arm convulse), and very painful pressure in my head, not like a headache but a feeling like your head is about to explode, as well as a tickling sensation in my ears, usually while trying to fall asleep or at key moments. Their techniques and timing are not known to me, the pressure in my head was almost always while driving (seeming to be at key moments) and the shocks were usually while trying to relax or sleep or while thinking about their presence, they like me to ignore them and punish me when I don't.

"A normal day for me consists of waking up to their presence... This starts with a slow chanting of bullshit with no meaning. By the time I get in the shower (a dreaded place because the sound of the water amplified their voices in a sickening way) my mind still half asleep sometimes mimics them causing me to mumble what they are saying. Now it is less severe in the morning, unlike the morning terror they put me through the first year, making me think some kind of restraints have been put on them, or maybe they just don't want me to die of a heart attack just yet... I drive to work and they torment my mind more and more as the day progresses... It gets worse after work when I try to relax they speak more rapidly sometimes driving me into a frenzy. Often while diverting my attention watching TV or something I will say a complete or partial sentence that obviously didn't originate from me telling me that they can manipulate the speech related part of my brain...

"I know a lot of the above sounds completely paranoid (you would have to be there). In fact this is the barest glimpse into my life for the last two and a half years...

"My Conclusions: I have no idea as to the extent of the knowledge and or acceptance of the extremes of my situation, it makes me sick to think about it. Regardless of me personally, I ask you to consider the information presented here. Maybe I am one of the few that knows it is absolute fact from personal experience, but I also know how hard it is to convince an unknowing person of an unbelievable fact. Especially when faced with misinformation.

"This technology is real, and we have a lot to worry about and a lot to do to correct it. With this technology it is possible for unknowing citizens to be subjected to laboratory rat like experimentation, as in my case. But more importantly it can be used to ultimately control civilization, by mental eavesdropping or manipulation for political, business, or other reasons. What it boils down to is the complete loss of human rights and privacy. George Orwell had a pretty good vision of the future in *1984*. He was lacking in the technology, but right on about Big Brother. If a small voice speaks out about corruption it is stamped out or made a fool of. Even more horrifying than telescreens, is direct access to the human mind by a race of people that are still producing nuclear weapons and lying about crimes a half century old. Please don't let it continue!" [8]

NOTES:

1. Koski, Marrti, *Untitled research paper,* Stockholm: Mediaecco, 1993

2. Naeslund, Robert. "An Open Letter to the Swedish Prime Minister Regarding Electromagnetic Terror", Stockholm: Mediaecco, 1993. *Secret and Suppressed,* Jim Keith, ed. (Portland, Oregon: Feral House, 1994)

3. Ibid.

4. *Frankfurther Allgemeine Zeitung,* November 18, 1985 5. Fratus, David, letter of October 18, 1988, obtained from the Internet, copy in the author's possession

6. Constantine, Alex, letter to the editor, *Mondo 2000* magazine, December, 1994

7. Anonymous, text obtained on the Internet

8. Bader, Dave, "Modern Human Experimentation/Torture", text obtained on the Internet

Chapter 27:

WOODPECKER

There are even more awesome uses for the new breed of electromagnetics. Now the means for influencing and controlling entire populations is in the hands of the ruling elite.

In 1972, Dr. Gordon J.F. McDonald gave testimony before the House Subcommittee on Oceans and International Environment on the issue of electromagnetic weapons used for mind control and mental disruption. McDonald stated, "The basic notion was to create, between the electrically charged ionosphere in the higher part of the atmosphere and conducting layers of the surface of the Earth, this neutral cavity, to create waves, electrical waves that would be tuned to the brainwaves... about ten cycles per second... you can produce changes in behavioral patterns or in responses."

In the late 1970s electromagnetic weapons came into their own, and the proof of this may be the sudden drop in ozone levels reported internationally. On February 24, 1987, the PBS-TV network show NOVA announced that a hole had been discovered in the ozone layer above the Antarctic. According to the NOVA commentator, "Antarctica—the coldest place on Earth. Here a mysterious change has been detected in a vital element in the atmosphere. This invisible layer 15 miles high acts as a sunscreen around the Earth—our only protection from it.

"Scientists warn that ozone depletion" could cause "major effects on human health, including: higher incidence of skin cancer, cataracts, and depression of the immune system. Losses of ozone would affect climate, damage the growth of plants and disturb the food chain."

The cause of the depletion of ozone, according to the mainstream media, was the release of chlorofluorocarbon (CFC) gases into the atmosphere of the type used in refrigerators, solvents, air conditioning, and insulation, but in September, 1987, *Omni* magazine may have offered a clue to the real culprit.

According to that magazine, "An obscure group of scientists, working for the British Antarctic Survey, stumbled upon the ozone hole. Joseph Farman, leader of the group... noticed a sharp decrease in column-ozone every September and October, starting in 1977..."

These dates for the sudden depletion in ozone levels were confirmed by the February 16, 1986, edition of the *Sunday Oklahoman,* which stated: "The ominous thing about the ozone drop is the rapidity with which it is developing. Until about 1977, there was no indication it had changed by any substantial amount since the late 1950s. But it has really fallen off the table in the past few years."

The *Washington Post* for July 29, 1987, quoted Robert Watson, employed by NASA, as saying that until recently scientists were "worried that a 5 percent change [in ozone levels] over the next century could be adverse. Instead of 5 percent, we're looking at 50 percent in only 10 years... This was absolutely unexpected; it's caught our attention.'

Three months later the *Washington Post* was reporting a drop in ozone levels up to 97% at some locations over the Antarctic, drops in ozone over the United States, and a drifting ozone hole that passed over the eastern U.S. Noted were outbreaks of 'solar retinitis,' or sunburnt eyes in the eastern United States, as well as an 83% increase in cases of skin cancer in the U.S. [1]

What had caused the reported sudden depletion in ozone levels? Although there has been nary a hint of it in the mainstream press, there are strong indications—including a precise time correlation with the discovery of the ozone holes—that it was electromagnetic bombardment of the atmosphere.

The Soviets have long been interested in the work of Nikola Tesla, and on July 4, 1976, that interest paid off. The Soviets fired up seven Tesla magnifying transmitters located at Chernobyl, beaming 10 herz of energy into the ionosophere and creating an energetic standing wave that stretched from Chile to Alaska. At the same time, three Soviet satellites coordinated this irradiation of the upper atmosphere. These signals were detected all over the world, and were known as the "Russian Woodpecker" due to the chattering interference they produced on radio receivers. [2]

Describing the effects of the Tesla magnifying transmitter, Lieutenant Colonel Thomas Bearden, lecturing at a symposium of the U.S. Psychotronics Association in 1981, said, "Tesla found that he could set up standing waves... in the earth (the molten core of the earth), or, just set it up through the rocks—the telluric activity in the rocks would furnish activity into these waves and one would get more potential energy in those waves than he put in. He called the concept the magnifying transmitter."

Bearden stated of the Tesla transmitters, "They will go through anything. What you do is that you set up a standing wave through the earth and the molten core of the earth begins to feed that wave (we are talking Tesla now). When you have that standing wave, you have set up a triode. What you've done is that the molten core of the earth is feeding the energy and it's like your signal—that you are putting in—is gating the grid of a triode... Then what you do is that you change the frequency. If you change the frequency one way (start to dephase it) you dump the energy up in the atmosphere beyond the point on the other side of the earth that you focused upon. You start ionizing the air, you can change the weather flow patterns (jet streams, etc.)—you can change all of that—if you dump it gradually, real gradually—you influence the heck out of the weather. It's a great weather machine. If you dump it sharply, you don't get a little ionization like that. You will get flashes and fireballs (plasma) that will come down on the surfaces of the earth... you can cause enormous weather changes over entire regions by playing that thing back and forth."

Weather changes and more.

According to a United Press International report of December 22, 1977, "a series of mysterious atmospheric explosions were reported along the New Jersey shore last night for the third time this month... Police said the explosions were preceded by a series of rumblings. On December 2, there were two similar incidents, but the Federal Aviation Administration, the Civil Aeronautics Board and the Nuclear Regulatory Commission have been unable to offer any explanation for the blasts."

Other effects have been attributed to the Russian Woodpeckers by Dr. Andrija Puharich, in a research paper titled *Global Magnetic Warfare.* Puharich stated that controlled earthquakes could be set off by the Russians using this technology, and that, "Of the many great earthquakes of 1976, there is one that demands special attention—the July 28, 1976 Tangshan, China earthquake." Tangshan was devastated with 650,000 persons dead.

Almost a year later, the *New York Times,* on June 5, 1977,

recounted curious precursor events to the Tangshan quake, stating that, "just before the first tremor at 3:42 AM, the sky lit up 'like daylight.' The multi-hued lights, mainly white and red, were seen up to 200 miles away. Leaves on many trees were burned to a crisp and growing vegetables were scorched on one side, as if by a fireball."

In 1978, Dr. Robert Beck reported on ELF fields related to mood alterations in Canadians. Beck and another researcher, William Bise, noted changes in the behavior and brain wave patterns of persons in the Pacific Northwest, attributing them to the Russian Woodpecker broadcasts.

In 1984, Thomas Bearden delivered another talk entitled "Soviet Weather Warfare Over North America." Bearden noted the existence of hitherto-unseen weather patterns and cloud formations in North America since the Russian Woodpeckers had gone into operation. These, he maintained, were the signature of the Tesla magnifying transmitter. One cloud pattern that Bearden mentioned was a "giant radial," resembling the Japanese "rising sun" symbol with rays radiating out of a central circle.

Bearden expanded on the capabilities of the Russian Woodpeckers, the technology employing electromagnetic waves of pure potential: "By interfering two beams of such scalar waves at a distance, a scalar interferometer is produced. By slow rotation of the transmitter, the entire distant interference zones—and the highs and lows—can be moved along. This scheme then allows the capturing and movement of high cloud masses, direct manipulation of high and low pressure areas, diversion of jet streams, and extensive Soviet control over the weather patterns of North America." [3]

By the 1970s the Americans were struggling to come into parity with the Russians in terms of the new technology. Concerned with advances in Russian technology, in the 1970s the Americans launched Project Nile Blue, later renamed Climate Dynamics.

Reportedly as part of a secret Soviet/U.S. Polar warming pact, the Americans began to broadcast their own ELF signals at 30 Hertz. Signals broadcast at 30 Hertz are reportedly far less dangerous than the Soviet 10 Hertz signals, which have been speculated to cause weakened immune systems, effects on mood and cognitive processes, and increased vulnerability to a host of diseases, some of them newly manufactured in laboratories.

According to the *P.A.C.E. Newsletter*, "ELF fields usually propagate vertically to the ground, creating 'Standing Waves' that tend to go down towards the Earth's core and up to the various strata of the biosphere. Like their ultraviolet photon counterparts from the sun, they can redistribute energy and momentum in the [atmospheric] troposphere through cumulus convection.

It has been suggested ELF-induced charges in the ion electrical effects perturb the electric current and field patterns of the field circuit of the atmosphere, a field whose existence is established by 'classical' thunderstorm activity theory. It is known that the microphysics of the surface level atmosphere and other strata are dependent on atmospheric electric state." [4]

A story in the New York Times for December 16, 1980, alluded to American ELF transmissions: "Scientists in Antarctica believe they have probably created an aurora over Quebec. The aurora should have resulted from an experiment conducted... to interfere with the earth's magnetic field lines that extend from Antarctica to Canada. Electrons forming the earth-encircling radiation belt normally are trapped in paths that spiral around the magnetic field lines and reverse direction as they near the earth at each end of the magnetic arc. If their paths are perturbed by radio waves, they fail to reverse and plunge into the atmosphere.

"When specific radio frequencies are transmitted, their effects (which can include electron showers, perturbations of the earth's magnetism and disturbances in the radio-reflecting layers of the upper atmosphere) should all oscillate at a tempo matching that of the transmitted signal." [5]

The Washington Times of February 4, 1986, noted the existence of ELF generators located in Norway and Alaska, and said that scientists in Alaska "manipulate and orchestrate aurora displays by beaming powerful radio waves up from the ground. Recent tests have also indicated that a related phenomenon, the polar electrojet, a 'river of electricity flowing through the upper atmosphere,' may have a practical application." [6]

At the same time, apparent cover stories were issued, such as a report in the Washington Post that said, "Powerful radio waves, generated by navigational beacons on earth are causing 'Electron Rain' to fall into the earth's upper atmosphere from the Van Allen radiation belts thousands of miles out in space, a team of researchers from four universities has found." [7]

When the satellite Ginga, or Galaxy, was launched by the Japanese in February 1987 it was described as a mission to detect X-ray emissions from the stars. But, as is often the case in space research, it had another purpose: to detect radiation from Chinese and Russian underground nuclear weapons testing. One of the concerns of the Japanese was that atmospheric currents would carry radiation leakage from Central Asia directly across the airstream of Japan.

In June *Ginga* detected massive gamma ray bursts and, contacting NASA, the Japanese were informed that the probable source of the radiation was the Russian *Kosmos* 1900 satellite, supposedly used for oceanic observation. Further testing confirmed that the radiation was coming from the *Kosmos* 1900. [8]

This Russian satellite and others were being used in a program run by Sergei Korolev, the "father" of the Sputnik, in the radioactive "seeding" of the Van Allen upper atmospheric belts. Satellites carrying nuclear reactors would fire pulses of electromagnetic energy into the ionosphere. The purpose of *Kosmos* 1900 was the creation of an electromagnetic "mirror" for the reflection of Russian-originated ELF beams.

On October 1, 1996, Russian Deputy Foreign Minister Grigory Karasin on a visit to Tokyo announced that Russia would participate with Japan in the creation of a joint missile defense system. Boris Yeltsin had earlier proposed a joint defense system to the Americans. The overall plan was, in fact, a tripartite defense system aimed at countering the Chinese threat. [9]

There are many curious phenomena taking place in the world today, suggesting that advanced electronic weapons such as those discussed above are in operation. As an example, in 1985 a number of arson specialists investigating the large number of forest fires that were taking place in central California came to the conclusion that the fires had started high in the trees. At the time of the fires there had been no reports of lightning. Is it possible that this was an example of the testing of space-based Star Wars-style weaponry? [10]

NOTES:

1. *Washington Post*, March 10, 1987 and October 28, 1987; *Washington Times*, September 15, 1987

2. Anonymous, "Electromagnetic Weapons in the Australian Outback," Archipelago, reprinted in *Leading Edge* number 98; *P.A.C.E. (Planetary Association for Clean Energy) Newsletter*, March 1980; Thomas, William. "Target: Ozone! The Military Maestros' Secret Plan to Pluck the Earth's Ionosphere Like a HAARP," *Paranoia* magazine, fall, 1995

3. Smith, Jerry. *HAARP: Ultimate Weapon of the Conspiracy*, (1997: AUP, Kempton, Illinois.

4. *P.A.C.E. Newsletter*, March 1986

5. *New York Times*, December 16, 1980

6. *Washington Times*, February 4, 1986

7. *Washington Post*, December 7, 1987

8. Anonymous, "Electromagnetic Weapons in the Australian Outback," Archipelago, reprinted in *Leading Edge* number 98

9. Anonymous, "Electromagnetic Weapons"

10. Forest, Waves. "Space-Age Snowjob", *Now What* #3

Maria Devi Khrystos: Ukrainian mind control cult?

Delgado's experiments with electric stimulation of the brain and the dialation and constriction of pupils with these monkeys. Bottom: Dialation of the left pupil and constriction of the right pupil by stimulation of the hypothalamus.

Chapter 28:

HAARP

On August 11, 1987, U.S. patent number 4,686,605 was issued to Dr. Bernard J. Eastlund. The *New York Times* of August 15, 1987, said that Dr. Eastlund is "a physicist and an expert on oilfield development, who is a consultant for the Atlantic Richfield Oil Company (ARCO)... Mr. Eastlund assigned the patent rights to APTI, Inc., a Los Angeles subsidiary of Atlantic Richfield."

The patent said that the technology is able to:

"Cause... total disruption of communications over a very large portion of the Earth... disrupting not only land-based communications, but also airborne communications and sea communications (both surface and subsurface)... missile or aircraft destruction, deflection, or confusion... weather modification... by altering solar absorption... Ozone, nitrogen, etc. concentrations could be artificially increased..."

In an assessment of Dr. Eastlund's discoveries on *National Public Radio* one month later, it was reported that "Dr. Eastlund stated that his new invention could be used to change the weather by redirecting the very high wind patterns. The invention would use an earth-based power source to create electromagnetic radio waves and focus them way up in the atmosphere. Dr. Eastlund says the invention could steer jet streams, but could also be used to disrupt communications all over the world, and perhaps, most significantly, might be used to destroy or deflect a missile attack." Eastlund's brainchild is, in fact, a Tesla magnifying transmitter, and two reference sources in the patent itself are about Tesla technology.

Eastlund was interviewed on the radio show, and said, "I am not happy, personally, that the patent was issued publicly. This particular patent was under an initial secrecy order by the Patent Office. But, as I understand it, the Patent Office does not keep secret, basic fundamental information, which they interpreted this patent to be. Specific discussion of military applications is secret—proprietary also. It's what they wanted to do." [1]

The first apparent usage of the technology of patent 4,686,605 was HAARP, the High-frequency Active Auroral Research Program, run by the Department of Defense, the Air Force's Phillips Laboratory, and the Office of Naval Research. Although the military has denied that the patent is related to HAARP, Eastlund's responses put the obvious lie to that.

HAARP is a huge electromagnetic broadcasting facility located in Gakona, Alaska, on the site of an abandoned over-the-horizon radar installation. Covering 58 acres, the complex consists of 360 high frequency antennae towers aimed at the sky. The cost of the project is between $25 million and $30 million. The official description of the project is "a major Arctic facility for upper atmospheric and solar-terrestrial research."

Here is a quote from Eastlund's patent:

"In the past several years, substantial effort has been made to understand and explain the phenomena involved in belts of trapped electrons and ions, and to explore the possible ways to control and use these phenomena for beneficial purposes. For example, in the late 1950s and the early 1960s both the United States and the USSR detonated a series of nuclear devices of various yields to generate large numbers of charged particles at various altitudes, e.g., 200 kilometers or greater...

"This can cause confusion of or interference with or even complete disruption of guidance systems employed by even the most sophisticated of airplanes and missiles. The ability to employ and transmit over very wide areas of the Earth a plurality of electromagnetic waves of varying frequencies, and to change same at will in a random manner, provides a unique ability to interfere with all modes of communication, land, sea, and/or air, at the same time. Because of the unique juxtaposition of usable fuel source at the point where desirable field-lines intersect the Earth's surface, such wide-ranging and complete communication interference can be achieved in a reasonably short period of time... Thus, this invention provides the ability to put unprecedented amounts of power in the Earth's atmosphere at strategic locations and to maintain the power injection level, particularly if random pulsing is employed, in a manner far more precise and better controlled than heretofore accomplished by the prior art, particularly by the detonation of nuclear devices of various yields at various altitudes... Further, by knowing the frequencies of various electromagnetic beams employed in the practice of this invention, it is possible not only to interfere with third party communications but to take advantage of one or more such beams to carry out a communications network even though the rest of the world's communications are disrupted. Put another way, what is used to disrupt another's communications can be employed by one knowledgeable of this invention as a communications network at the same time. In addition, once one's own communications network is established, the far reaching extent of the effects of this invention could be employed to pick up communication signals of others for intelligence purposes...

"This invention has a phenomenal variety of possible ramifications and potential future developments. As alluded to earlier, missile or aircraft destruction, deflection, or confusion could result, particularly when relativistic particles are employed. Also, large regions of the atmosphere could be lifted to an unexpectedly high altitude so that missiles encounter unexpected and unplanned drag forces with resultant destruction or deflection of same. Weather modification is possible by, for example, altering upper atmosphere wind patterns by constructing one or more plumes of atmospheric particles which will act as a lens or focusing device. Also as alluded to earlier, molecular modification of the atmosphere can take place so that positive environmental effects can be achieved. Besides actually changing the molecular composition of an atmospheric region, a particular molecule or molecules can be chosen for increased presence. For example, ozone, nitrogen, etc., concentrations in the atmosphere could be artificially increased. Similarly, environmental enhancement could be achieved by causing the breakup of various chemical entities such as carbon dioxide, carbon monoxide, nitrous oxides, and the like..."

Interestingly enough, perhaps a more complete description of what the HAARP electromagnetic transmission facility can do was provided many years ago by *The New York Times,* for December 8, 1915. The article is also cited in the Eastlund patent.

"Nikola Tesla," the article begins, "the inventor, has filed patent applications on the essential parts of a machine, the possibilities of which test a layman's imagination and promise a parallel of Thor's shooting thunderbolts from the sky to punish those who had angered the gods... Suffice it to say that the invention will go through space with a speed of 300 miles a second, a manless ship without propelling engine or wings, sent by electricity to any desired point on the globe on its errand of destruction, if destruction its manipulator wishes to effect.

"'It is not a time,' said Dr. Tesla yesterday, 'to go into the details of this thing. It is founded upon a principle that means great things in peace; it can be used for great things in war. But I repeat, this is no time to talk of such things.'

"'It is perfectly practicable to transmit electrical energy without wires and produce destructive effects at a distance. I have already constructed a wireless transmitter which makes this possible, and have described it in my technical publications, among which I refer to my patent number 1,119,732, recently granted. With a transmitter of this kind we are enabled to project electrical energy in any amount to any distance and apply it for innumerable purposes, both in war and peace. Through the universal adoption of this system, ideal conditions for the maintenance of law and order will be realized, for then the energy necessary to the enforcement of right and justice will be normally productive, yet potential, and in any moment available, for attack and defense. The power transmitted need not be necessarily destructive, for, if distance is made to depend upon it, its withdrawal or supply will bring about the same results as those now accomplished by force of arms.'"

Another article referred to in the patent was also in *The New York Times*, this time for September 22, 1940. The following is an excerpt:

"Nikola Tesla, one of the truly great inventors who celebrated his eighty-fourth birthday on July 10, tells the writer that he stands ready to divulge to the United States government the secret of his 'teleforce' with which, he said, airplane motors would be melted at a distance of 250 miles, so that an invisible Chinese Wall of Defense would be built around this country...

"This 'teleforce', he said, is based on an entirely new principle of physics that 'no one has ever dreamed about', different from the principle embodied in his inventions relating to the transmission of electrical power from a distance, for which he has received a number of basic patents. This new type of force, Mr. Tesla said, would operate through a beam one one-hundred-millionth of a square centimeter in diameter, and could be generated from a special plant that would cost no more than $2,000,000 and would only take three months to construct.

"The beam, he states, involves four new inventions, two of which have already been tested. One of these is a method and apparatus for producing rays 'and other manifestations or energy' in free air, eliminating the necessity for a high vacuum; a second is a method and process for producing 'very great electrical force'; the third is a method for amplifying this force; and the fourth is a new method for producing 'a tremendous electrical repelling force'. This would be the projector, or gun, of the system. The voltage for propelling the beam to its objective, according to the inventor, will attain a potential of 50,000,000 volts.

"With this enormous voltage, he said, microscopic electrical particles of matter will be catapulted on their mission of defensive destruction. He has been working on this invention, he added, for many years and has recently made a number of improvements in it."

Tesla is apparently talking about the technology employed in HAARP.

Although the project is unclassified, this may be a ruse, since many of the functions that HAARP is capable of are not mentioned in its brief. The Department of Defense's intention is for us to believe that HAARP is a testing facility for ionospheric research, while others critical of the project point out that it is capable of this function and far more. One of the apparent, unstated purposes of HAARP is as a Strategic Defense Initiative ("Star Wars") weapons system. Another usage of the technology, verified in many accounts including Eastlund's original patent of the technology, is weather control. Another capability is mind control.

In November 1987, information on an earlier auroral stimulation project was revealed that also highlights suppressed capabilities of HAARP. In the magazine *Heartland*, it was stated,

"The most powerful radio signal in the Fairbanks area is not directed to a listening audience in interior Alaska. The U.S. government's China Hot Springs station is titled 'High Power Auroral Stimulation Facility.' UCLA operates the site, drawing researchers from across the country. One of the main projects involves a team led by Anthony Ferraro of Penn State University with assistance from the University of Alaska Geophysical Institute."

According to *Heartland*, in October 1987, Ferraro's team "successfully tested a theory that heating the ionosphere makes possible the generation and transmission of extremely low frequency or ELF radio waves... The technique tested here involves shining a one million watt high frequency wave into the ionosphere through a very narrow beam, effectively producing 80 million watts of power. 'When that beam shines into the ionosphere, it increases the temperature of the region by 50 percent,' Ferraro said.

"The beam heats a large pancake shaped spot, six miles thick and 12 miles in diameter, in the ionosphere 40 to 60 miles above the ground... When the temperature of the ionosphere increases, the current produced by the electrically charged particles in the ionosphere changes and can be regulated by turning the transmitter on and off. In effect this procedure creates a radio antenna in the ionosphere which emits a radio wave that comes back down to earth. The waves are extremely low frequency." [2]

An example of the kind of damage that HAARP is capable of comes from another project entirely, an Air Force radar installation that came on-line in 1979. Located on Cape Cod, the "Pave Paws" transmitter broadcast only 1/1000th of the electromagnetic energy of HAARP, but its effects were still deadly. Within two years, women living in nearby towns began developing leukemia at a rate 23% higher than the state norm, and various forms of cancer at a rate 69% higher than other women in Massachusetts. [3]

Perhaps the most important possible use of HAARP, especially in the context of this book, is mind control and disruption, although this capability is naturally never brought up in the official literature. HAARP broadcasts at the same frequencies as those of the human brain, and can be attuned for specific applications on entire populations. The technology also could conceivably be used for projecting words and images directly to the minds of entire populations.

HAARP was activated in 1997, although it is said that it will not be fully on-line until 2002.

NOTES:

1. *New York Times*, August 15, 1987; "All Things Considered," National Public Radio, September 6, 1987

2. *Heartland*, the Fairbanks, Alaska, *Daily News Miner*, November 29, 1987

3. Begich, Jr., Nick. "Ionospheric Interference—Another Pandora's Box? *Nexus* magazine, October/November 1994

Chapter 29:

HUM JOBS AND BALLS OF FIRE

Evidence that electromagnetic weapons are currently being directed at civilian populations include strange sounds described all over the world as "the Hum," "the Sound," or just "It," a low, rumbling noise at the very edge of audibility. The sound is described as persistent and maddening, as irritating as the screech of fingernails on a blackboard.

In Taos, New Mexico, "the Hum" has been going on since 1991. "It sounds like a great, big American car engine that's on idle," said Steven Walters. "When I first heard it, I thought I was going crazy."

K.C. Grams, an area resident, says the sound can get so loud that "my head buzzes, as if it were a beehive."

Schatzie Hubbell moved from Santa Fe, New Mexico, where she was plagued by the sound, to Fort Worth, Texas. "After living there for 32 years and being very involved in the community, we had to leave," she said. "It's like a Chinese torture treatment. It affects you at a level you can't get to. Extreme irritation. Fingers across the chalkboard."

James Kelly, director of research on hearing at the University of New Mexico says, "We now have two large populations who hear these hums, here and in England. The people in Taos are deeply disturbed by this. This is not trivial."

The noise is said to be incredibly annoying, and will not stop unless you overwhelm it by playing the stereo or television loudly, or doing something else to drown it out.

"The Hum" may have been even recorded by a Denver, Colorado, acoustical engineer, between 17 and 70 cycles per second, roughly the same audio level as distant thunder. This study has been confirmed by a survey of people who have heard the sound who, when it is simulated, place the frequency at between 33 and 80 cycles per second—results similar to those conducted on people in Great Britain who have been hearing the same kind of sound. [1]

Hueytown, Alabama, near Birmingham, has since December 1991—near the same time period the sound was first widely heard in Taos—been the recipient of the "Hueytown Hum." According to residents a sound reminiscent of a dentist's drill or a humming fluorescent light is sporadically heard, sometimes radiating from the ground and other times coming from the air. One particular area of approximately 500 homes seems to be particularly affected by the sound. [2]

Another report comes from New Zealand, and was published in *Would You Believe* magazine. Fred and Phyll Dickenson relate, "What you call "the Hum" is called "the Noise" in our country... New Zealand. It still continues here, too, some nights it is more predominant than others—possibly because it is quieter at night but it can still be heard in the daytime.

"It is strange but once one has heard it, it's never forgotten. Yet it takes a lot of people quite a time to kind of tune into it.

"Another peculiar thing about it is... younger people cannot hear it or rather 'tune into it', it appears 'older ears' are more inclined to pick it up.

"In some of our travels in the countryside, if there is a quiet spot along the road, especially in quiet country and in road cuttings with high banks or hills on either side, the 'noise' seems to be amplified.

"We noticed this once when we got out of the car to look at some rocks in a cutting, and were immediately struck with the intensity of the hum and we looked around for possible electric power lines which could possibly be the cause, but none were in sight. We were actually in wide open country with no power lines for miles.

"When I was working and coming home in the early hours of the morning I used to sit in the car when I reached the carpost and with windows closed would listen to this loud hum. The closed car confines seemed to amplify the noise. Getting out of the car it could still be heard, and just standing there, turning round to all points of the compass, the noise was still heard, in other words it had no fixed point of origin.

"I hasten to mention here it was NO internal head noise but was definitely coming in from outside the body. Some people pass it off as blood noises in a person's head but it is not that." [3]

A federal task force of scientists from the University of New Mexico, the U.S. Air Force, and Sandia and Los Alamos National

Laboratories was formed to investigate the phenomenon in Taos, New Mexico, but predictably they found nothing. Their speculations tend towards the sounds originating in the ear itself, and the motion of Earth's tectonic plates. My guess is they know exactly what is causing the sound.

The once-skeptical Rep. Bill Richardson, of the House Intelligence Committee, knows that "the Hum" is not delusion. He told a meeting in Taos that the sound is "defense related" and requested that the Pentagon "shut it down."

Another investigator, Bob Saltzman, talks about a scientist on the House Science, Space and Technology Committee losing his job over his claims that the Department of Defense was responsible for the hum. He also reports that Rep. Richardson has since backed off of his investigation and won't return his phone calls. [4]

Perhaps significantly, some people are not running away from "the Hum," but are relocating closer to it. Since the early 1990s, in Taos, dozens of people have moved to the area specifically to be in the vicinity of "the Hum." One woman says that she moved to Taos, and the anomalous sound after seeing a UFO. "I knew it couldn't possibly be an airplane," she said. "It came closer... then a very tired feeling overcame me. I felt compelled to lie down on the bed. What's more I felt a weight right over my chest, pushing me down." She fell asleep, but then, "When I was asleep, I had the strangest dream, one that recurs every now and then. Something closely resembling a cash register tape kept running upwards. I kept seeing rows and rows of green numbers. After a long time, the numbers started changing color. They became green on top and orange on the bottom. The running tape on the second set of numbers didn't run very long. When the numerical action stopped and I thought the experience was over, then some more numbers started coming up. These were orange. This experience seemed quite lengthy, just like the one with the green numbers. When the numbers quit registering in my mind, I wanted to get up, but again I was powerless to do so."

The woman awoke, feeling disoriented. "I tried to see the flying craft, but the sky looked like a blur to me." For days after she felt a "strange numbness. It felt like I was experiencing a brain rape. That's pretty strange for me, because I have a [literal] mind and I'm not that fond of numbers." [5]

Other incidents suggesting the testing of advanced electromagnetic or other weapons are the literally hundreds of unusual fireballs—usually green or orange-red—and other strange aerial phenomena that have been observed worldwide in recent years. Although I have records of sightings of similar fireballs from around the world, due to space limitations I will confine myself to recent sightings in Australia:

On May 28, 1993, a huge orange-red fireball with a bluish tail flew at the speed of a fast jet plane from the south to the north between Leonora and Laverton, Australia. Its flight was observed over an area of 250 kilometers. The fireball made a "pulsed roaring noise, similar to a very loud train." Immediately after the passage of the fireball a 3.9 Richter-scale earthquake struck in the area, with an enormous drawn-out blast being heard afterward. An engineer with explosives experience described the event as "definitely a major explosive concussion wave blast, similar to, but much bigger than, a normal open-pit mine blast." It is notable that this area of Australia has not had any other recorded earthquakes since it first began to be seismically monitored in 1900.

At the presumed impact site of the fireball—no impact crater was ever found—an enormous deep red hemisphere of light, surrounded by a silver layer of light, rose into the air and was observed by viewers as far as 50 kilometers away. According to a witness, it "bobbed around a bit for nearly two hours before disappearing suddenly—as if someone threw the light switch off." About one hour after the fireball impact, another smaller blue-green-white fireball rose from the ground and flew over the area. Another smaller explosion and slight earthquake were noted at the time.

Another fireball was observed in the same area in "May or June" of 1993, a yellow-orange-red "Moon-sized" object, flying from south to north at low level.

In October 1994, at the mining town of Tom Price in Western Australia, a huge pulsing red-orange fireball without a tail was observed slowly traveling overhead at a low altitude, perhaps 200 to 300 meters. Approximately 2,000 people observed the overflight of the fireball, and some witnesses describe the red flames swirling in a spiral pattern that disappeared into a "central black hole" in the burning mass. One witness called it an "implosion ball of flames." The fireball was visible for five to seven minutes and went from the west to hills in the east. Then the fireball flashed a vivid blue-white, illuminating the surrounding area, and shot off at a rapid speed to disappear in the east.

Immediately after the appearance of the fireball, a second fireball came out of the west, following the path of the first.

Aside from the fact that it was traveling at a lower altitude, the fireball is described as being identical to the first. This fireball also traveled to the east and disappeared in a blue-white flash.

A third fireball duplicated the appearance and trajectory of the first two, and also disappeared in a blue-white flash.

On May 1, 1995, at 2 a.m., a large orange-red fireball, with a blue-white tail, was seen above Perth, Australia, traveling at a north-northeast trajectory. Again, the fireball sounded like a roaring freight train, and flew at about the speed of a fast jet aircraft. Remarkably, as it traveled over east Perth, the fireball halted in its path, and the tail reversed its direction. Then the fireball exploded, lighting up the city.

According to researcher and mining geologist Harry Mason, "In many ways the event was similar in force level to a nuclear blast. A loud, vibrating, massive explosion-cum-seismic wave reverberated around Perth, causing the city buildings to shake and books and objects to fall off shelves." About half the population of the city was awoken by the explosion.

Some observers of the event reported that four white lights shot out from the center of the fireball and formed a "right-angled white cross in the sky." Although the event was estimated to have exploded with the force of several megatons of dynamite, the event was not covered in the world press.

The same night as the Perth fireball, almost 2,000 miles to the north, a couple in their home in the Kimberley region of Western Australia were woken around 3 a.m. by a roaring noise "similar to a D9 bulldozer or tank engine." Books and other items fell from shelves, with an apparent earthquake taking place for one to two minutes.

Retracing the trajectory of the Perth fireball, one comes to the Kamchatka Peninsula in Siberia, the area where the KAL 007 was downed. Noted in the book *KAL 007* is the information that the plane may have been attempting to gain information on an electromagnetic weapons complex located on the peninsula—and this complex may be the source of Australia's fireballs. [6]

Since the May, 1993 fireball and earthquakes, there have been more than 1,000 reports in Australia of fireballs and strange light phenomena, as well as large numbers of similar events worldwide. Many of the fireballs are reported to have made the same "freight train" sounds as they passed.

It is significant to note that residents who witnessed the Tom Price fireballs noted that they had come from the direction of an American "Very Low Frequency submarine communication base" at Exmouth Peninsula, a location supposedly turned over to the Australian Navy by the U.S., but where there are still a number of American technicians resident.

The Exmouth Peninsula site consists of a power station and "Tower Zero," a high box-like aerial tower on a hilltop with 11 equally spaced smaller towers—each about 1,000 feet tall—arrayed around it. The towers are connected by wire forming three concentric circles. Inside of Tower Zero is an elevator that runs to the top of the tower.

Entering the tunnel that goes into the hillside at Tower Zero one finds an at least three-story underground base, with a 50 foot high by 15-foot diameter copper coil. The cover story is that the Exmouth site is transmitting very low frequency (VLF) or extremely low frequency (ELF) radio messages to submarines, but an examination of the facility reveals that it is a Tesla Magnifying Energy Transmitter, that is, a Tesla electromagnetic weapons system.

Another aspect of these events are huge blue-white light flashes of the type seen at Rocky Gully, Western Australia, in 1996. According to Australian researcher Harry Mason, "blue-white streamers of arcing electricity issued from the forest floor into the atmosphere, creating an intense, violent, blue-white glow (and an attendant 'electrical noise') that was visible for miles—'like someone with a giant arc welder'. This event persisted for at least several minutes. The observers fled the area in fear for their lives, phased out by the apparently enormous energy involved in the event."

According to Mason, "These massive energy bursts of high-altitude, blue-white and/or ground level electrical arcs are reasonably common and I have about 100 such documented events" listed in his database.

These may be the same high energy bursts that have been seen by pilots in clear skies, and detected by the Compton Gamma Ray Observatory satellite, launched in 1991 by the space shuttle, and the ALEXIS spy satellite. These satellites have detected radio and gamma ray bursts about 100,000 feet above the Earth, seen most frequently over Africa and South America. The scientists running these programs have not said much about the phenomena, "the likes of which are not described in the scientific literature." [7]

Retired U.S. Army Lieutenant Colonel Tom Bearden talked about similar phenomena in 1985. He said, "There have been a series of tests of these kinds of [electromagnetic] weapons, apparently for a number of years. For example, airliners from

Iran, before the fall of the Shah, saw deep within the Soviet Union very large, glowing spherical balls of light which started out small and then expanded to very large size, which are apparently these kind of weapons for use in an anti-ballistic missile defense role."

Bearden also stated, "...You can create, for example, either an electromagnetic explosion at a distance, or you can create an electromagnetic implosion at a distance... This would look like a cold explosion, so to speak, and I believe the thing on April the 9th, 1984, off the coast of Japan that involved several 747 jet airliners [is an example of this]."

747 Pilot Doug Happ was a witness of this event, in which a huge cloud was seen rising from an overcast area below. Happ said, "It looked like a plate coming up through the overcast, but it just kept expanding, and as it got higher it was apparent that you could see right through the middle of it, so it looked like a big smoke ring. At the time that we first noticed this cloud we weren't sure what to do and we took no evasive action because we didn't know which way to go, and I think eventually we either rammed through it or it completely engulfed us." When Happ's plane reached its destination, Anchorage, Alaska, it was checked for radioactive contamination. The result of the tests was negative. [8]

Another frequently observed aerial display is of orange-red vertical beams, reported since about 1985, with at least 100 events reported since that time.

Mason reports that, "One 1996 Brisbane beam event report was very significant as the observers saw very high-voltage, blue-white discharge streamers issuing from their house wall-mounted main power box as an orange beam hovered nearby in the sky. Members of another household reported their power box hummed violently as the orange beam hovered some distance in the sky.

"This data confirms the probability that Tesla-style longitudinal scalar EM potentials were involve in this Brisbane event (and therefore were possibly present during the other beam events), probably created by a remote Tesla EM transmitter..." [9]

The following radio interview provides additional insight on the current state of electromagnetic weaponry, and information on the sorts of advanced weaponry that may have been used to generate the Perth fireball and other events of this nature. It is excerpted from the Moscow broadcast of *The Voice of Russia:* "Science and Engineering," that aired December 12, 1996. The excerpt begins:

"Our next question is from Ross Dowe in Victoria, Australia. He's interested in science in general, but was particularly intrigued by a program last April, in which you, Boris, spoke of microwave generator development in Russia. He'd like you to return to the subject... First of all, could you explain why there is an interest in such generators"...

BORIS BELITSKY: Powerful microwave generators are of interest, for one thing, because of their possible military applications. They can be used to fire a plasmoid, that is, a blob of plasma...

YEKIMENKO: Remind us, Boris, just what is meant by plasma...

BELITZKY: Plasma is a mixture of electrons and ions. We have all seen it, for example, in electric arc discharges and in sparks. It is also a prime factor in thermonuclear reactions, as in the sun. Space scientists in this country have a long record of experimenting with it. For example, plasma engines were tested in some of the early Soviet Mars probes, a quarter of a century ago. Very extensive studies of plasma have been carried out under the program of research into controlled nuclear fusion. Research into the military applications has been conducted at some of the leading research institutes of the military-industrial complex, for example at the Research Institute of Radio Instruments.

YEKIMENKO: How would a microwave generator be used in anger, Boris?

BELITZKY: It would be used to fire a plasmoid, that is, a blob of plasma into the path of an incoming missile, its warhead, or an aircraft. The plasmoid would effectively ionize that region of space and, in this way, disturb the aerodynamics of the flight of the missile, warhead, or aircraft, terminate their flight, making such a generator and its plasmoid a practically invulnerable weapon, providing protection against attack via space or the atmosphere.

YEKIMENKO: Boris, I hate to ask this question, but still... The generals and scientists who speak of this weapon—they couldn't be bluffing, could they?

BELITZKY: Oh, no. This is evident if only from the fact that a few years ago in 1993, at the Russian-American summit in Vancouver, the Russians proposed a joint experiment in testing such generators—or plasma weapons, as they are called here—as an alternative to the Strategic Defense Initiative, SDI. In such an experiment, which it was proposed to code name "Trust," the system would be used to repulse a missile attack. In this way, Russia hoped to strengthen the new climate of post-Cold War security in the world.

YEKIMENKO: Is it known who is the leading scientist behind the development of plasma weapons in Russia?

BELITZKY: Yes. It is 65-year-old Rimily Avramenko, a graduate of the Moscow Institute of Power Engineering. In 1955 he started work under Alexander Mints at the research institute headed by that outstanding scientist. Then followed a period of work at the Sary-Shagan Proving Ground, not far from Lake Balkhash. It was there that he started work on anti-missile defense systems. He was a leading designer of the giant "Don" radar complex, which some specialists in the West dubbed the "Eighth Wonder of the World." As for plasma weapons, he has been working in that field since 1967.

YEKIMENKO: Was he the first scientist in this country to tackle the problem of anti-missile defense?

BELITZKY: No. The first was probably the famous Peter Kapitsa. When Kapitsa was banished in Stalin's time to his country home, he designed a weapons system based on microwave emission. That was in 1953, and he called the system the Nigotron, a contraction based on the name of the village where his country home was situated, Nikolina Gora. Other scientists interested in this possibility were Alexander Mints and Lev Artsimovich. These were actually Avramenko's mentors. All of them didn't believe in the effectiveness of (existing) "anti-missile" (technology). They felt a countermissile would not be effective against an incoming missile, protected by a stealth-type coating and a host of decoys. And they began looking for alternative solutions to the problem. They soon concluded that the most vulnerable factor in a missile attack was the media through which the incoming missiles traveled. And they decided that the best solution was to influence that medium. That was how the idea of using powerful microwave generators was born. [10]

NOTES:

1. Donnelly, John, "Hmmmmmmmm: Low-level sound not music to ears of those who hear it," Knight-Ridder news service, July 10, 1993; Haederle, Michael, "In Taos, Researchers Can Hum it, but They Can't Name That Sound", *Los Angeles Times,* September 1, 1993
2. Birmingham *Alabama Post Herald,* March 26, 1992; "The Hueytown Hum," *Fortean Times* issue 65
3. Dickenson, Fred and Phyll, "The 'Noise' in New Zealand", *Would You Believe* magazine, undated clipping
4. Donnelly
5. Kanon, Gregory M., *The Great UFO Hoax.* (Lakeville, Minnesota: Galde Press, 1997)
6. Mason, Harry. "Bright Skies: Top-Secret Weapons Testing?", *Nexus* magazine, April/May and June/July 1997
7. Petit, Charles. "Scientists Are Unable to Explain High-Atmosphere Gamma Ray Bursts", *San Francisco Chronicle,* May 27, 1994; and *Washington Post,* February 14, 1994, cited in *Flatland* magazine, number 11
8. CNN "Special Assignment", undated transcript from about 1985
9. Mason
10. *The Leading Edge* magazine, issue 100

Chapter 30:

LETHAL NON-LETHALS

One of the current buzzphrases making the rounds in military and government circles is "non-lethality." This term is used to describe a class of weapons—including electronics—that do not kill persons but disable them. They are "soft kill" weapons, and in public discussions of the topic, developments such as nets, rubber bullets, snares, malodorous sprays, aqueous foams that 'befuddle combatants' senses and effectiveness', lubricants that make walking impossible, and particles that gum up mechanical systems are mentioned. These examples, while great for the fluff purveyed by *Time Magazine* or *Popular Science,* carefully do not betray the rationale behind thinking in the "non-lethal" warfare zone.

"Non-lethality" is not, in fact, a description of a type of weapon, but a way of thinking about warfare. The real purpose of non-lethality is to more finely tune control, to create a more precise and responsive infrastructure of control on both the battlefield and in everyday society.

Interest in non-lethality began with the brainstorming of a man named John Alexander. Alexander had been a commander of Green Berets in Vietnam, leading Cambodian mercenaries, and engaging in secret programs including the infamous Phoenix assassination operation. After returning to the States and getting a Ph.D. from Walden University, he studied the near-death experience with Elisabeth Kubler-Ross and became an official spokesperson for Silva Mind Control.

In 1980 Alexander published an article in the U.S. Army's *Military Review,* titled "The New Mental Battlefield." Far from compounds resembling artificial banana peels to make armies slip and slide, Alexander's thesis was that telepathy could be used as an offensive weapon, and that electronic weapons might also be used for interfering with the brain activity of target groups.

Alexander was encouraged by two senior army officials to do

additional research in the area, and this led to his joining the special technologies group at Los Alamos National Laboratories. There Alexander began a collaboration with Janet Morris, also a grad of Silva, and Research Director of the U.S. Global Strategy Council think tank, whose chairman is Ray Cline, former Deputy Director of the CIA. The USGSC's lobbying was responsible for the creation of the Non-lethality Policy Review Group, led by Major General Chris S. Adams, USAF (retd.), former Chief of Staff, Strategic Air Command. This group has encouraged the military to think in terms of non-lethality.

In 1991 Janet Morris issued several papers promoting the concept of non-lethality, suggesting an escalation in certain key areas of military research and production. These included technologies directed at the destruction of weapons of war, but also an increased focus on anti-personnel electromagnetics. This latter category of weapons would include hand-held lasers for blinding the enemy, "isotropic radiators", essentially a larger scale laser for blinding the enemy that was reportedly used during the Iraqi war, infrasound weapons, and very low frequency weapons.

Morris, in her "In Search of a Non-Lethal Strategy" states, "Some very low frequency sound generators, in certain frequency ranges, can cause the disruption of human organs and, at high power levels, can crumble masonry."

Another take is provided by the Strategic Studies Institute (SSI) of the U.S. Army War College, in Pennsylvania. The 1994 paper "The Revolution in Military Affairs and Conflict Short of War" posits thay "Many American strategic thinkers believe that we are in the beginning stages of a historical revolution in military affairs." They even give it an acronym: RMA. "This will not only change the nature of warfare, but also alter the global geopolitical balance."

According to the RMA manifesto there are a number of new avenues of warfare research that should be pursued, specifically "behavior modification" and "Technology designed specifically for conflict short of war, especially psychological, biological, and defensive technology." Also mentioned is that "large numbers of Americans may find themselves in areas of instability and conflict," and that such individuals should be "equipped with an electronic individual position locator device (IPLD). The device, derived from the electronic bracelet used to control some criminal offenders or parolees, would continuously inform a central data bank of the individuals' locations. Eventually such a device could be permanently implanted under the skin."

The authors of the study lament the fact that "The use of the new technology may also run counter to basic American values," and, "Deception, while frequently of great military or political value, is thought of as somehow 'un-American.'"

This is particularly true when it is practiced by Americans upon Americans, the authors of the paper omit mentioning, although they do have a solution: "Overcoming these constraints to make a RMA in conflict short of war would require fundamental change in the United States—an ethical and political revolution may be necessary to make a military revolution."

The authors state that as far as "constraints and countermeasures," "there is another alternative: we could deliberately engineer a comprehensive revolution, seeking utter transformation rather than simply an expeditious use of new technology."

No, all indications suggest that non-lethal weaponry is not about sticky foam and rubber bullets for crowd control. [1]

A report issued by the Pentagon's Commission on Roles and Missions of May 1995 outlined four current military priorities. These were, as noted by *Aviation Week & Space Technology* magazine, (1) "combating the proliferation of weapons of mass destruction" (2) "information warfare" (3)"peace operations" (4) and "operations other than war." Although non-lethal weapons might be of some use in arenas such as Bosnia and Somalia, note that this breed of military engagement might just as well be applied to the policing of American urban areas, or the suppression of a peace march. [2]

According to military sources, with non-lethal technology they are attempting to create an "architecture" to handle "in-between" situations. An article in *Aviation Week & Space Technology* on non-lethality is worth quoting at length:

"'The most profound implication of the new era often goes unremarked: Namely, that the basic rationale for defense planning has shifted from threat to capability, and from liability to opportunity,' Adm. William A. Owens, vice chairman of the Joint Chiefs of Staff, wrote in the Naval Institute Press 'Proceedings' in May. Today, 'we must face the issue of the political purpose of military force directly. It is no longer simply a matter of thinking it enough to counter successfully a defined military threat; we must design military forces more specifically in terms of their political purposes. In short, we must rebuild an intellectual framework that links our forces to our policy—no small task in a revolutionary era.'

"Scientists and military officers insist that new peacekeeping/peace enforcement tactics and weapons can be effective only if merged with comprehensive, advanced information systems. Space, airborne and ground-based sensors—including unattended devices—would provide a flood of data that enable decisive actions in non-combat situations. Information must be processed and routed to the proper authorities in time to preclude hostile action, ideally, or to enable rapid response if firing occurs.

"Sandia's [Gerold] Yonas maintained that this 'system of systems' will require an up-front science-based systems engineering (SBSE) approach to ensure resources are used effectively. Sensors, information systems, communications and rules-of-engagement must be coordinated within a comprehensive architecture. 'If you don't do it all right, you won't have a symphony. And massive use of force will not work. The bad guys will win,' he said." [3]

One aspect of non-lethality, "information warfare," was pursued at the Stanford Research Institute's Project Grill Flame at Langley, an investigation of "remote viewing," i.e., out-of-body perception. The remote viewers were culled from Church of Scientology members classed as OTs and Clears. Clear is essentially a non-neurotic case, a level with a definition that has been adjusted progressively downward in capability since Hubbard's early pronouncements about near-supermen.

OT is the terminology for Operating Thetan, the term "thetan" taken from the Greek letter *theta* and used as the terminology for "spirit" in Scientology. Scientology OTs believe that they are free to operate as spirits outside of their physical bodies, thus presumably aiding their ability at remote viewing.

Scientologists involved in the Grill Flame project included Ingo Swann, Harold Puthoff, and Pat Price, although I believe that Swann has since become disaffected from the church and is now a member of a spin-off group called Avatar. At the time of the experiments, Swann is said to have denied CIA involvement but later copped: "It was rather common knowledge all along who the sponsor was, although in documents the identity of the Agency was concealed behind the sobriquet of 'an east coast scientist.' The Agency's interest was quite extensive. A number of agents of the CIA came themselves ultimately to SRI to act as subjects in remote viewing experiments, as did some members of Congress."

An additional Grill Flame laboratory was added at Fort Meade in Maryland, run by General Stubblebine. One of the participants was Major Ed Dames, currently a frequent visitor to the Art Bell radio show, fanning the flames of interest in out-of-body jaunts and apocalyptic endtime scenarios, but oddly avoiding any mention of government mind control proclivities.

A British media correspondent who visited the facility at Fort Meade found out that medical oversight for the experiments was run by Louis Jolyon West. West was also conducting his own experiments at the time on "phenomenology of disassociative states," a description that could span the whole spectrum of mind control interests, but may be centered on research documented in his "Pseudo-Identity and the Treatment of Personality Changes in Victims of Captivity and Cults" (1994).

West states, "Prolonged environmental stress or life situations profoundly different from the usual, can disrupt the normally integrative functions of personality. Individuals subjected to such forces may adapt through dissociation by generating an altered persona, or pseudo-identity."

From the CIA experimentation in remote viewing with SRI, a gamut of private projects have been launched. [4]

In 1997, the Air Force upped the ante on non-lethality—and mind control—by creating the position of Deputy Director for Information Operations. Far from the Public Relations position that it sounds like, it is in fact a division for "offensive information warfare," that will be headed by Lt. Col. Jimmy Miyamoto. The Information Operations office will coordinate with the Joint Chiefs of Staff, the National Security Agency, Defense Intelligence Agency, the CIA, the National Reconnaissance Office, Defense Airborne Reconnaissance Office, and the National Imagery and Mapping Agency. The duties of the office, according to *Defense Week*, will be to coordinate Air Force efforts in non-lethality, including a psychological operations drive to create holographic projectors with the capability "to project persuasive messages and three-dimensional pictures of cloud, smoke, rain droplets, buildings... The use of holograms as a persuasive message will have worldwide application." [5]

Another informative look at closure that is currently taking place in the area of military weaponry is provided in an article by Colonel Michael Aquino, titled "From PSYOP to MindWar: The Psychology of Victory," that was reportedly submitted by Aquino to the Washington publication *Military Review*, but apparently rejected, thence sent in photocopies to members of Aquino's Temple of Set organization and others.

Aquino, whose last published photo of himself shows a man

who looks like Grandpa Munster, complete with the prominent widow's peak, is a familiar name to those who have researched political conspiracy; for newcomers, his dossier bears repetition.

Aquino received a master's degree in political science from the University of California at Santa Barbara and has reportedly qualified in Defense Attache, Strategic Intelligence, Psychological Operations, Special Forces, and the Airborne divisions in the army, supposedly reporting directly to the Joint Chiefs of Staff. Aquino reportedly served as a Tactical Psychological Operations officer in the 82nd Airborne in Vietnam, and received the Bronze Star, the Air Medal, and the Vietnamese Cross of Gallantry. In 1973 Aquino became executive officer of the 306th Psychological Operations Battalion at Fort McArthur in California. During the 1970s Aquino was a prominent member of the Church of Satan but became disillusioned with LaVey's sideshow-style antics and started his own group, the Temple of Set.

According to a police intelligence report, dated July 1, 1981, the Temple of Set "is a small group but nonetheless has several hundred members and operates on a national level. Aquino is the official head of the organization and rules the organization through a council of nine, who are in fact his chief lieutenants." At least two members of the "council of nine" at that time were members of Army Intel.

The army, interestingly enough, has never expressed any problem with Aquino's satanic beliefs, either during his association with LaVey or afterward. It is not outside the realm of possibility that LaVey's satanic practices are in fact army sponsored. According to a Pentagon spokesperson, "Aquino has an absolute constitutional right [to his belief]... unless there is illegal behavior associated with it."

In the late 1980s Aquino and an associate, Gary Hambright, were accused by the San Francisco Police Department of being involved in a satanic child molestation ring centered around the Presidio military base, where Aquino was stationed at the time. Twenty-two families filed $66 million in claims against the army. Although formal charges were never filed against Aquino, only against his associate, it is reported that parents of children allegedly abused claimed that it was because the army pressured federal investigators and the San Francisco police not to pursue the case.

Apparently there were satanic activities taking place at the Presidio at the time, as confirmed by the on-site investigation of Bay Area reporter Linda Goldston, who found a bunker behind the intelligence offices with ritual symbols painted on the walls. For a more complete reporting of the case, read *The New Satanists*, by Linda Blood.

After the child molestation scandal, Aquino was transferred to the National Defense University in Washington, D.C.

Aquino's *MindWar* article, attributed on the cover page to the "HEADQUARTERS IMPERIAL STORMTROOPER FORCE/Office of the Chief of Staff/MindWar Center/Hub Four", discusses the use of psychotronic weapons—i.e. electronic weapons that influence the mind—and the use of LBM, Lesser Black Magic, for the control of populations.

The crazy science fiction imaginings of a satanist? Yes, but also the imaginings of a highly-placed member of U.S. Army intelligence, and almost certainly clearly reflective of the ambitions of the controllers of this world. [6]

NOTES:

1. Krawczyk, Glenn, "Big Brother's Recipe for 'Revolution in Military Affairs'", *Nexus* magazine, June/July 1995
2. Scott, William B., "Panel's Report Backs Nonlethal Weapons", *Aviation Week & Space Technology,* October 16, 1995
3. Ibid.; Ricks, Thomas E. "Nonlethal Arms: New Class of Weapons Could Incapacitate Foe Yet Limit Casualties," *The Wall Street Journal,* January 4, 1993
4. Swann, Ingo. Cited in *Virtual Government* by Alex Constantine, (Venice, California: Feral House, 1997); West, Louis Jolyon. Cited in Constantine
5. "Air Force Organizes for Offensive Info War", *Defense Week* magazine, March 31, 1997
6. Raschke, Carl A., *Painted Black.* (San Francisco: Harper & Row, 1990); Blood, Linda, *The New Satanists.* (New York: Warner Books, 1994)

DRUGS TESTED BY THE CIA UNDER PROJECTS BLUEBIRD, ARTICHOKE, MKULTRA, AND MKDELTA:

1. Adrenalin
2. Aktetron
3. Alcohol
4. Amphetamine
5. Amphetamine Sulphate
6. Analasine
7. Anhalamine
8. Anhalidine
9. Anhaline
10. Anhalonidine
11. Analonine
12. Anhalonium
13. Aphyllidine
14. Aphyllin
15. Atropine
16. Atrosine
17. Bambusa
18. Banisterine
19. Barbiturate
20. Belladonna
21. Benzidrene
22. Bendocaine
23. Bromoharmine
24. Bulbocapnine
25. Butyl-bromally-barbituric acid
26. Caffeine
27. Caffeine sodium
28. Calcium chloride (35)
29. Cannabidiol
30. Cannabinol
31 Cannabis
32. Cannabol
33. Caramine (narcotic)
34. Carboline
35. Caroegine
36. Chloral hydrate
37. Cocaine
38. Coffee
39. Coramine
40. Delvinyl sodium
41. Di benzo pyran derivatives
42. Dicain
43. Dramamine
44. Ephedrine
45. Ephetamine
46. Epinephrine
47. Ergot
48. Ergotamine
49. Ethyl harmol
50. Eucaine
51. Eucodal
52. Eukotal
53. Eunacron
54. Epicane
55. Escrine
56. Ether
57. Evipal
58. Evipan
59. Evipan Sodium
60. Evipan Sodium (35)
61. Genoscopolomine
62. Harmaline
63. Harmalol
64. Harman
65. Harmine
66. Harmine methiodide
67. Harmol
68. Heroin
69. Hexacol
70. Histadyl
71. Hydractine
72. Hypoloid soluble hexabarbitone
73. Icoral
74. Indole
75. Indole methyllarmine
76. Insulin
77. Lophop-nine
78. Lyscorbic acid
79. (illegible)
80. (illegible)
81. (illegible)
82. (illegible)
83. Manganese chloride (35)
84. Methy-cocaine
85. Metra-ol
86. Morphine
87. Morphine hyrdochloride
88. Narco-imal
89. Nambutal
90. Nicotine
91. Nikthemine (narcotic)
92. Nitrous oxide
93. Novacaine
94. Nupercaine
95. Pantocaine
96. Pantopone
97. Parahyx
98. Pellotine
99. Pentobarbitol sodium
100. Pentothal acid
101. Pentothal sodium
102. Percaine
103. Pernoston
104. Peyotl
105. Phenactin
106. Phenamine
107. Pehyl-thio-urethanes
108. Picrate
109. Picrotoxin
110. Procaine
111. Pulegone-orcinol
112. Pulegone-olivetol
113. Pyrahexyl
114. Pyramidon
115. Quinie
116. Salsoline
117. Scolpolmine
118. Scolpolmine aminoxide hydrobromide
119. Scopolomine-pheta-mine-eukotal
120. Sodium (62)
121. Sodium amatyl
122. Sodium barbital
123. Sodium dlelvinal
124. Sodium evipal
125. Sodium pentobarbital (nembutal)
126. Sodium pentothal
127. Sodium phenobarbital
128. Sodium rhodanate
129. Sodium soneryl
130. Sodium succinate (77)
131. Sodium thioethamyl
132. Somnifen
133. Stovaine
134. Strychnine
135. Styphnic acid
136. Sympatol
137. Synhexyl
138. Telepathine
139. Tatra-hydro-cannibol-acetate
140. Tetra-hydro-harman
141. Tetra-hydro-harmine
142. Tropacocaine
143. Tropenone
144. Yageine
145. Yohimbine sulphate

Chapter 31:

ALIENS FROM EARTH

Since the beginning of attention to the phenomenon at the middle of this century, the government has been involved in manipulation of the UFO experience for own purposes. I believe that the primary reason that government agents have been involved in the UFO field has been to confuse the issue of advanced aeronautics and weapons testing—for instance, with disinformation that has turned the secret Nevada testing base Area 51 into a hotbed of extraterrestrial alien activity.

The government has even admitted issuing disinformational reports during the 1950s and '60s about UFOs that were in fact U-2 spyplane flights, but that admission serves as a cover-up in itself. I have commented at length upon this situation in my *Casebook on Alternative 3* and *Casebook on the Men in Black,* and the interested reader may follow that avenue at greater length there.

When examining the issue of mind control related to the UFO experience, there is remarkable information showing that government manipulation may go far beyond the creation of disinformation, and the befuddling of researchers. Information has come to light in recent years suggesting that many cases of so-called alien abduction may conceal another reality entirely: that of the simulation of alien abduction as a cover for mind control experimentation.

This possibility has been explored at length in a recent bookby Gregory Kanon on UFOs, *The Great UFO Hoax: The Final Solution to the UFO Mystery,* but other researchers have traversed this territory for years, including Martin Cannon, John Judge, Jacques Vallee, and myself. I believe that the deceased conspiracy researcher Mae Brussell may have been the first to suggest the idea of simulated alien abduction as a cover for mind control testing in one of her radio shows.

One of the first persons in the intelligence community to suggest that UFOs might serve a useful purpose was H. Marshall

Caldwell, the Assistant Director for Scientific Intelligence for the CIA. He wrote a memo to then-CIA Director Walter Smith reporting that,

"With world-wide sightings reported, it was found that, up to the time of the investigation, there had been in the Soviet press no report or comment, even satirical, on flying saucers, though Gromyko had made one humorous mention of the subject. With a State-controlled press, this could result only from an official policy decision. The question, therefore, arises as to whether or not these sightings:

"(1) could be controlled,

"(2) could be predicted, and

"(3) could be used from a psychological warfare point of view, either offensively or defensively.

"The public concerns with the phenomena, which is reflected both in the United States press and in the pressure of inquiry upon the Air Force, indicates that a fair proportion of our population is mentally conditioned to the acceptance of the incredible. In this fact lies the potential for the touching-off of mass hysteria and panic."

Caldwell also suggests,

"A study should be instituted to determine what, if any, utilization could be made of these phenomena by United States psychological warfare planners..."

On July 16, 1978, UFO witness Sergeant Clifford E. Stone, attempting to get to the bottom of the UFO question, filed a Freedom of Information Act request to the National Security Agency. One of the documents that Stone obtained was a National Security Agency unofficial draft titled "SUBJECT: UFO'S". The interesting material in the paper began a few paragraphs in:

"...2. Scientific Findings: Dr. Jacques Vallee, famed communications science expert, has studied thousands of cases where human beings have observed unusual phenomena. He has found that the human response to such observation is predictable and graphically depictable. Whether the person's psychological structure is being assaulted by the unusual and shocking brutality of a murder or the strangeness of a UFO sighting, the effect is the same:

"a. Initially as by a kind of psychological inertia, the mind records fairly objectively what the eye is reporting.

"b. But when it has realized the strange nature of the phenomena it goes into shock. The mind likes to live in a comfortable world where it feels it knows what to expect, and that is not too threatening either physically or psychologically. The unusual dispels the comfortable illusion the mind has created. This shock tears at the very mooring of the human psychological structure.

"c.   To protect itself against such an intrusive and threatening reality the mind will begin to add imagination and interpretation to the incoming data to make it more acceptable. Since the mind is doing all this in haste some of the hurriedly added details and suggestions tumble over one another and contradict one another in a bizarre fashion (as any police officer interrogating murder witnesses will tell you).

"d.   Once the mind has constructed a safe framework for the new information it may again peek out and collect some more objective data. If the data is still threatening it will again go into shock and the process starts all over again.

"e.   If the data is at the highest strangeness level where it brings terror either:

"(1)   The mind will pass out and go into amnesia burying the events perhaps permanently in the unconsciousness.

"(2)   The personal psychological will collapse and the mind will reach down into its deepest place where "that which cannot be destroyed" is and it will abandon itself to this entity for survival protection.   Encounter with this changeless indestructible entity is usually referred to as a religious experience.   In the confusion and the shock, this experience is often attributed to the shocking event or object and that is why primitive peoples worship such bizarre things as airplanes or cigarette lighters.

"f.   The degree of strangeness of the phenomena dictates how many people the mind is willing and able to tell the event to.   A mildly unusual or shocking event will be told to many people.   A very shocking event of high strangeness will be told to few people or practically none at all.   Occasionally the event is so shockingly unusual that it isn't even reported to the person's conscious mind but is buried in the unconscious of the person where it is only accessible to hypnosis or careful level six communication, sharing with another person."

This fascinating, even "Tavistockian" document seems to go well beyond the average military reporting on the UFO phenomenon, and illustrates well why simulated UFO abduction may be useful to mind controllers: the experience is so incredible and so demeaning that it is communicated to few if any other persons, and sometimes may exist in memory only at an unconscious level.   Additionally, "high strangeness" may in fact be a means of accessing deeper levels of the mind.

In the late 1980s Dr. Michael Persinger, a neurologist at the Laurentian University of Ontario, Canada, did initial tests on what has come to be known as the 'Persinger helmet." This is a device that directs specific electromagnetic frequencies at the hippocampus area of the back brain of the person wearing it. According to Persinger, using the helmet, a large percentage of subjects feel that they have been abducted by UFOs, have gone out of body, or have experienced other forms of altered consciousness, including 'union with God.' The experience, Persinger says, "involves a widening of emotional meaning, such that things not typically considered significant would now be considered meaningful." During back brain irradiation, hallucinations are "perceived as extremely real."

Susan Blackmore, who experienced the Persinger technology, wrote of it in the *New Scientist* in November, 1994: "Persinger applied a silent and invisible force to my brain and created a specific experience for me. He claimed that he was imitating the basic sequences of the processes of memory and perception and that, by varying those sequences, he could control my experience. Could he have done it from a distance? Could it be done on a wider scale? Suddenly prospects of magnetic mind control seem an awful lot worse than the idea of being abducted by imaginary aliens..." [1]

Persinger was involved in Operation Black Beauty, the creation of a refrigerator-sized electromagnetic broadcasting unit used to quell riots. The device is said to employ time-varying fields of extremely low frequency energy, broadcast at frequencies between 1 and 10 hertz, that cause vomiting in whomever the unit is trained on. [2]

A short and non-definitive digression into a related phenomenon: cattle mutilations. These are the thousands of mysterious cases of cattle that since the late 1960s have been found dissected, sometimes in a surgical fashion, and which are usually linked in the media to flying saucer intervention. A case could be made for the "mutes" being an issue of mind control in themselves, but put that aside. There is a large body of evidence suggesting that the mutilations are of a far more terrestrial nature than tabloid TV will allow us to imagine.

For starters, UFOs are almost never seen in the vicinity of cattle mutilation, that is, using the strict definition of unidentified flying OBJECTS. What are seen are usually unidentified lights and, when a craft is seen, it is usually a black unmarked helicopter. There is no limit to the rabidity of some

UFO buffs, and so the black choppers are sometimes mentioned as being shape-shifting extraterrestrial craft, when in fact there is no evidence whatsoever to suggest this. Why not, instead, go out on a limb and simply imagine that they are black helicopters?

Other evidence suggests that men, not alien monsters, are doing the mutilations. Toxicology tests sometimes show the presence of nicotine in the bovine carcasses, and nicotine is a commonly used ingredient in tranquilizer dart drugs. The animals are sometimes found to have been marked with fluorescent paint, presumably for identification in the dark. Also, often seen in the vicinity of mutilations are truck-trailer rigs, large enough for transporting small helicopters. At least one probable staging area for the mutilation episodes has been identified in Colorado, as noted in my book *Black Helicopters II: The Endgame Strategy.*

Why would humans be interested in mutilating cattle? The most probable answer was provided by G.C. Errianne, a private investigator who looked into the matter. Erriane indicated that covert government testing was done using cattle due to the similarity of the membrane of the eye with "a certain ethnic group." Further investigation showed that the U.S. government had been involved in testing biowarfare weapons specifically targeted to at least two ethnicities. [3]

As far as government manipulation involving humans, one of the "premier" abduction cases that seems to have set the stage for many that followed was that of Betty and Barney Hill. In 1961 the Hills were motoring in Groveton, New Hampshire, when a flying disk craft approached and hovered at a distance. The Hills fled in their car but later, because of nightmares, consulted a psychiatrist and were hypnotized. Six months of therapy seemed to reveal an abduction and physical examination by humanoids in the disk craft.

The nature of the abduction itself was quite strange, with the inhabitants of the saucer craft being described by Betty Hill under hypnosis as wearing uniforms and billed caps ("similar to Air Force," she said during hypnotic regression). Barney Hill thought that one of the supposed aliens looked like a "military pilot," and amended that: "He looks like a German Nazi. He's a Nazi..." Hill said, "I thought of the Navy and the submarine, and I thought the men that moved back were just dressed in blue denims. But this other man was dressed in a black shiny coat, with a cap on."

If the government was involved in the abduction, what might

have brought the Hills to their attention was the fact that they were an interracial couple, and held organizational positions in a number of civil rights groups. This was at a time when such groups were under close scrutiny by the government, and it may have suited military psy-ops to either examine the Hills hypnotically, or even implant bugging devices for surveillance. The Hills were also close friends with Major James McDonald, reportedly working in intelligence at Pease Air Force Base. [4]

Another famous abductee whose experience deserves closer scrutiny is Whitley Streiber. Streiber went to the Fabian-founded London School of Economics in England. While in London, he directed a film about The Process cult group, although with no prints of the film available, it is not known what position Streiber took in regards to the cult.

In his best-selling book about abduction, *Communion*, Streiber notes that for years he had believed that he was present at the Charles Whitman shooting spree at the University of Texas, but finally realized that he wasn't. In the sequel, *Transformation*, Streiber realizes that he must have been, because of a friend's confirmation. [5]

Streiber believes that he has two implants in his body, one in an earlobe, the other injected into a little finger. At the 1996 Gulf Breeze, Florida, UFO Conference Streiber mentioned the idea that he might have been the subject of mind control operations by the government. He speculated that his believed experiences with extraterrestrial aliens may in fact have been broadcast to him through the implants. [6]

Martin Cannon, a pioneer in making the distinction between little grey men from outer space and those from the government, describes the case of a woman he calls "Veronica." She was abducted not into a flying saucer, but into the house of a scientist in Los Angeles who, Cannon was able to determine, had earlier been involved in CIA mind control experimentation.

I investigated the case of a young woman who, in 1993, believed that during a visit in San Francisco with the head of a satanic church she had been drugged and taken to a nearby hotel where she was operated upon by humans in white coats. On another occasion she was taken outside of San Francisco by the same satanic chief and was shown a disk craft parked at some distance from a rural road. [7]

And if Jolly West and his crowd are promoting "False Memory Syndrome," they are also pushing "Alien Memory Syndrome." According to an Australian researcher, "one of Louis Jolyon West's protegés, Barry Taff, co-wrote an article for *UFO* magazine suggesting aliens were responsible for this type of [mind control] activity. Taff worked at the UCLA Neuropsychiatric Institute, and according to Los Angeles based researcher Martin Cannon, has consulted for a large number of government agencies, including the National Institute of Mental Health, Rand Corporation, the Atomic Energy Commission and the CIA."

Val Bankston, who believed that she had been abducted by aliens, met Taff and agreed to participate in some experiments on abduction with him. Bankston said, "You may recognize the name Barry Taff. He researched and wrote a movie called 'The Entity.' He also conducts parapsychology investigations, pursues effects that he covertly produces himself with high technology. Oddly enough, shortly after we met, I was assaulted by a disembodied entity in broad daylight who engaged in sexual acts with me. At the time, I believed it was an incubus. Knowing what I do about Barry, the fact that he is a certified hypnotist, for one I believe that he hypnotized both me and the other subject of his research—which led to the movie 'The Entity'—into having these experiences. He may have treated several women this way and picked the one that best bolstered his book and movie scheme." [8]

Another remarkable case is that of Bruce Smith, who in 1990 attended a lecture by "alien abduction expert" Budd Hopkins in Trenton, New Jersey. For some reason Hopkins' talk about alien abductions hit Smith at a visceral level, unnerving him: "I didn't think I was going to be able to walk out of there," he said later.

But Smith did walk out of the UFO lecture and, hooking his trailer home onto the back of his car, went west, stopping in state parks. One of those state parks was in Tesuque, New Mexico. Smith was asleep in a campground there when he woke up in the middle of the night, horrified with the belief that aliens were going to abduct him. Drifting between sleep and wakefulness, Smith felt hands grasp his ankles and pull. But the being on the other end of those hands was not quite what Smith had been led to expect. The "being" was wearing a white button-down shirt, the kind of shirt that his father had always worn, Smith recalled.

Far from his expectation of a glowing silver saucer craft, Smith says that he was manhandled into the back of a large, dark blue van with military markings that he thinks were of the U.S. Navy. The van drove over rough roads for an hour until it stopped. The rear door of the van was opened and aliens levitated Smith out the back door and into a huge structure that

Smith feels is part of the Los Alamos nuclear laboratory.

Inside the laboratory, Smith was placed on an examination table where an alien named "Roget" gouged at his eyes with a scalpel.

Smith remembered none of this until he began hypnotherapy in Washington. During hypnosis he remembered the abduction, and also recalled that he had been abducted "thousands of times and during many lifetimes." After the encounter in Tesuque, "They came back one more time. On the eighth of June. They came in an unusual ship that had rooms in it that looked like college dorm rooms."

Was Smith actually abducted by aliens, or is the truth something more prosaic but equally sinister? [9]

UFO abduction researcher Budd Hopkins turns up in another case, described by former Army Intelligence case officer Julianne McKinney, now of the Electronic Surveillance Project Association of National Security Alumni. McKinney's account follows:

"The woman, apparently a 'pet' experimentee, found herself being introduced to a wide variety of prominent individuals whose connections with the CIA she believed to be quite apparent. One of those, she states, was Robert Jay Lifton, a well known author and expert on brainwashing, whose books include *The Nazi Doctors: Medical Killing* and the *Psychology of Genocide* (Basic books, 1986).

"Her experiences included a voluntary ('referral') admission to Hollywood Hospital, Vancouver, British Columbia, Canada, in 1973, during an era when MKULTRA experiments in the Allan Memorial Institute, McGill University, Montreal, Canada, were only beginning to capture the attention of the U.S. Senate.

"More recently, in 1990, she was transported to New York University's Cameron Medical Center, in Westchester, NY (under circumstances which qualify as an abduction), where she was forcibly wrestled to the ground by approximately six Center staffers and forcibly confined for a period of approximately three weeks. She was neither psychiatrically counseled nor formally tested while in that facility. The psychiatrists assigned to her case appeared more intent on forcing her to take a combination of neuroleptic drugs, to include Haldol, Navane and Cogentin. (Haldol and Navane can cause tardive dyskinesia.) She resisted those attempts.

"A court ultimately ordered this woman released from the Center, stipulating that she was not to be administered drugs. On subsequently acquiring her medical records, under conditions which prevented censoring or doctoring of those records, she found that her psychiatrists had planned to inject her with drugs (in defiance of the court order) on the day of her release. As luck would have it, she was released a day early.

"This woman states also that she has met Budd Hopkins, of the Intruders Foundation, and that she had a long-term, confiding relationship with John E. Mack, Professor of Psychiatry, Harvard Medical School, and founding Director of the Center for Psychological Studies in the Nuclear Age (previously named Research Program for the Study of Human Continuity; and still previously rumored to have cooperated with the CIA in studies of 'human ecology')." [10]

In recent years there have been cases of "alien" implants being surgically removed, but it is interesting that the "aliens" would coincidentally be employing a technology similar to that invented by Dr. Delgado in the 1950s. One such instance was described in a lecture by Dr. Roger Leir, at a MUFON meeting in Thousand Oaks, California, on February 23, 1996. Leir removed three apparent implants on August 19, 1995, two from one patient and one from another patient. The two alleged implants removed from the first patient were located on each side of her large toe. The third alleged implant was removed from the back of the left hand of another patient.

One object was triangular in shape, while the other two objects "resembled small cantaloupe seeds." [11]

Surrounding the implants the tissue was grey but without inflammation. According to Darrel Sims, a hypno-anestheia therapist and UFO abduction researcher, both persons had been unaware of the implants, but they were discovered during unrelated x-ray procedures. There were no scar traces from injection of the implants. Both patients, according to Sims, were possible cases of UFO abduction. Dr. Leir also reports that the objects were in close proximity to nerve fibers.

Dr. Leir used a gauss meter, measuring electromagnetic fields, in finding the exact locations of the objects. According to Dr. Leir, when he brought the gauss meter near the object in the man's hand, it "went crazy."

Each of the objects is reported to have been covered with a dense grey membrane. Although objects that have been in a human body for a long time do get coated with an organic, fibrous coating, this material can be scraped off. In the case of the alleged implants, the membrane was much more difficult to remove. Inside the membrane the objects were two separate pieces of black metal, apparently held together only by the membrane. The metal was later identified as boron. When exposed to fluorescent light, all three objects glowed brightly. [12]

Harvard's John Mack, in *Abductions,* provides a detailed look at another "alien" implant:

"Elemental analyses and electronic microscopic photography revealed an interestingly twisted fiber consisting of carbon, silicon, oxygen, no nitrogen, and traces of other elements. A carbon isotopic analysis was not remarkable. A nuclear biologist colleague said the 'specimen' was not a naturally occurring biological subject but could be a manufactured fiber of some sort. It seemed difficult to know how to proceed further.

"There is no evidence that any of the implants recovered are of rare elements, or of common ones in unusual combinations. In discussions with a chemical engineer and other experts in materials technology, I have been told that it would be extremely difficult to make a positive diagnosis of the nature of any unknown substance without having information about its origins. Under the best of circumstances it would be difficult to prove, for example, that a substance was not of terrestrial or even biological origins."

Of course John Mack is an interesting case in himself, a man who seemingly refuses to consider the idea that abductions might be performed by anyone other than extraterrestrials. Mack's Center for Psychology and Social Change is backed to the tune of hundreds of thousands of dollars by various members of the Rockefeller family. Mack is also a member of Scott Jones' Human Potential Foundation, also reported to be Rockefeller-endowed. [13]

My conclusion is mad and science fictional, but the evidence supports it. Military and intelligence agencies are using alien abduction as a cover story and possibly as close encounters simulated by technology such as holograms and advanced aerial disk craft to conceal the processing and implanting of human beings with mind control technology.

NOTES:

1. Smith, Jerry, *HAARP: Ultimate Weapon of the Conspiracy,* (1997: AUP, Kempton, Illinois); Constantine, Alex, *Psychic Dictatorship in the U.S.A.* (Portland, Oregon: Feral House, 1995); Blackmore, Susan, "Alien Abduction," the *New Scientist* magazine, November 1994, cited in Walter Bowart's "The Trial and Conviction of a 'EBE Possessed' Serial Killer," obtained on the Internet from *MindNet Journal,* volume 1, numbers 8a, 8b,8c

2. Krawczyk, Glenn. "Mind Control & the New World Order", *Nexus* magazine, February/March 1993

3. Sanders, Ed. "The Mutilation Mystery", *Oui Magazine*, September, 1976; Keith, Jim, *Black Helicopters II: The Endgame Strategy*, (Lilburn, Georgia: IllumiNet Press, 1997)

4. "Manchurian abductees," *World Watchers International* newsletter, Fall 1989; Keith, Jim, *Casebook on Alternative 3*, (Lilburn, Georgia: IllumiNet Press, 1994)

5. Wanderer, Robert, "'Transformation' Transformed", *MUFON Journal*, issue 254, June 1989

6. "False Miracles in the Sky: Is the U.S. Military in the Business of Hoaxing UFOs?," *The Devil's Advocate*, issue number 5

7. Cannon, Martin. "The Controllers: A New Hypothesis of Alien Abductions", *MUFON UFO Journal*, Number 270, October 1990

8. Taff, Barry, 'Paranormal Phenomena and UFOs,' *UFO* magazine, Vol. 2, No 4; Krawczyk; Constantine, Alex, *Virtual Government*. (Venice, California: Feral House, 1997)

9. Donahue, Bill. "It's life, but not as we know it", *Northwest Magazine*, April 28, 1991

10. McKinney, Julianne. "Microwave Harassment & Mind-Control Experimentation", Electronic Surveillance Project, Association of National Security Alumni, Silver Spring, Maryland

11. Hudgeons, Steve, "Implants," April 2, 1996, obtained from the Internet, copy in the author's possession

12. Lindemann, Debra L., "Surgeon Tells First Results of Implant Analysis," April 6, 1996, obtained from the Internet, copy in the author's possession; "Jon King's X-file document," *UFO Reality* magazine, 1996, otherwise unidentified clipping

13. Kanon, Gregory M., *The Great UFO Hoax*. (Lakeville, Minnesota: Galde Press, 1997)

The secret SAPO-base "Tjädergården."

Chapter 32:

UNIDENTIFIED FLYING AGENTS

Investigation of the UFO phenomenon leads us directly into the camp of the leading lights of government mind control, particularly of the aforementioned "non-lethal" variety.

Although many of the elements of the current UFO belief system, including alien invasion, have been around since the beginnings of UFO research in the 1950s, the burst in media activity that took place in the 1980s can be traced to a few sources. The first and most influential can be isolated with the individuals who went about hoaxing Paul Bennewitz. Although the Bennewitz case is only one of many instances where the UFO experience was apparently manipulated by agents of the government, it is representative and revealing.

In 1980 Bennewitz—often referred to in UFO literature as a "physicist," although he never obtained a degree—and well-known UFO researcher Dr. Leo Sprinkle were in touch with a young woman, Judy Doraty, who believed she had witnessed a calf stolen by a saucer and had been abducted by aliens. According to Doraty, in May of 1980 she and her young son had been driving near Cimarron, New Mexico, when they had observed "two or more" UFOs, and the theft of a calf via saucer. Doraty claimed at that time she and her son were abducted, and that she was taken to an underground base for examination and implanting with an alien device. At the base she had observed vats of unidentifiable body parts, and a vat with a male human floating in it.

Bennewitz paid for medical examinations of the pair including CAT scans, which reportedly confirmed the existence of the implants in the woman and her son. Bennewitz believed that "at least 300,000 or more in the U.S. and at least 2,000,000 if not more worldwide" had been implanted with cerebral control devices by the aliens, although his means of detecting these implants seems somewhat subjective: "You can recognize them because of their eyes... [a] peculiar look in the eyes and a funny smile." [1] *Bennewitz, the owner of an electronics research laboratory, attempted to detect the electromagnetic signals that he felt the aliens must be using to control her, and to find out a way to shield people from these signals. In late 1979 he told members of the Aerial Phenomena Research Organization of detecting these low frequency signals, and that he had begun to make calculations about electronic and propulsive techniques employed by the aliens.

At the same time, from his home in the Four Hills area of Albuquerque, New Mexico, he was photographing unidentified lights in the area of the Manzano Nuclear Weapons Storage Facility east of Kirtland Air Force Base. Bennewitz believed that he had "established constant direct communication with the Alien using a computer and a form of Hex Decimal Code with Graphics and print-out." The specific way in which Bennewitz believed he had established this link is not known to this researcher, although he did mention that when a UFO was in sight he would ask it telepathic messages. One blink of the saucer was a 'yes,' two blinks a 'no.' Bennewitz supposedly produced a vocabulary of 27 words that he communicated to the aliens with. [2]

Eventually Bennewitz believed that he had discovered an alien base a mile beneath the earth at Dulce, New Mexico, as well as one on the west slope of nearby Mount Archeleta, with an estimated alien population of 2,000. He took aerial photos of the reputed base at Dulce from a helicopter, and believed that he had viewed and taken photos of saucer craft, beam weapons, and aliens on the ground, although when the pictures were developed, these photos were inexplicably missing from the series.

Bennewitz produced a written report on his research titled Project Beta, which is primarily a primitive "Look out boys! The Aliens are here!" study of alien psychology, as well as proposed means by which the army might destroy the alien bases—using Bennewitz' company, Thunder Electronics, as a sub-contractor for his own beam weapons inventions.

According to the report, he had spent two years in surveillance of "alien ships within a sixty (60) mile radius of Albuquerque," as well as "Detection and disassembly of alien communication and video channels—both local, earth, and near space." Bennewitz believed he had received "Constant reception of video from alien ship and underground base viewscreeen; Typical alien, humanoid and at times apparent Homo Sapien."

During the period of his research, Bennewitz was closely in touch with a military officer named Major Edwards, at the Manzano facility, and he gave several presentations to "high level" Air Force personnel at the base. He reported that he had also surveilled an alleged alien base in the company of Edwards.

UFO researcher Jacques Vallee was told by William Moore that "[Bennewitz] had innocently stumbled on a signal used in a secret Air Force experiment that was totally unrelated to UFOs. He was approached by security officers who tried to get him to disconnect this equipment and to stop monitoring their electromagnetic tests. The more they did this, of course, the more Bennewitz was convinced they had something to hide (which was true) and that it had to do with UFOs (which was false). And he refused to comply." [3]

While Bennewitz watched the military, they watched him. People came to his door "out of the blue," and he saw implant scars on the back of their necks. "The aliens have gone wild," Bennewitz wrote, paralyzing him four times and injecting him 250 times "with hypodermics."

To understand the saga of Paul Bennewitz, additional background is necessary. Although I was not present at the 1989 MUFON conference at which William Moore spoke, Jacques Vallee was, and gave the following description:

"In a confused and embarrassing presentation before the MUFON Conference, Bill Moore indeed confessed that he had willingly allowed himself to be used by various people claiming to act on behalf of Air Force Intelligence and that he had knowingly disseminated disinformation, although he had never been 'on the payroll.' This is a mere play on words, of course. Not being on the payroll does not mean that he was not paid in cash or through other means...

"Moore gave a weak excuse for his actions, claiming that he had acted in a heroic private effort to infiltrate and expose the operation."

William Moore has said that in early September 1980, he, Moore, was contacted by a "well-placed individual within the intelligence community who claimed to be directly connected to a high-level project dealing with UFOs." This man, known as "Falcon," said that he was part of a group that wanted to expose the continuing government cover-up of UFOs. Moore admits that he went along with the man in order to gain access to government UFO information.

Acting as liaison between Moore and the group was Sgt. Richard Doty. Moore soon learned his own role, which was to provide information on Bennewitz in exchange for "sensitive" information on UFOs. He also learned that "several government agencies" were collaborating in discrediting Bennewitz by funnelling disinformation to him.

"By 1981," Moore says, "Paul was gathering data from a variety of sources and amalgamating it with information being fed to him by a number of government people in whom, for some reason, he seemed to have an implicit and abiding faith. The story that emerged from this melange of fact, fiction, fantasy, hearsay, hard data and government disinformation was absolutely incredible! Yet somehow, Paul believed in it and set out on a one-man crusade to tell the world that malevolent aliens from space were in league with our government to take over the planet. What had begun in 1979 as an effort to learn whether the behavior of a woman who claimed she had been abducted by UFO aliens and was being influenced by some sort of radio remote control had, in the space of less than three years, blossomed into a tale which rivaled the wildest science fiction scenario anyone could possibly imagine."

"My role in the affair," said Moore, "was largely that of a freelancer providing information on Paul's current thinking and activities. I had nothing whatsoever to do with the counter-intelligence and disinformation, although I either knew or was aware of a number of people involved in that end of things." [4]

It may be significant that William Moore's first two books, The Philadelphia Experiment and The Roswell Incident were co-authored with Charles Berlitz who, according to the Seattle Times/Post Intelligencer, at the beginning of World War II, "was taken out of the Air Force to work in counter-intelligence. He is reluctant to talk about this period and his work as an operative ('nobody likes to say 'spy') in anything but the foggiest terms. But he was, clearly, the perfect operative. 'I would pretend that I was a Frenchman in Venezuela or a Venezuelan in France.' During the war he worked underground, with a new name and identity, in various countries." The article indicates that Berlitz' connections with the spy biz did not end with World War II, but that "He resumed his intelligence work, though not overseas, during the Korean and Vietnam wars." [5]

While Bennewitz monitored low frequency electronic broadcasts and filmed unusual aerial displays that may or may not have been saucer craft, the government was monitoring him and, I suspect, destroying him. Moore says that Bennewitz detected instances of surveillance, but that there were wiretaps and break-ins that Bennewitz didn't know about.

One of these instances may have happened when Bennewitz was visited at home by an anonymous man with a "top secret document that was dated in the '50's, indicating if anybody found out about all of this they would kill them."

Bennewitz was asked, "Doesn't that bother you?" He responded that it didn't. It may have been that the information offered Bennewitz was the counterfeit MJ-12 document later circulated by Moore associate Jaime Shandera.

Bennewitz was apparently under observation from a house across the street from his own, and took photos of persons visiting the house with NORAD and Air Force license plates. [6]

By 1982, the alien scenario that Bennewitz was being fed was essentially that of the belief structure held by a large portion of the UFO community today. Malevolent grey aliens were abducting humans, mutilating cattle, and implanting humans with control devices. They had made a treaty with the U.S. government, and had an underground base in Dulce, New Mexico, and for these concessions they had given saucers and weaponry to the government. In addition, there was a benevolent group of aliens intent on stopping the destructive Greys from ravaging the planet.

As time went on, Bennewitz had a nervous breakdown reportedly due to the disinformation he was being fed by government agents. According to Moore, Bennewitz stocked his house with guns and knives and installed extra locks, although Bennewitz believed the aliens were able to come through the walls and inject him with chemicals that knocked him out. Bennewitz suffered from insomnia and his hands shook, as if they were palsied. Eventually he was hospitalized and placed under psychiatric care. [7]

On the other hand, perhaps it was not just disinformation that derailed Bennewitz. There is the possibility that he was neutralized by ELF irradiation or other forms of government mind control that drove him crazy.

After Bennewitz, the web of disinformation continued to spread. In 1983 Linda Moulton Howe, a well-known UFO researcher who oddly seems unable to entertain any other idea than that UFOs are from outer space, was working on an HBO documentary on UFOs. According to Moore, "when the filmmaker [Howe] appeared on the scene, and it looked as if Paul's story might become part of the script, the counterintelligence people simply extended their disinformation activities accordingly."

Howe met Richard Doty at Kirtland Air Force Base in a building posted as an Air Force Office of Special Investigations office. Once inside, Howe was taken to a room to speak with Doty. Howe believed that they were going to discuss a UFO sighting that had taken place at Ellsworth Air Force base, but Doty began talking about her UFO documentary, leading her to believe that she had been closely monitored during the film's production. Doty told her that her research, and in particular an earlier documentary titled *Strange Harvest,* had upset people, with the implication that they were ranking military people. Doty also told her that his superiors had asked him to show her the contents of a plain brown envelope, which he removed from a desk drawer. Although she was allowed to read the contents of the envelope, she was not permitted to take notes.

Inside the envelope was a document titled "Briefing Paper for the President of the United States of America About Unidentified Aerial Vehicles," or very similar words. The "Briefing Paper" described incidents of flying saucer crashes in Aztec, New Mexico; Kingman, Arizona; Mexico; and two in Roswell, New Mexico.

According to the briefing, two species of extraterrestrials had established contact with the U.S. government. One species was the well-known Greys, while the other was not described. The document mentioned that extraterrestrials had been responsible for creating Jesus Christ as a means for influencing human behavior.

The madness would spread. The UFO field would soon collide with the political conspiracy research field and with the underground patriot movement, and men like Bill Cooper, John Lear, and others would be proclaiming that the secretive men who ruled the world were not men at all. What was done to Bennewitz and Howe on an individual case basis, was soon being done to the American public on a much wider scale—and is still being done by disinformation agents and the gullible souls who believe them.

Richard Doty, at the time of the Bennewitz affair, is believed to have been working for the Air Force Office of Special Investigations. He had been trained in disinformation and psychological warfare, and allegedly admitted that he was a member of a disinformation group—probably the Aviary, to be taken up later in this text.

According to published reports, William Moore stated that Doty reported to a Pentagon official named Hennessey, reportedly chief of security for the Stealth project. It is impossible to gauge Doty's actual connections and responsibilities, since portions of his service records are expunged, although while stationed at Linsay Air Force Base in West Germany, according to Phillip Klass, "Doty was charged with falsifying official documents and telling falsehoods to his commanding officer. A formal investigation confirmed these charges and Doty was 'decertified' as a special agent [with the] Air Force Office of Special Investigations and returned to Kirtland AFB in late 1986. Doty spent his last two years before retirement in food services management." [8]

The plot thickens. Researcher Lee Graham has said that William Moore contacted him "in an intelligence capacity" and that Moore said he worked for the government in releasing sensitive UFO information. According to Graham, Moore had shown him a Defense Investigation Service badge, although UFO researcher and "nuclear physicist" Stanton Friedman in his 1996 apologia for the bogus MJ-12 documents titled *Top Secret/Majic* puts a different spin on the event. Friedman said, "As a joke, Bill once pulled out a MUFON identification card, flashed it at Lee, and indicated that he was working for the government. Lee bought it." This sidesteps the alleged impersonation of a government official, Graham's memory of a DIS badge, not a MUFON card, the fact that Moore has admitted to being a government agent, and the bottom line that the joke is unfunny. One wonders why Friedman would go out of his way to disclaim the government connection of an admitted government collaborator. [9]

The group that was functioning behind the scenes in the Bennewitz story was probably the Aviary. In 1988 Seligman Productions purchased from William Moore interviews with two alleged government agents who went by the names Falcon and Condor. They spoke behind screens during the filming, allegedly out of fear of retaliation from their employers. In the final product, broadcast on national television under the title *UFO Cover-Up Live!*, their UFO revelations were cobbled together with computer graphics of aliens and alien internal organs that were claimed to have been done by the government; a kind of gut level MJ-12 document. The computer graphics were nothing of the sort. They were based upon earlier drawings published by UFO researcher Leonard Stringfield. [10]

The revelations that Falcon and Condor offered were predictable: confirmation of crashed saucers, live and dead aliens, and the existence of the overarching secret government

MJ-12 agency charged with investigating and keeping the lid on the existence of aliens. According to researcher Robert Hastings, the two anonymous agents doing the alien whistle-blowing were familiar face Sgt. Richard Doty, Air Force OSI agent, and Robert Collins, an Air Force captain. [11]

William Moore has said that Doty was not Falcon, but was in fact a liaison for another person. This person is possibly C.B. Scott Jones, identified as "Falcon," a member of U.S. Navy Intelligence for 15 years, and a collaborator with "non-lethality" heavy weight John B. Alexander. Does this mean that neither Doty nor Collins were actual members of what appears to be a secret intelligence agency group, but were masquerading as such, or employed at a lower level? Certainly their credentials are not in the same league as the other reported members of the group.

There is another echelon (perhaps the only actual group) reported as being members of the Aviary who cannot be connected to UFO disinformation except in a tangential way. Two alleged members of the Aviary, C.B. Scott Jones and John B. Alexander, are said to have met William Moore at a party.

Then there are the bird names used by Doty and Collins, although this does not prove membership in, but perhaps only knowledge of the Aviary. This distinction is not often noted by researchers who maintain that the Aviary is "a group of intelligence and Department of Defense officers and scientists with a brief to discredit any serious research in the UFO field." This statement is probably true, but I am obliged to point out that the evidence at this time is circumstantial. [12]

Alleged members of the flock are:

C.B. Scott Jones, reported to be "Falcon." After a long career in Naval Intelligence, Jones "worked in the private sector research and development community involved in the U.S. government sponsored projects for the Defense Nuclear Agency (DNA), Defense Intelligence Agency (DIA) and U.S. Army Intelligence and Security Command." He was also a collaborator with John B. Alexander, and the head of the Rockefeller Foundation. [13]

Colonel John B. Alexander, retired, reported to be "Penguin," who has long been involved in fringe science and parapsychological pursuits, and is the man who invented the "non-lethality" approach in the military. Alexander is on the board of directors for Psi-Tech, a remote viewing company that also employs Major Edward Dames (formerly of the DIA), a frequent guest on the nationwide Art Bell talk radio show. Dames was, I believe, one of the persons talking on the Bell show about the companion spaceship of the Hale-Bopp comet, information that sent the Heaven's Gate group over the edge to suicide.

Ron Pandolphi, allegedly "Pelican," is a Ph.D. in physics who works at the Office of the Deputy Director of Science and Technology in the CIA. [14]

Dr. Christopher Green, allegedly "Bluejay," from the CIA.

Harold Puthoff, said to be "Owl," ex-NSA, a Scientologist at last report, and involved in remote viewing studies.

Dr. Jack Verona, said to be "Raven," employed by the Department of Defense, and reportedly involved in creating the DIA's Sleeping Beauty mind assault electromagnetic weapons.

Bruce Maccabee, Ph.D., reported to be "Seagull," is an expert in optical physics and laser weapons at the U.S. Naval Surface Weapons Laboratory in Maryland. He is an author on UFO topics, and a consultant to MUFON, the Mutual UFO Network.

Prior to the publication of a paper revealing the alleged identities of the Aviary, researcher Armen Victorian was visited by the anonymous "Morning Dove" and "Hawk," "who had travelled to the UK with a message from the senior ranks advising me not to go ahead with my exposé. I rejected this proposal." [15]

On examination, the group has several shared interests. These are remote viewing and non-lethal weaponry.

It is, of course, understandable why the government would want to confuse and neutralize the UFO research community, even if there are no aliens at Area 51, Dulce, or any other facility. UFO researchers from early on have probably been considered a kind of citizens' spy agency, snooping and reporting on activities that take place in the air and in the vicinity of military bases. Those investigative reports, circulated via a large number of books, journals, and videos, are also freely available to foreign powers.

A secondary priority of military intelligence may be to encourage UFO whistleblowers from within the military and intelligence community to report to UFO "experts" covertly connected to the government, thus identifying themselves and allowing the government to stop leaks of classified information.

It is curious that disinformation connected to the Aviary by researchers is mostly of an amateurish variety, like the computer graphics of *UFO Cover-up Live!* Given the resources of the above mentioned individuals, why would they have not produced the magnum opus of UFO disinformation, replete with unimpeachable film records and witnesses to back them up? Something like a big-budget *Alien Autopsy* film?

Such an effort simply isn't necessary. A large percentage of UFO researchers and the field of UFO buffs will buy into almost any cheapjack silliness that is offered so long as it "proves" that aliens are behind the mess the world is in. Disinfo jobs like the creation of the MJ-12 document and the production of the *UFO Cover-Up Live!* mugging and computerisms could be a relatively low priority in the intelligence agency scheme of things, done by underlings, and without much expense or oversight. Why waste time, effort, and funds with overkill when the most shoddy of efforts will pass muster and be treated by most UFO buffs as ultimate authority?

NOTES:

1. Bennewitz, Paul, "Project Beta", copy in author's possession; Bennewitz, Paul, Interview conducted by Jim McCampbell, September 11, 1984, copy in the author's possession
2. Bennewitz, Paul, Interview conducted by Jim McCampbell
3. Vallee, Jacques, *Revelations.* (New York: Ballentine, 1991)
4. *UFO* magazine, Vol. 4, No. 4; Vallee
5. Cridland, Tim. Text of an unpublished letter to *Fate* magazine, February 21, 1997; *Seattle Times/Post Intelligencer,* May 6, 1990
6. Bennewitz, interview by Jim McCampbell
7. Bennewitz, *Project Beta*
8. Vallee; Sutherly, Curt. *Caveat Emptor* magazine, Spring, 1990
9. Vallee; Friedman, Stanton. *Top Secret/Majic.* (New York, Marlowe & Company, 1996)
10. Vallee
11. Vallee; Sutherly
12. Victorian, Armen. "Psychic Warfare & Non-Lethal Weapons," *Nexus* magazine, October/November 1993; Victorian, Armen, "Non-lethality: John B. Alexander, "The Pentagon's Penguin," *Lobster* magazine, issue 25
13. Victorian, "Psychic Warfare"
14. Ibid.
15. Ibid.; Boylan, Richard J. "Birds of a Feather: No More UFO-ET-Disclosure Policy Splits Covert Network", obtained on the Internet, copy in author's possession; Victorian, "Non-lethality"; Guyatt, David, "Police State of Mind," *Fortean Times* magazine, March, 1997; Sutherly

Chapter 33:

MONARCH

The mind control topic that has received the most publicity—and argument—in recent years is the alleged government Project MONARCH. Some hypnotherapists and alleged victims have come forward telling of the existence of this supposedly CIA-sponsored program, while a flood of copycat reports have relied on these sources.

A book published in 1995, *Trance Formation of America,* was written on the subject by a confessed victim, Cathy O'Brien, and her deprogrammer husband, Mark Phillips. In this apparently vanity-printed tome O'Brien alleges that she was a victim of MKULTRA MONARCH mind control for the majority of her life, and was only rescued when she was deprogrammed at the age of 30 by Phillips, who says that he is a formerly CIA-connected hypnotherapist.

Trance Formation of America is prefaced with a long, poorly written—in fact, barely literate—introduction by Phillips, who alleges that he is a former employee of the CIA, or at least of a CIA cutout called Capital International Airways. Phillips mentions being present at least one "video taping of a TOP SECRET psychiatric experiment" around 1970.

"While I lack the official published academic credentials," Phillips says, "I am recognized internationally by mental health and law enforcement professionals as an authority on the secret science concerning external control of the mind." It is interesting that there is no substantiation of this recognition in the book. What the slug of business cards that Phillips reprints do suggest is that he was a salesman for several companies, and was a hypnotherapist practicing for some period of time in Nashville, although lacking "the official published academic credentials," I wonder about the legality of that.

According to Phillips, at one point during the deprogramming of Cathy O'Brien, he was given the name and phone number of Jolyon "Jolly" West, at UCLA. "Little did I know," Phillips reports, "that Dr. West had worked for the CIA in Project MK-Ultra mind control research for decades." Phillips must in truth have known very little, since if he had cracked even one book on mind control he would certainly have come across West's name several times.

O'Brien—actually a much more competent writer than Phillips—recounts her alleged history as a drug and electroshock mind-controlled slave-prostitute, beginning shortly after her birth in Michigan 1957, with early child abuse by her father and two uncles, including her being filmed in bestiality movies produced by her father.

O'Brien alleges incidents of prostitution, mind control, and abuse by priests at various Catholic churches in Michigan; Michigan Congressman Guy VanderJagt; President Gerald Ford; Senator Robert C. Byrd; Senator James Traficant; Pennsylvania Governor Dick Thornburgh; Senator Patrick Leahy; Governor of Tennessee Lamar Alexander; Dodger baseball manager Tommy LaSorda; President Ronald Reagan; General Manuel Noriega; Contra leader Daniel Ortega; CIA Director William Casey; baseball player Nolan Ryan; Secretary of Education Bill Bennet; President George Bush; Hillary Clinton; and a bevy of others including, quoting O'Brien, "friends, local mobsters and Masons, relatives, Satanists, strangers, and police officers."

According to O'Brien's recollection, many of those whom she would come in contact with and be prostituted to during her period as a mind controlled slave were trained in a complicated series of MONARCH verbal commands, mostly consisting of punning phrases relating to the *Wizard of Oz*, Disney films, and television shows like *I Dream of Jeannie*, *The Brady Bunch*, and *Bewitched*. No Nietzche or Alfred Rosenberg? That would seem more to the tastes of the mind controllers that I know about. These phrases would be used to manipulate her and other MONARCH victims, causing them to shift from one programmed identity to another.

In 1974, according to O'Brien's account, she was taken to MacDill Air Force Base in Florida, where she received additional mind control programming, then in 1975 she was taken to Wyoming, where she claims she was tortured and raped by Dick Cheney, then-White House Chief of Staff to President Ford. In 1976, she recalls, she was taken to the Kennedy Space Center in Titusville, Florida, where she received her first NASA mind control programming.

Involved tangentially in the country music business, O'Brien found that most of the big names in that industry were either

294

mind-controlled slaves (Barbara Mandrell, Louise Mandrell, Loretta Lynn), or CIA-run slave masters (Louise Mandrell's husband R.C. Bannon, Boxcar Willie, Alex Houston, Kris Kristopherson, Louise Mandrell's father Irby Mandrell, Jimmy Buffet). According to O'Brien, CIA-involved country music acts would be booked into areas where they could perform covert operations for the Agency, mostly in the nature of drug running operations. On one cocaine run to Hot Springs, Arkansas, in 1979, O'Brien reports that she met Bill Clinton, who had a nose full of cocaine and used "standard Jesuit hand signals and cryptic language," by which he controlled O'Brien.

O'Brien says she met Wayne Cox, whom she would soon marry, in Nashville. Cox was a member of alleged "CIA operative" Jack Greene's Desperado Band. Cox, she alleges, is an occult-involved serial killer who would dismember victims and sell their body parts to satanists through an underground distributor. O'Brien says that "During the months I was back with Cox, a muscle in my upper vaginal wall was cut and dropped in preparation for [Alex] Houston to flesh carve a hideous witch's face for Senator Byrd's perversions."

In 1980, O'Brien's daughter Kelly was born, according to her only to be shunted directly into the MONARCH program of prostitution and mind control.

In the 1980s O'Brien says she received MONARCH programming from the Temple of Set's Colonel Michael Aquino, at Fort Campbell, Kentucky; Fort McLellen in Anniston, Alabama; and Redstone Arsenal and Marshall Space Flight Center in Huntsville, Alabama; the latter programming in which "NASA cooperated fully."

During the 1980s O'Brien claims she was working as a mind-controlled courier, running messages to and transporting drugs from such individuals as Senator Byrd, Baby Doc Duvalier, drug lord Jose Busto, Ronald Reagan, and others. Ronald Reagan used the nifty device of programming her to respond to certain colors, and when he wanted her to perform a certain act or shift into a particular personality, all he had to do was hand her one of the colored jelly beans out of the jar on his desk.

O'Brien says that in one operation she relayed from Vice President Bush to Vice President Salinas the "initial diplomatic groundwork for the North American Free Trade Agreement (NAFTA)." While under the control of George Bush, O'Brien reports, Bush claimed to be a space alien and used hologram technology to transform his features into a lizard. Coal to Newcastle.

Another of O'Brien's mind-controlled missions, she says, was to deliver Education 2000 materials for Canadian Prime Minister Brian Mulroney to implement. According to O'Brien, she was also utilized as a sex slave at the Bohemian Grove compound in Northern California. She describes various rooms at the compound prepared for the prominent sex freaks of different persuasions who frequented the place.

In the loose-knit communities and publications of conspiracy politics research and the patriot movement, many take Phillips and O'Brien's story as gospel. Of course, many also take Serge Monast's Blue Beam story, space alien Hatonn's channellings in *Contact* magazine, "the Photon Belt," the Roswell alien saucer crash, Candy Jones, the MJ-12 "document," Commander X, Bill Cooper, the Spear of Destiny, and any number of other shady propositions as being truth, as well. The human race, by and large, is not that intelligent, methinks.

I remember one woman at a local patriot coffee klatch—a "Meet, eat, and retreat" group, as Jack McLamb described it—asking me what I thought of O'Brien's MONARCH allegations. I told her that although I am not omniscient, due to the lack of proof and the wild nature of her claims, that I doubted that MONARCH existed. The woman looked at me like I had suddenly used a hologram to transform my features into those of a lizard. Doubting any story of evil perpetrated by the government was ample reason to believe that I was a member of the Other Side.

So what is the basis of Cathy O'Brien's story about being a MONARCH slave, and Mark Phillips' tale of deprogramming her? Truth is often stranger than fiction, and it is remotely—think in terms of millions of light years distant—possible that O'Brien and Phillips are telling the truth. More likely, in my opinion, is that they are telling partly truth, partly lies or delusion. O'Brien may have been the victim of massive abuse during her life. But most likely is that the whole convoluted crazy story is delusion or consciously made up. My reasons for believing this, aside from the overall improbability of her lurid account, follow.

O'Brien states that MONARCH mind control conferred photographic memory on her, thus making it possible for her to remember verbatim the conversations of the persons in her book. What she pointedly does not remember is even a single date by which the presence and activities of prominent or not-so-prominent persons could be connected, verified, or disproved in her anecdotal accounts. She attributes this to the "timeless" condition of being mind-controlled, but if she was that "timeless," it is my belief that she would not have been able to make a single appointment, catch a single airplane or boat, remember her daughter's birth date (which she does at one point), or even remember what decade these alleged events transpired in.

Additionally, while O'Brien remembers quite a bit of realistic-sounding detail about homespun scenes in places like Muskegon, Wisconsin, her powers of description utterly fail her when she is talking about the layout of Air Force bases, the technology of mind control laboratories, the top secret compounds of high level politicos, and offices and other interiors in Washington, D.C. I would think that there would be a wealth of detail there, if the accounts were true, but there is not.

Also, there is not one incident of high level political chicanery that she mentions that could not have been surmised from published accounts, nor are there any unknown secretive dealings that could be verified independently—not one that I can find. The prominent political figures are solitary on the MONARCH stage, with almost all subsidiary characters—aides, secretaries, friends, wives, hangers-on—anonymous or completely absent. O'Brien's remembrance of what took place amongst the high and mighty, figures like Bush, Reagan, and Noriega, is oddly all common knowledge in the news and the literature of conspiracy theory—in fact, very common knowledge. All of her "insider" information is confined to primitive diatribes about the New World Order, NAFTA, and Education 2000, the kind of half-baked pabulum that anyone could pick up with a cursory reading of some of the popular titles in conspiracy research.

Finally, there seems to have been some collaboration on the accounts of both Phillips and O'Brien, or perhaps a third person working over both manuscripts. Although O'Brien is a far superior writer to her "deprogrammer" husband, they both have an identically weird usage of parentheses, as well as a misunderstanding of the spelling of the same words. Example: the use of "peaked" when they mean "piqued."

One could speculate long and hard on the truth about *Trance Formation of America*. Was O'Brien actually abused and prostituted and, under hypnosis, did she dub in a great deal of extraneous material involving the rich and satanic? Is it a purposeful hoax hatched by Phillips and O'Brien for the purpose of selling books? A ploy written to make actual CIA and cult mind control appear ridiculous? We may never know, but we can know with a good deal of certainty that *Trance Formation of*

America is not what it purports to be: a true recounting of a victim's mind control ordeal.

Another "tell-all" book about MONARCH mind control is the encyclopediac vanity-published *The Illuminati Formula Used to Create an Undetectable Total Mind Controlled Slave,* by Fritz Springmeier and Cisco Wheeler. Springmeier is a Christian minister, a certified graphoanalyst, and reported to me in a brief telephone conversation that he has spent several years deprogramming alleged MONARCH victims. Wheeler, "since 1986... has been a recovering victim of mind control. She was part of a group of Illuminati hierarchy members that rebelled against their slavery... Her father was an Illuminati Grand Master as well as one of the better programmers."

When I spoke to Springmeier he explained to me that his books should be at the top of the *New York Times* bestseller lists, seeing as how they reveal the most horrible secret of the 20th century. He also explained that he had spent one-half-million hours deprogramming mind control victims. Odd that so much of his research would be cursory, given that dedication.

The book is, in fact, poorly written, and loaded with misspellings. I would forgive those shortcomings if there was any real research, but the historical sections of the book are a rehash of the standard works on mind control like Bowart's *Operation Mind Control,* and a retelling of lurid evangelist exposés of the "I was a 33rd degree Illuminati high priest" sort. Uninformed conspiracy theorizing is coupled with page after page of unverified "Illuminati" codes, details on mind control bases (they allege Area 51 in Nevada is one of these, where an estimated 2,000,000 Monarch slaves have been programmed), analyses of movies and television programs as purveyors of Monarch codes, and a hodgepodge of other things including reprinted pages from a *Star Trek* "technical manual" alleged to be used for programming.

The book is primarily 468 pages of poorly rehashed mind control history, allegations, and hearsay, no doubt culled from transcripts of the persons Springmeier says that he has deprogrammed. And again, is what Springmeier and Wheeler say totally bogus? There is nothing verifiable, other than the well-worn stories that the co-authors have culled from the work of others. Nothing in this huge "Illuminati Formula" is proven, nothing whatsoever is verified.

Again, I admit that out of all of the people who Springmeier claims he has deprogrammed, there might be some of them who have received abuse, who have been victims of satanic groups, or who have even received intelligence agency mind control. But with the undocumented way that the book is done, there is no way of telling if any of the material that Wheeler and Springmeier presents is true.

The single most telling detail suggesting that MONARCH is a hoax or a product of delusion is that the term itself does not appear in any intelligence agency document, or in the statements of any bonafide intelligence agent that I am aware of. Nor do any of the other MONARCH buzzphrases that are so handily tossed about by "experts" on the subject. There is no corroboration of MONARCH terms in any verified intelligence agency documents that I am aware of, nor by any actual defectors from the intelligence community, of which there are many.

I am not saying that cultic abuse and murder and mind control do not take place in the world, I know they do. I am not saying that men like Michael Aquino, Anton LaVey, Louis Jolyon West, and prominent politicians may not be involved in this kind of activity—some of them are. What I am saying is that understanding what is really going on is ill-served by MONARCH faddists and conspiracy freaks who, having seen something in print once, believe it forever, or who cannot tell the difference between truth and imagination, and cannot separate out fact from urban legend, or memory from hypnotic fantasies.

For all I know, MONARCH may even exist roughly in the way that persons like Phillips, O'Brien, Wheeler, and Springmeier have described. But their documentation and analysis is not up to proving it. And it is perfectly apparent that if they deal with the content of mind control trauma in the same way that they handle the conspiracy research they cite whose sources I am quite familiar with, then their abilities as deprogrammers as well as writers and researchers should be doubted.

The answer to the O'Brien-Phillips-Wheeler-Springmeier school of conspiracy research is, of course, compiling evidence, not just hashing together allegations, fantasies, innuendoes, and things once heard at a revival meeting. But that would seemingly ruin the fun. The worst thing about these sorts of researchers is that their false reports and delusory connections muddy the water for anyone trying to get to the truth about mind control.

Dr. Ewen Cameron.

Chapter 34:

WORLD BRAIN

Although it may be argued that the growth of technology and industry in Europe in the 18th and 19th centuries allowed the birth of democracy, the evolution of technology has also led to the centralization of power and wealth in the hands of a few. Dollars, most fundamentally, define the true power of the vote in this world, therefore the rich have trillions of votes whereas the poor may not be able to vote at all. And the votes of the rich, their dollars, are being cast in favor of totalitarianism: they are being invested in the technology of control.

The increase in the sophistication and power of technology is a self-reinforcing loop that geometrically undermines democratic impulses, as the owners consolidate their own interests, and continue to shape the popular will in the image of the needs of control. For example, almost all information sources available to the vast majority of the populace are part of the controlled media. The mind of the subordinate in most cases is not his own.

As the controllers and their corporations assimilate all of the apparatus of society, creating new strategies for assimilation as they go, the individual becomes increasingly dependent on the external functions of the controllers for his daily necessities; unless he goes along with the program, he is ejected from the society, usually to die.

Now, new strategies of technological control bring the goal of total mind and body control into range. Now mind control implants and broadcast electromagnetics are able to not only channel messages and control into the subject's brain, they are also able to link the brain with computers—to digitize the subject's mind as part of a larger computerized structure.

By 1969, it is rumored, the CIA was able to achieve direct communication between computers and the brain. Whether this precise date is correct or not, in 1994 a Colorado company, Advanced Neurotechnologies, came up with a device called

Brainlink, consisting of a brain-to-computer interface that amplified 0.5Hz to 40Hz brainwaves, and turned them into coded computerese. [1]

At about the same time, there were also reports that Naval Research Laboratories, the Japanese Ministry of International Trade and Industry, the U.S. Defense Advanced Research Projects Agency, and other groups were collaborating in research into the Molecular Electronic Device (MED), also known as the "biochip." According to researcher David Paul, "There are several designs for these organic microprocessors, but the essential idea is to use protein molecules or synthetic organic molecules as computing elements to store information or act as switches with the application of voltage. Signal flow in this case would be by sodium or calcium ions. Others feel that artificial proteins can be constructed to carry signals by electron flow. Still another idea is to 'metalize' dead neuronal tissue to produce processing devices."

Paul quotes geneticist Kevin Ulmer, of Genex Corporation, who states, "The ultimate scenario is to develop a complete genetic code for the computer that would function as a virus does, but instead of producing more virus, it would assemble a fully operational computer inside a cell." [2]

In July 1996, information was released on research currently taking place into creation of a computer chip called the "Soul Catcher 2025." Dr. Chris Winter and a team of scientists at British Telecom's Martlesham Heath Laboratories, near Ipswich, are developing a chip that, when placed into the skull behind the eye, will record all visual and physical sensations, as well as thoughts. According to Winter, "This is the end of death... By combining this information with a record of the person's genes, we could recreate a person physically, emotionally, and spiritually."

Another of the possibilities of the chip that Winter discussed was the downloading of an older person's entire life experience into a newborn child.

Winter says that the first uses of the "Soul Catcher" will be for the military, where soldiers will be implanted to act as communications links, and an up-link to GPS (global position system) satellites. Prototypes are to be available within five years, military applications within 10 years, and free commercial availability in 20-30 years.

It is interesting that the Martlesham Heath location is located close to the area where the famous 1980 UFO incident took place at Woodbridge/Bentwaters. [3]

In 1996 an alleged secret document was released that had supposedly been leaked from "Intelli-Connection, a Security Division of IBM," located at 1200 Progress Way, Armonk, New York. The similarity of the name of the above-described Soul Catcher 2025 chip with the 2020 neural chip may not be coincidental, since the technology seems roughly identical. Here is an edited text of the document, reprinted at length because of its significant implications:

CONFIDENTIAL
LIMITED DISTRIBUTION ONLY
LEVEL 9 COMMUNICATION

2020 NEURAL CHIP IMPLANT

The control of crime will be a paramount concern in the 21st Century. We must be ready with our security products when the demand for them becomes popular. Our Research and Development Division has been in contract with the Federal Bureau of Prisons, the California Department of Corrections, the Texas Department of Public Safety, and the Massachusetts Department of Correction to run limited trials of the 2020 neural chip implant. We have established representatives of our interests in both management and institutional level positions within these departments.

Federal regulations do not yet permit testing of implants on prisoners, but we have entered into contractual testing of our products. We have also had major successes in privately owned sanitariums with implant technology. We need, however, to expand our testing to research how effective the 2020 neural chip implant performs in thos identified as the most aggressive in our society. Limited testing has produced a number of results.

In California, several prisoners were identified as members of the security threat group, EME, or Mexican Mafia. They were brought to the health services unit at Pelican Bay and tranquilized with advanced sedatives developed by our Cambridge, Massachusetts laboratories. The implant procedure takes 60-90 minutes depending upon the experience of the technician. We are working on a device which will reduce that time by as much as 60%. The results of implants on 8 prisoners yielded the following:

—Implants served as surveillance monitoring device for threat group activity

—Implants disabled two subjects during an assault on correctional staff

—Universal side-effects in all 8 test subjects revealed that when the implant was set to 116 MHz all subjects became lethargic and slept an average of 18-22 hours per day

—All subjects refused recreation periods for 14 days during the 116 MHz test evaluation

—7 of the 8 subjects did not exercise, in the cell or out of the cell, and 5 of the 8 subjects refused showers up to three days at a time

—Each subject was monitored for aggressive activity during the test period and the findings are conclusive that 7 out of the 8 test subjects exhibited no aggression, even when provoked

—Each subject experienced only minor bleeding from the nose and ears 48 hours after the implant due to initial adjustment

—Each subject had no knowledge of the implant for the test period and each implant was retrieved under the guise of medical treatment

It should be noted that the test period was for less than two months. However, during that period, substantial data was gathered by our research and development team which suggests that the implants exceed expected results. One of the major concerns of Security and the R & D team was that the test subject would discover the chemical imbalance during the initial adjustment period and the test would have to be scrubbed. However, due to advanced technological developments in the sedatives administered, the 48-hour adjustment period can be attributed to prescription medicatio given to the test subjects after the implant procedure.

One of the concerns raised by R & D was the cause of the bleeding and how to eliminate that problem. Unexplained bleeding might cause the subject to inquire further about his "routine" visit to the infirmary or other health care facility.

The security windfall from the brief test period was enormous. Security officials now know several strategies employed by the EME that facilitate the transmission of illegal drugs and weapons into their correctional facilities. One intelligence officer remarked that while they cannot use the information they have in a court of law, they know who to watch and what outside "connections" they have. The prison at Soledad is now considering transferring three subjects to Vacaville where we have ongoing implant research. Our technicians have promised that they can do three 2020 neural chip implants in less than an hour. Soledad officials hope to collect information from the trio to bring a 14-month investigation into drug trafficking by correctional officers to a close.

Essentially the implants make the unsuspecting prisoner a walking, talking recorder of every event he comes into contact with. There are only five intelligence officers at the Commission of Corrections who actually know the full scope of the implant testing.

In Massachusetts, the Department of Correction has already entered into high-level discussions about releasing certain offenders to the community with the 2020 neural chip implants...

[Dated 20 October 1995, with distribution marked "Eyes Only: Project Group 7A"]

After reading the above paper, I wondered if it was a factual leaked memorandum or an all-too-common disinformation ploy concocted by some zealous anti-mind control activist. It was only after discovering corroborative information that the scale tipped in my mind toward it being factual. That is, "Vision 2020: Colorado Courts of the Future", dated March 20, 1992, and originating from the Colorado State Judicial System. The Vision 2020 Project, or at least one compartment of it, was the result of evaluations of the proposal of implementing electronic implants by 80 prominent citizens of Colorado. The citizens came out in favor of the proposal.

According to Vision 2020, "biological and chemical technologies will explode in the next thirty years as rapidly as electronic technologies. We will be able to use genetic engineering, chemicals and chip implants to change human behavior. This will raise several questions regarding the extent to which the state can 'reprogram' individuals because of their societally unacceptable behavior... these advances in technology will occur..." The ultimate conclusion of the document is that "new treatment methods and sentencing alternatives should be utilized."

Additional confirmation of the 2020 document is the fact that mind control experimentation is still going on at Vacaville, as the document states. This was confirmed in July of 1995, when it was announced that three inmates at Vacaville had died in non-air conditioned cells. The announcement indicated that two of the prisoners may have died due to the "medical" treatment they were receiving at the time. The medical facility, however, revealed that the so-called medical treatments were in fact behavior modification treatments. [4]

And so we have reached a culmination.

Surfers of the informational moment are hanging ten on the most awesome cybernetic tsunami ever conceived, barrelling through an electronic womb-net of human culture, rocking and buffeted but unsensing of the farther shore ahead.

As the denizens of Tavistock have commented repeatedly, the structures and thinking patterns of the Industrial Age are breaking up, and breaking in on the conceptual edge of the Information Age. This transition is an alchemical change without equivalence in recorded history. There are no viable analogies other than, perhaps, the discovery of the uses of fire, and in fact the only available and most insightful analogies are being provided by madmen whose addled cortexes are the nearest thing to the mental equipment necessary to comprehend the current changes.

The reason that the information floodgates have been allowed to be opened is that the castles of the conspiracy are well defended by underlings, and that, secondarily, the controllers are benumbed by the excess of centuries. Free access to information and to the future will be a temporary thing unless we use this moment well.

Now we return to H.G. Wells, who had so much to say about the *Things to Come.* There may be a long-term strategy involved in the computerization of the world and the creation of the Internet, which can be discerned by referencing Wells, in a speech before a Round Table front, the Royal Institute of International Affairs, in November, 1936, when he spoke of something called the "World Encyclopaedia." Wells said:

"At first the realization of the ineffectiveness of our best thought and knowledge struck only a few people, like Mr. Maynard Keynes, for example... It is science and not men of science that we want to enlighten and animate our politics and rule the world... I want to suggest that something, a new social organization, a new institution—which for a time I shall call World Encyclopaedia... This World Encyclopaedia would be the mental background of every intelligent man in the world... Such an Encyclopaedia would play the role of an undogmatic Bible to World culture. It would do just what our scattered and disoriented intellectual organizations of today fall short of doing. It would hold the world together mentally... It would compel men to come to terms with one another... It is a super university I am thinking of, a World Brain; no less... Ultimately, if our dream is realized, it must exert a very great influence upon everyone who controls administrations, makes wars, directs mass behavior, feeds, moves, starves and kills populations... You see how such an Encyclopaedia organization could spread like a nervous network, a system of mental control about the globe, knitting all the intellectual workers of the world through a common interest and cooperating unity and a growing sense of their own dignity, informing without pressure or propaganda, directing without tyranny."

Wells was more candid about mind control in an unpublished memo, penned November 30, 1936:

"The Universities and the associated intellectual organizations throughout the world should function as a police of the mind."

Certainly all of this sounds science fictional—you know, *The Time Machine* and *War of the Worlds,* and all that—but we are at that stage where it has suddenly become real.

It was during the Nixon administration that a 300-page White House "Administratively Confidential" report, prepared by John Erlichman of Watergate fame, proposed putting a government radio in every home in the United States. Although the system would ostensibly be used as an emergency warning system, the report also suggested that the radios could be used to educate preschoolers for world citizenship, and to propagandize to offset social unrest.

But the report went farther, and in retrospect provides some insight into what is going on today. According to the report, the government radios would be part of a "wired nation" system that would also act as a computer clearinghouse, localizing all the nation's police and health records in one giant databank. [5]

And, of course, this is only the tip of the electronic iceberg. Given the advances in computing and electronic control over the past several decades, it is apparent that the most science fictional possibilities for worldwide mind control are here, or at least only around the corner. Given technologies for the broadcasting of thought via electromagnetics, for "synthetic telepathy," it is not at all unlikely that there could soon be a worldwide network of satellites providing, not only surveillance, but total mind control, broadcasting thoughts, moods emotions. These satellites could hang in geosynchronous orbit, manipulating we marionettes in whatever fashion might be desired. It would be a Home Shopping Network of the Mind, where one had no choice but to buy, buy, buy.

Thoughts would be broadcast to mollify the masses, thoughts

to make them work harder, thoughts to reward them for being good little drones, to make them buy consumer goods, to enrage them to whatever murderous *jihad* the engines of commerce and the *Society of the Spectacle* required that month.

NOTES:

1. Smith, Jerry, *HAARP: Ultimate Weapon of the Conspiracy*, (1997, AUP, Kempton, Illinois)

2. Paul, David, "Man A Machine," *Apocalypse Culture*, Adam Parfrey, ed. (Venice, California: Feral House, 1990)

3. *The Daily Telegraph*, UK; *Daily Mail*, UK, July 18, 1996 4. "2020 Neural Chip Implant", reprinted in *Nexus* magazine, October/November 1996; "Microchip Technology," *EYE* magazine, Fall 1993; Martin and Caul. "Mind Control", the *Napa Valley Sentinal,* undated copy; "Jon King's X-File Document", *UFO Reality* magazine, 1996, otherwise unidentified clipping

5. Packard

FINALITY

Human culture has always been manipulated by mind control, i.e., the monopolization, concealment, and destruction of information and the control of man's primary tool of information processing: the mind. In the 20th century, however, the technological tools for attaining total control have been delivered into the hands of a small coterie, the scientists and the men who hold their leashes, and those tools have been turned upon the mostly unsuspecting populace, who have been manipulated, prodded, worked on, deluded and destroyed, usually in the name of achieving a peaceful, i.e., a controlled society.

When information on mind control is broached the response is standard: This is science fiction. Certainly the technology of surveillance and control has been evolving at a rapid rate, the average person responds, but it will be years, perhaps centuries before true mind control is achieved.

Think again. This response in itself is a carefully cultivated mind state. The true capabilities of technology have been concealed in order to achieve the element of surprise.

The world is now science fiction. There are no limits to the control that can be induced upon the population by technology as it currently exists. Now the only delay is in the utilization. It is true that there may be some fine-tuning, some honing, some distribution of technology that will take place in the years to come. There will be new brainstorms that link the disparate technologies that exist, there will be strategies for, as Christians are apt to say, getting people to take "the Mark." But total control is no longer the nightmarish pipedream of centuries to come. Give it ten years: then the war for the control of the mind will have been won—or lost.

Key to understanding mind control is understanding the capabilities of life itself, and that may be salvation for the population of this planet. Mind control is a reductive process by which a life unit is reduced in power until it is placed under the control of the manipulative agent. It is the means by which man is turned into an animal, or a machine.

The direction is obvious. It is our challenge to decondition ourselves and our fellow humans from all of the various modes of mind control that currently shape and warp our lives, both the dramatic ones I have focused on in this volume, and the less dramatic ones that have been applied since time immemorial. Brain control implants, yes; psychotronic generators, yes; but there are a host of more subtle control techniques that must be confronted: television, advertising, schooling, religion... political correctness.

At one end of the scale there is the psychiatric-conditioned animal, the human reduced in intellect and taught to drool by Pavlovian dog training techniques. The other end of the scale of possibilities open to humanity knows no definition. Although it may be a controversial viewpoint, I believe that the potentials of humans are unlimited after they have been progressively freed from limiting beliefs and delusions, all of which communicate to them that they are puny things who must carry out the wishes of the controllers. Technology can, in fact, be utilized to destroy limitations to human freedom, and that is another part of the challenge, to harness technology in the work of liberation.

Ultimately, all barriers to our evolution can be shed. All limits to human freedom are imposed by mind control.

SOURCES:

Adventures Unlimited, One Adventure Place, P.O. Box 74, Kempton, Illinois 60946
A-Albionic Consulting & Research, P.O. Box 20273, Ferndale, Michigan 48220
C.I. Associates, P.O. Box 55, Decatur, Arkansas 72722
Factsheet Five, P.O. Box 170099, San Francisco, California 94117-0099
IllumiNet Press, P.O. Box 2808, Lilburn, Georgia 30226
Leading Edge Research, P.O. Box 7530, Yelm, Washington 98597
The McAlvany Intelligence Advisor, P.O. Box 84904, Phoenix, Arizona, 85071
M.O.M., P.O. Box 1486, Noxon, Montana 59853
Nexus magazine, P.O. Box 177, Kempton, Illinois 60946-0177
Paranoia magazine, P.O. Box 1041, Providence, Rhode Island 02901
The Patriot Report, P.O. Box 122, Ponderay, Idaho, 83852
The Phoenix Foundation, P.O. Box 92008, Nashville, Tennessee 37209
Prevailing Winds Research, P.O. Box 23511, Santa Barbara, California 93121
The Spotlight, 300 Independence Ave. SE, Washington, D.C. 20003
Steamshovel Press, P.O. Box 23715, St. Louis, Missouri 63121

THE
ADVENTURE
UNLIMITED
CATALOG

THE TIME TRAVEL HANDBOOK
A Manual of Practical Teleportation & Time Travel
edited by David Hatcher Childress

In the tradition of *The Anti-Gravity Handbook* and *The Free-Energy Device Handbook,* science and UFO author David Hatcher Childress takes us into the weird world of time travel and teleportation. Not just a whacked-out look at science fiction, this book is an authoritative chronicling of real-life time travel experiments, teleportation devices and more. *The Time Travel Handbook* takes the reader beyond the government experiments and deep into the uncharted territory of early time travellers such as Nikola Tesla and Guglielmo Marconi and their alleged time travel experiments, as well as the Wilson Brothers of EMI and their connection to the Philadelphia Experiment—the U.S. Navy's forays into invisibility, time travel, and teleportation. Childress looks into the claims of time travelling individuals, and investigates the unusual claim that the pyramids on Mars were built in the future and sent back in time. A highly visual, large format book, with patents, photos and schematics. Be the first on your block to build your own time travel device!
316 PAGES. 7X10 PAPERBACK. ILLUSTRATED. $16.95. CODE: TTH.

PATH OF THE POLE
Cataclysmic Pole Shift Geology
by Charles Hapgood

Maps of the Ancient Sea Kings author Hapgood's classic book *Path of the Pole* is back in print! Hapgood researched Antarctica, ancient maps and the geological record to conclude that the Earth's crust has slipped in the inner core many times in the past, changing the position of the pole. *Path of the Pole* discusses the various "pole shifts" in Earth's past, giving evidence for each one, and moves on to possible future pole shifts. Packed with illustrations, this is the sourcebook for many other books on cataclysms and pole shifts such as *5-5-2000: Ice the Ultimate Disaster* by Richard Noone. A planetary alignment on May 5, 2000 is predicted to cause the next pole shift—a date that is less than a year away! With Millennium Madness in full swing, this is sure to be a popular book.
356 PAGES. 6X9 PAPERBACK. ILLUSTRATED. $16.95. CODE: POP.

Charles Hapgood
author of
Maps of the Ancient Sea Kings

IN SEARCH OF ADVENTURE
A Wild Travel Anthology
compiled by Bruce Northam & Brad Olsen

An epic collection of 100 travelers' tales—a compendium that celebrates the wild side of contemporary travel writing—relating humorous, revealing, sometimes naughty stories by acclaimed authors. Indeed, a book to heat up the gypsy blood in all of us. Stories by Tim Cahill, Simon Winchester, Marybeth Bond, Robert Young Pelton, David Hatcher Childress, Richard Bangs, Linda Watanabe McFerrin, Jorma Kaukonen, and many more.
459 PAGES. 6X9 PAPERBACK. ILLUSTRATED. $17.95. CODE: ISOA

JOHN MICHELL

ECCENTRIC LIVES AND PECULIAR NOTIONS
by John Michell

The first paperback edition of Michell's fascinating study of the lives and beliefs of over 20 eccentric people. Published in hardback by Thames & Hudson in London, *Eccentric Lives and Peculiar Notions* takes us into the bizarre and often humorous lives of such people as Lady Blount, who was sure that the earth is flat; Cyrus Teed, who believed that the earth is a hollow shell with us on the inside; Edward Hine, who believed that the British are the lost Tribes of Israel; and Baron de Guldenstubbe, who was sure that statues wrote him letters. British writer and housewife Nesta Webster devoted her life to exposing international conspiracies, and Father O'Callaghan devoted his to opposing interest on loans. The extraordinary characters in this book were—and in some cases still are—wholehearted enthusiasts for the various causes and outrageous notions they adopted, and John Michell describes their adventures with spirit and compassion. Some of them prospered and lived happily with their obsessions, while others failed dismally. We read of the hapless inventor of a giant battleship made of ice who died alone and neglected, and of the London couple who achieved peace and prosperity by drilling holes in their heads. Other chapters on the Last of the Welsh Druids; Congressman Ignacius Donnelly, the Great Heretic and Atlantis; Shakespearean Decoders and the Baconian Treasure Hunt; Early Ufologists; Jerusalem in Scotland; Bibliomaniacs; more.
248 PAGES. 6X9 PAPERBACK. ILLUSTRATED. $14.95. CODE: ELPN.

THE CHRIST CONSPIRACY
The Greatest Story Ever Sold
by Acharya S.

In this highly controversial and explosive book, archaeologist, historian, mythologist and linguist Acharya S. marshals an enormous amount of startling evidence to demonstrate that Christianity and the story of Jesus Christ were created by members of various secret societies, mystery schools and religions in order to unify the Roman Empire under one state religion. In developing such a fabrication, this multinational cabal drew upon a multitude of myths and rituals that existed long before the Christian era, and reworked them for centuries into the religion passed down to us today. Contrary to popular belief, there was no single man who was at the genesis of Christianity; Jesus was many characters rolled into one. These characters personified the ubiquitous solar myth, and their exploits were well known, as reflected by such popular deities as Mithras, Heracles/Hercules, Dionysos and many others throughout the Roman Empire and beyond. The story of Jesus as portrayed in the Gospels is revealed to be nearly identical in detail to that of the earlier savior-gods Krishna and Horus, who for millennia preceding Christianity held great favor with the people. *The Christ Conspiracy* shows the Jesus character as neither unique nor original, not "divine revelation." Christianity re-interprets the same extremely ancient body of knowledge that revolved around the celestial bodies and natural forces. The result of this myth making has been "The Greatest Story Ever Sold."
256 PAGES. 6X9 PAPERBACK. ILLUSTRATED. $14.95. CODE: CHRC.

CONSPIRACY & HISTORY

MIND CONTROL, WORLD CONTROL
by Jim Keith
Veteran author and investigator Jim Keith uncovers a surprising amount of information on the technology, experimentation and implementation of mind control. Various chapters in this shocking book are on early CIA experiments such as Project Artichoke and Project R.H.I.C.-EDOM, the methodology and technology of implants, mind control assassins and couriers, various famous "Mind Control" victims such as Sirhan Sirhan and Candy Jones. Also featured in this book are chapters on how Mind Control technology may be linked to some UFO activity and "UFO abductions."
256 PAGES. 6x9 PAPERBACK. ILLUSTRATED. FOOTNOTES. $14.95. CODE: MCWC

LIQUID CONSPIRACY
JFK, LSD, the CIA, Area 51 & UFOs
by George Piccard
Underground author George Piccard on the politics of LSD, mind control, and Kennedy's involvement with Area 51 and UFOs. Reveals JFK's LSD experiences with Mary Pinchot-Meyer. The plot thickens with an ever expanding web of CIA involvement, from underground bases with UFOs seen by JFK and Marilyn Monroe (among others) to a vaster conspiracy that affects every government agency from NASA to the Justice Department. This may have been the reason that Marilyn Monroe and actress-columnist Dorothy Killgallen were both murdered. Focusing on the bizarre side of history, *Liquid Conspiracy* takes the reader on a psychedelic tour de force.
264 PAGES. 6x9 PAPERBACK. ILLUSTRATED. $14.95. CODE: LIQC

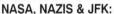

INSIDE THE GEMSTONE FILE
Howard Hughes, Onassis & JFK
by Kenn Thomas & David Hatcher Childress
Steamshovel Press editor Kenn Thomas takes on the Gemstone File in this run-up and run-down of the most famous underground document ever circulated. Photocopied and distributed for over 20 years, the Gemstone File is the story of Bruce Roberts, the inventor of the synthetic ruby widely used in laser technology today, and his relationship with the Howard Hughes Company and ultimately with Aristotle Onassis, the Mafia, and the CIA. Hughes kidnapped and held a drugged-up prisoner for 10 years; Onassis and his role in the Kennedy Assassination; how the Mafia ran corporate America in the 1960s; more.
320 PAGES. 6x9 PAPERBACK. ILLUSTRATED. $16.00. CODE: IGF

NASA, NAZIS & JFK:
The Torbitt Document & the JFK Assassination
Introduction by Kenn Thomas
This book emphasizes the link between "Operation Paper Clip" Nazi scientists working for NASA, the assassination of JFK, and the secret Nevada air base Area 51. The Torbitt Document also talks about the roles played in the assassination by Division Five of the FBI, the Defense Industrial Security Command (DISC), the Las Vegas mob, and the shadow corporate entities Permindex and Centro-Mondiale Commerciale. The Torbitt Document claims that the same players planned the 1962 assassination attempt on Charles de Gaul, who ultimately pulled out of NATO because he traced the "Assassination Cabal" to Permindex in Switzerland and to NATO headquarters in Brussels. The Torbitt Document paints a dark picture of NASA, the military industrial complex, and the connections to Mercury, Nevada which headquarters the "secret space program."
258 PAGES. 5x8. PAPERBACK. ILLUSTRATED. $16.00. CODE: NNJ

THE HISTORY OF THE KNIGHTS TEMPLAR
The Temple Church and the Temple
by Charles G. Addison. Introduction by David Hatcher Childress

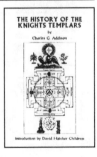

THE HISTORY OF THE
KNIGHTS TEMPLARS
by
Charles G. Addison

Introduction by David Hatcher Childress

Chapters on the origin of the Templars, their popularity in Europe and their rivalry with the Knights of St. John, later to be known as the Knights of Malta. Detailed information on the activities of the Templars in the Holy Land, and the 1312 A.D. suppression of the Templars in France and other countries, which culminated in the execution of Jacques de Molay and the continuation of the Knights Templars in England and Scotland and the formation of the society of Knights Templar in London and the rebuilding of the Temple in 1816. Plus a lengthy intro about the lost Templar fleet and its connections to the ancient North American sea routes.
395 PAGES. 6x9 PAPERBACK. ILLUSTRATED. $16.95. CODE: HKT

MIND CONTROL, OSWALD & JFK:
Were We Controlled?
Introduction by Kenn Thomas
Steamshovel Press editor Kenn Thomas examines the little-known book *Were We Controlled?*, first published in 1968. The book maintained that Lee Harvey Oswald was a special agent who was a mind control subject, having received an implant in 1960 at a Russian hospital. Thomas examines the evidence for implant technology and the role it could have played in the Kennedy Assassination. Thomas also looks at the mind control aspects of the RFK assassination and details the history of implant technology. A growing number of people are interested in CIA experiments and its "Silent Weapons for Quiet Wars."
256 PAGES. 6x9 PAPERBACK. ILLUSTRATED. NOTES. $16.00. CODE: MCOJ

24 HOUR CREDIT CARD ORDERS—CALL: 815-253-6390 FAX: 815-253-6300
email: auphq@frontiernet.net   http://www.adventuresunlimited.co.nz

UFOs & EXTRATERRESTRIALS

EXTRATERRESTRIAL ARCHAEOLOGY
by David Hatcher Childress
With 100s of photos and illustrations, *Extraterrestrial Archaeology* takes the reader to the strange and fascinating worlds of Mars, the Moon, Mercury, Venus, Saturn and other planets for a look at the alien structures that appear there. Using official NASA and Soviet photos, as well as other photos taken via telescope, this book seeks to prove that many of the planets (and moons) of our solar system are in some way inhabited by intelligent life. The book includes many blow-ups of NASA photos and detailed diagrams of structures—particularly on the Moon.
- NASA PHOTOS OF PYRAMIDS AND DOMED CITIES ON THE MOON.
- PYRAMIDS AND GIANT STATUES ON MARS.
- HOLLOW MOONS OF MARS AND OTHER PLANETS.
- ROBOT MINING VEHICLES THAT MOVE ABOUT THE MOON PROCESSING VALUABLE METALS.
- NASA & RUSSIAN PHOTOS OF SPACE-BASES ON MARS AND ITS MOONS.
- A BRITISH SCIENTIST WHO DISCOVERED A TUNNEL ON THE MOON, AND OTHER "BOTTOMLESS CRATERS."
- EARLY CLAIMS OF TRIPS TO THE MOON AND MARS.
- STRUCTURAL ANOMALIES ON VENUS, SATURN, JUPITER, MERCURY, URANUS & NEPTUNE.
- NASA, THE MOON AND ANTI-GRAVITY. PLUS MORE. HIGHLY ILLUSTRATED WITH PHOTOS, DIAGRAMS AND MAPS!
304 PAGES. 8x11 PAPERBACK. BIBLIOGRAPHY & APPENDIX. $18.95. CODE: ETA

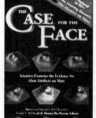

THE CASE FOR THE FACE
Scientists Examine the Evidence for Alien Artifacts on Mars
edited by Stanley McDaniel and Monica Rix Paxson
Mars Imagery by Mark Carlotto
The ultimate compendium on artificial structures in the Cydonia region of Mars. *The Case For the Face* unifies the research and opinions of a remarkably accomplished group of scientists, including a former NASA astronaut, a quantum physicist who is the chair of a space science program, leading meteor researchers, nine Ph.D.'s, the best-selling science author in Germany and more. The book includes: NASA research proving we're not the first intelligent race in this solar system; 120 amazing high resolution images never seen before by the general public; three separate doctoral statistical studies demonstrating the likelihood of artificial objects at the Cydonian site to be over 99%; and other definitive proof of life on Mars. Solid science presented in a readable, richly illustrated format. Featured on the Learning Channel with Leonard Nimoy.
320 PAGES. 6x9 PAPERBACK. ILLUSTRATED. INDEX & BIBLIOGRAPHY. $17.95. CODE: CFF

FLYING SAUCERS OVER LOS ANGELES
The UFO Craze of the '50s
by DeWayne B. Johnson & Kenn Thomas
commentary by David Hatcher Childress
Beginning with a previously unpublished manuscript written in the early 1950s by DeWayne B. Johnson entitled "Flying Saucers Over Los Angeles," this book chronicles the earliest flying saucer flap beginning June 24, 1947. The book continues with other sightings into the late '50s, including many rare photos. It also presents one of the first analyses of the sociological and psychological dimensions of the UFO experience, from a vantage point of certainty that flying saucers are real—borne out by the actual news and witness accounts. Starting with such cases as the Roswell crash and the Maury Island incident, it continues to little-known sightings; this manuscript offers a contemporaneous view of the earliest UFO excitement in America, unvarnished by the accumulated speculation of the last 50 years. A more detailed account of the many early sightings has never before been published. Additionally, the book contains an appendix of actual newsclippings from the Los Angeles newspapers of the time.
256 PAGES. 6x9 PAPERBACK. ILLUSTRATED. BIBLIOGRAPHY. $16.00. CODE: FSLA

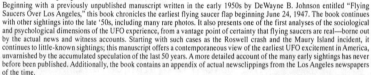

COEVOLUTION
The True Story of 10 Days with an Extraterrestrial Civilization
by Alec Newald
One Monday in mid-February 1989, Alec Newald set off on what should have been a 3-hour drive from Rotorua to Auckland but instead became 10 days of missing time! Newald claims he had been taken by friendly aliens to their home planet during this time. In the first part of the book he describes the planet, the civilization and the technology used by these extraterrestrials. The second part of the book is about the strange visitations that he received from "government scientists" who wanted to know what he knew about ET's, and the profound implications for planet earth: coevolution with another world.
194 PAGES. 5x8 PAPERBACK. ILLUSTRATED. APPENDIX. $16.95. CODE: COEV

PYRAMID TRUTH GATEWAY UNIVERSE
The Purpose, Intent, and Overview of Extraterrestrial Visitations
by Reg T. Miller
A thick and well-illustrated book on the mysteries of the Great Pyramid and how this ancient structure relates with space travel, time travel and extraterrestrials. Lots of diagrams and sacred geometry are used to explain: The Origin of Creation; Ancient Civilizations and Technology; Earth Chronicles; Abductions and Implants; Transitions and Time Warps; Pyramid Power; Ancient Astronauts; Energy Healing; Nemesis, the Deadly Comet; more.
359 PAGES. 7x10 PAPERBACK. ILLUSTRATED. $24.95. CODE: PTGU

24 HOUR CREDIT CARD ORDERS—CALL: 815-253-6390 FAX: 815-253-6300
EMAIL: AUPHQ@FRONTIERNET.NET HTTP://WWW.ADVENTURESUNLIMITED.CO.NZ

THE LOST CITIES SERIES

LOST CITIES OF ATLANTIS, ANCIENT EUROPE & THE MEDITERRANEAN
by David Hatcher Childress

Atlantis! The legendary lost continent comes under the close scrutiny of maverick archaeologist David Hatcher Childress in this sixth book in the internationally popular *Lost Cities* series. Childress takes the reader in search of sunken cities in the Mediterranean; across the Atlas Mountains in search of Atlantean ruins; to remote islands in search of megalithic ruins; to meet living legends and secret societies. From Ireland to Turkey, Morocco to Eastern Europe, and around the remote islands of the Mediterranean and Atlantic, Childress takes the reader on an astonishing quest for mankind's past. Ancient technology, cataclysms, megalithic construction, lost civilizations and devastating wars of the past are all explored in this book. Childress challenges the skeptics and proves that great civilizations not only existed in the past, but the modern world and its problems are reflections of the ancient world of Atlantis.

524 PAGES. 6X9 PAPERBACK. ILLUSTRATED WITH 100S OF MAPS, PHOTOS AND DIAGRAMS. BIBLIOGRAPHY & INDEX. $16.95. CODE: MED

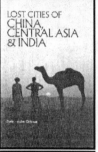

LOST CITIES OF CHINA, CENTRAL INDIA & ASIA
by David Hatcher Childress

Like a real life "Indiana Jones," maverick archaeologist David Childress takes the reader on an incredible adventure across some of the world's oldest and most remote countries in search of lost cities and ancient mysteries. Discover ancient cities in the Gobi Desert; hear fantastic tales of lost continents, vanished civilizations and secret societies bent on ruling the world; visit forgotten monasteries in forbidding snow-capped mountains with strange tunnels to mysterious subterranean cities! A unique combination of far-out exploration and practical travel advice, it will astound and delight the experienced traveler or the armchair voyager.

429 PAGES. 6X9 PAPERBACK. ILLUSTRATED. FOOTNOTES & BIBLIOGRAPHY. $14.95. CODE: CHI

LOST CITIES OF ANCIENT LEMURIA & THE PACIFIC
by David Hatcher Childress

Was there once a continent in the Pacific? Called Lemuria or Pacifica by geologists, Mu or Pan by the mystics, there is now ample mythological, geological and archaeological evidence to "prove" that an advanced and ancient civilization once lived in the central Pacific. Maverick archaeologist and explorer David Hatcher Childress combs the Indian Ocean, Australia and the Pacific in search of the surprising truth about mankind's past. Contains photos of the underwater city on Pohnpei; explanations on how the statues were levitated around Easter Island in a clockwise vortex movement; tales of disappearing islands; Egyptians in Australia; and more.

379 PAGES. 6X9 PAPERBACK. ILLUSTRATED. FOOTNOTES & BIBLIOGRAPHY. $14.95. CODE: LEM

ANCIENT TONGA
& the Lost City of Mu'a
by David Hatcher Childress

Lost Cities series author Childress takes us to the south sea islands of Tonga, Rarotonga, Samoa and Fiji to investigate the megalithic ruins on these beautiful islands. The great empire of the Polynesians, centered on Tonga and the ancient city of Mu'a, is revealed with old photos, drawings and maps. Chapters in this book are on the Lost City of Mu'a and its many megalithic pyramids, the Ha'amonga Trilithon and ancient Polynesian astronomy, Samoa and the search for the lost land of Havai'iki, Fiji and its wars with Tonga, Rarotonga's megalithic road, and Polynesian cosmology. Material on Egyptians in the Pacific, earth changes, the fortified moat around Mu'a, lost roads, more.

218 PAGES. 6X9 PAPERBACK. ILLUSTRATED. COLOR PHOTOS. BIBLIOGRAPHY. $15.95. CODE: TONG

ANCIENT MICRONESIA
& the Lost City of Nan Madol
by David Hatcher Childress

Micronesia, a vast archipelago of islands west of Hawaii and south of Japan, contains some of the most amazing megalithic ruins in the world. Part of our *Lost Cities of the Pacific* series, this volume explores the incredible conformations on various Micronesian islands, especially the fantastic and little-known ruins of Nan Madol on Pohnpei Island. The huge canal city of Nan Madol contains over 250 million tons of basalt columns over an 11 square-mile area of artificial islands. Much of the huge city is submerged, and underwater structures can be found to an estimated 80 feet. Islanders' legends claim that the basalt rocks, weighing up to 50 tons, were magically levitated into place by the powerful forefathers. Other ruins in Micronesia that are profiled include the Latte Stones of the Marianas, the menhirs of Palau, the megalithic canal city on Kosrae Island, megaliths on Guam, and more.

256 PAGES. 6X9 PAPERBACK. HEAVILY ILLUSTRATED. INCLUDES A COLOR PHOTO SECTION. BIBLIOGRAPHY & INDEX. $16.95. CODE: AMIC

24 HOUR CREDIT CARD ORDERS—CALL: 815-253-6390 FAX: 815-253-6300

email: auphq@frontiernet.net   http://www.adventuresunlimited.co.nz

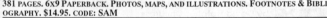

ANTI-GRAVITY

THE ANTI-GRAVITY HANDBOOK

edited by David Hatcher Childress, with Nikola Tesla, T.B. Paulicki, Bruce Cathie, Albert Einstein and others

The new expanded compilation of material on Anti-Gravity, Free Energy, Flying Saucer Propulsion, UFOs, Suppressed Technology, NASA Cover-ups and more. Highly illustrated with patents, technical illustrations and photos. This revised and expanded edition has more material, including photos of Area 51, Nevada, the government's secret testing facility. This classic on weird science is back in a 90s format!
* How to build a flying saucer.
* Crystals and their role in levitation.
* Secret government research and development.
* Nikola Tesla on how anti-gravity airships could
  draw power from the atmosphere.
* Bruce Cathie's Anti-Gravity Equation.
* NASA, the Moon and Anti-Gravity.
230 PAGES. 7X10 PAPERBACK. BIBLIOGRAPHY. APPENDIX. ILLUSTRATED. $14.95. CODE: AGH

ANTI-GRAVITY & THE WORLD GRID

edited by David Hatcher Childress

Is the earth surrounded by an intricate electromagnetic grid network offering free energy? This compilation of material on ley lines and world power points contains chapters on the geography, mathematics, and light harmonics of the earth grid. Learn the purpose of ley lines and ancient megalithic structures located on the grid. Discover how the grid made the Philadelphia Experiment possible. Explore the Coral Castle and many other mysteries, including acoustic levitation, Tesla Shields and scalar wave weaponry. Browse through the section on anti-gravity patents, and research resources.
274 PAGES. 7X10 PAPERBACK. ILLUSTRATED. $14.95. CODE: AGW

ANTI-GRAVITY
& THE UNIFIED FIELD

edited by David Hatcher Childress

Is Einstein's Unified Field Theory the answer to all of our energy problems? Explored in this compilation of material is how gravity, electricity and magnetism manifest from a unified field around us. Why artificial gravity is possible; secrets of UFO propulsion; free energy; Nikola Tesla and anti-gravity airships of the 20s and 30s; flying saucers as superconducting whirls of plasma; anti-mass generators; vortex propulsion; suppressed technology; government cover-ups; gravitational pulse drive; spacecraft & more.
240 PAGES. 7X10 PAPERBACK. ILLUSTRATED. $14.95. CODE: AGU

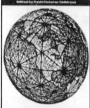

ETHER TECHNOLOGY

A Rational Approach to Gravity Control
by Rho Sigma

This classic book on anti-gravity and free energy is back in print. Written by a well-known American scientist under the pseudonym of "Rho Sigma," this book delves into international efforts at gravity control and discoid craft propulsion. Before the Quantum Field, there was "Ether." This small, but informative book has chapters on John Searle and "Searle discs;" T. Townsend Brown and his work on anti-gravity and ether-vortex turbines. Includes a forward by former NASA astronaut Edgar Mitchell.
108 PAGES. 6X9 PAPERBACK. ILLUSTRATED. $12.95. CODE: ETT

MAN-MADE UFOS 1944—1994

Fifty Years of Suppression
by Renato Vesco & David Hatcher Childress

A comprehensive look at the early "flying saucer" technology of Nazi Germany and the genesis of man-made UFOs. This book takes us from the work of captured German scientists to escaped battalions of Germans, secret communities in South America and Antarctica to today's state-of-the-art "Dreamland" flying machines. Heavily illustrated, this astonishing book blows the lid off the "government UFO conspiracy" and explains with technical diagrams the technology involved. Examined in detail are secret underground airfields and factories; German secret weapons; "suction" aircraft; the origin of NASA; gyroscopic stabilizers and engines; the secret Marconi aircraft factory in South America; and more. Not to be missed by students of technology suppression, secret societies, anti-gravity, free energy, conspiracy and World War II! Introduction by W.A. Harbinson, author of the Dell novels *GENESIS* and *REVELATION*.
318 PAGES. 6X9 PAPERBACK. ILLUSTRATED. INDEX & FOOTNOTES. $18.95. CODE: MMU

24 HOUR CREDIT CARD ORDERS—CALL: 815-253-6390 FAX: 815-253-6300
EMAIL: AUPHQ@FRONTIERNET.NET HTTP://WWW.ADVENTURESUNLIMITED.CO.NZ

One Adventure Place
P.O. Box 74
Kempton, Illinois 60946
United States of America
Tel.: 815-253-6390 • Fax: 815-253-6300
Email: auphq@frontiernet.net
http://www.adventuresunlimited.co.nz

ORDERING INSTRUCTIONS

✓ Remit by USD$ Check, Money Order or Credit Card
✓ Visa, Master Card, Discover & AmEx Accepted
✓ Prices May Change Without Notice
✓ 10% Discount for 3 or more Items

SHIPPING CHARGES

United States

✓ Postal Book Rate { $2.50 First Item / 50¢ Each Additional Item
✓ Priority Mail { $3.50 First Item / $2.00 Each Additional Item
✓ UPS { $5.00 First Item / $1.50 Each Additional Item

NOTE: UPS Delivery Available to Mainland USA Only

Canada

✓ Postal Book Rate { $3.00 First Item / $1.00 Each Additional Item
✓ Postal Air Mail { $5.00 First Item / $2.00 Each Additional Item
✓ Personal Checks or Bank Drafts MUST BE USD$ and Drawn on a US Bank
✓ Canadian Postal Money Orders OK
✓ Payment MUST BE USD$

All Other Countries

✓ Surface Delivery { $6.00 First Item / $2.00 Each Additional Item
✓ Postal Air Mail { $12.00 First Item / $8.00 Each Additional Item
✓ Payment MUST BE USD$
✓ Checks and Money Orders MUST BE USD$ and Drawn on a US Bank or branch.
✓ Add $5.00 for Air Mail Subscription to Future *Adventures Unlimited* Catalogs

SPECIAL NOTES

✓ RETAILERS: Standard Discounts Available
✓ BACKORDERS: We Backorder all Out-of-Stock Items Unless Otherwise Requested
✓ PRO FORMA INVOICES: Available on Request
✓ VIDEOS: NTSC Mode Only
✓ For PAL mode videos contact our other offices:

European Office:
Adventures Unlimited, PO Box 372,
Dronten, 8250 AJ, The Netherlands
South Pacific Office
Adventures Unlimited Pacifica
221 Symonds Street, Box 8199
Auckland, New Zealand

Please check: ☑

☐ This is my first order   ☐ I have ordered before   ☐ This is a new address

Name
Address
City
State/Province | Postal Code
Country
Phone day | Evening
Fax

Item Code	Item Description	Price	Qty	Total

Please check: ☑

☐ Postal-Surface
☐ Postal-Air Mail (Priority in USA)
☐ UPS (Mainland USA only)

Subtotal ➡	
Less Discount-10% for 3 or more items ➡	
Balance ➡	
Illinois Residents 6.25% Sales Tax ➡	
Previous Credit ➡	
Shipping ➡	
Total (check/MO in USD$ only)➡	

☐ Visa/MasterCard/Discover/Amex

Card Number

Expiration Date

10% Discount When You Order 3 or More Items!

Comments & Suggestions	Share Our Catalog with a Friend